"A must read, not only for company leaders but for anyone who wants the secret of career success: to get ahead you have to sometimes break the rules and forget everything 'they' told you to do."
—Kate White, editor in chief of *Redbook* and author of *Why Good Girls Don't Get Ahead . . . But Gutsy Girls Do*

"A great book! Elevates the technology of change to a new level. *Change-Ready* people and organizations will lead the race into the twenty-first century."
—Daniel Burrus, author of *Technotrends*

"Every small business owner/operator should insist that his management team read SACRED COWS. The resulting rise in profitability and efficiency will easily be measured on the bottom line . . . where it counts."
—Tom Du Pont, Chairman, *Du Pont Registry* magazine

"I really liked my sacred cow burger but think a lot of readers will find theirs to be a little bitter at first but sweeter with every bite. That is a lot like change."
—Tom Reece, President and CEO, Dover Corporation

"Spotting, rounding up, and slaughtering sacred cows is important work for the leader of any organization. Kriegel has a unique way of putting his finger on important and timely ideas and communicating them in a way that makes them sink in and stick."
—Gregory Faherty, President, Siplast

"Full of ready-to-use ideas! We love it!"
—Stew Leonard, Jr., CEO, Stew Leonard's

"Electric! Rediscovers *people* as the No. 1 technology and *change* the vehicle for success. Throw away the textbooks and breathe Kriegel's fresh air."
—Frank Pacetta, author of *Don't Fire Them, Fire Them Up*

"Light up the grill. Kriegel shows American business why the old rules no longer apply. To successfully compete in the twenty-first century, this book is a must."
—Connie Glaser, coauthor of *Swim with the Dolphins*

"A great follow-up to *If It Ain't Broke . . . BREAK IT!* There's no question that the degree of an organization's *Change-Readiness* foreshadows its future vitality. Your focus on the sacred cows of the gatekeepers of change is right where it should be."
—C. Robert Henrikson, Executive Vice President, MetLife®

"A common-sense approach [that] offers practical solutions to effect change."
—Gregory S. Campbell, Executive Vice President,
Coldwell Banker Corporation

"A great title, an extraordinary book. After reading it, I called a company barbecue to slaughter our sacred cows."
—Tony Alessandra, Ph.D., author of *Non-Manipulative Selling* and
The Platinum Rule

"At last, a diet book for corporate America. Kriegel shows us that sacred cows are to corporations what cholestrol is to the rest of us. While there is plenty of meat in this trim-the-fat book, if you want to know an effective way to streamline, buy SACRED COWS MAKE THE BEST BURGERS."
—Jaclyn Kostner, Ph.D., author of *Virtual Leadership* and CEO,
Bridge the Distance, International

SACRED COWS MAKE THE BEST BURGERS

SACRED COWS
MAKE THE BEST
BURGERS

PARADIGM-BUSTING STRATEGIES FOR DEVELOPING

CHANGE-READY PEOPLE AND ORGANIZATIONS

ROBERT KRIEGEL AND DAVID BRANDT

WARNER BOOKS

A Time Warner Company

Warner Books, Inc., 1271 Avenue of the Americas, New York, N.Y.
10020
 A Time Warner Company

Printed in the United States of America
First Printing: February 1996
10 9 8 7 6 5 4 3 2 1

ISBN: 0-446-51840-9
LC: 95-62343

Illustrations by Bryce Browning

To my father, Stanley Brandt, who understood that those who embrace change never get old. His life inspired many of the ideas in this book.

—DB

To Marilyn, my wife, lover, coach, best friend, adviser, business partner, and soul mate, without whom I would be a sacred cow.

—RK

THANKS!, THANKS!, THANKS!, THANKS!, THANKS!, THANKS!
for all your input, inspiration, and intelligence:

Laurie and Kate Brandt, Marilyn and Otis Kriegel, Jim Eaneman, Ken Jenny, Lynn Henriksen, Lisa Taunton, LaVonne Brooks, Bryce Browning, Susan Suffes, John and Katinka Brockman, Steven Ball, Bob Nye, Steven Cristol, Peller Marion, Doug Biederbeck, Art Gingold, David Smith, Ron Tilden, and all the people who participated in our seminars and workshops.

Contents

SACRED COWS
MAKE THE BEST
BURGERS

One

Cows and Gatekeepers

sacred cow \'kaù\ *n, plural* sacred cows
1. a plodding, bovine mammal of numerous stomachs and dubious intelligence regarded in some climes as holy in origin and therefore immune from ordinary treatment
2. Business: **a.** An outmoded belief, assumption, practice, policy, system, or strategy, generally invisible, that inhibits change and prevents responsiveness to new opportunities

They're out there. Herds of sacred cows grazing on your profits and choking off your productivity. Old, mildewed, obsolete ideas that no longer work in a business climate that demands cutting-edge thinking and bold, imaginative solutions. Even ideas that just a few years ago made millions are now staler than last week's sourdough.

Cows trample creative, innovative thinking. They inhibit quick response to change and cost money and time. They roam every-where—in the halls, boardrooms, and offices, and in people's minds. Sometimes they're obvious, other times invisible, simply background like the wall behind a Rembrandt.

Yet many organizations continue to worship their sacred cattle. They're afraid to abandon what once made them successful, and they extract a heavy fine from those cow hunters who would "pasture-ize" them.

Remember the classic "cows" from the last few decades: the 40 hour workweek, job security and the 25-year gold watch, retirement at age 65, management by objectives, command-and-control organizations, top-down decision-making, single-paycheck households.

CORPORATE WEATHER REPORT

In a stable environment, sacred cows have a long half-life. What worked yesterday will work today and probably tomorrow. But that's not what is going on out there. It's hurricane season for American business. Winds of change are barreling in from all directions. Competition is tougher than ever and coming from places you least expected. The customer is more sophisticated and demanding. Technological changes are incessant. Government regulations are tougher. And everyone is restructuring, reorganizing, reinventing, downsizing, outsourcing—all at an ultrasonic pace.

Don't look for a safe harbor to wait out the storm, because these winds are unrelenting. If anything, they're getting stronger and coming faster, blowing the shutters off corporate headquarters and small businesses alike.

The weather report? More of the same.

LOOKING BACK THREE YEARS

To get an idea of the speed of change, try this exercise: Look back on your job three years ago. Remember what you used to do and how you did it. Whom did you work for and with? Who were your competitors? What technologies did you use? How was your organization structured? What about the size of your workload?

On a scale of 1 to 10, how would you rate the level of change that has occurred in this relatively short time? Over 80 percent of the people in our programs rate changes at work between 7 and 10. And there are always a few 12s and 15s!

Now project three years into the future. How would you rate the changes you think will occur in that period of time?

Future changes will be bigger and come faster because the rate of change grows exponentially, not incrementally. So get ready for the storm of your life. The hurricane season has just begun.

FAD OF THE MONTH

American business isn't just watching from the bunkhouse as this storm shakes up everything and everybody. New programs, processes, and strategies have been introduced to help you keep ahead of these changes and eliminate sacred cows. In fact, they're emerging almost as fast as the changes themselves.

Everywhere you go you hear the latest buzzwords: *reengineering, total quality, virtual teams, "horizontal" corporate structures* . . .

WHY CHANGE FAILS

Most of these strategies look good, sound great, and make sense— *on paper.* The problem lies in implementation. When it's time to turn these ideas into action, trouble begins.

Says reengineering guru Mike Hammer, "Coming up with the ideas is the easy part, but getting things done is the tough part. The place where these reforms die is . . . down in the trenches."[1]

The result: Though it's predicted that U.S. corporations will spend $34 billion on reengineering,[2] most efforts will flop. "Reengineering is not a bed of roses. . . . Some statistics say seven out of ten reengineering initiatives fail," notes Leo Lewis, president of the Tandy Computer Users Group.[3] And a recent study by consulting giant

McKinsey found that a majority of companies researched achieved less than a 5 percent change due to reengineering.[4]

TOTAL QUALITY ISN'T

TQM (total quality management) was supposed to be the elixir of the eighties. It didn't turn out that way. Surveys indicate that two-thirds of American managers think TQM has failed in their companies. And the number of applicants vying for the Malcom Baldridge Award, the Holy Grail of quality, has fallen sharply since its peak year in 1991.[5]

"The 'Q' word has become cheap currency," says David Snediker, vice president for quality at Battelle Memorial Institute. "I wish I could think of a new title, a new name for my office, and start over."[6]

LIP SERVICE

"You name it and we've tried it: total quality, reengineering, empowerment, independent work teams. We've done them all, and at all levels," an executive for one of the major chemical companies told us. "If you gave our managers a test on these theories, they'd pass with flying colors.

"But if you look around our plants, we're still operating pretty much the same way we did ten years ago. Same structures, same top-down culture. Nothing much has changed except our terminology. Can you blame me or the workers for being cynical when some new panacea comes down the pike?"

The president of a small electronics distributor who supplies major high tech manufacturers says, "I sell to the people who are the case studies you read about in all the books and magazines. They're always talking about teamwork with the suppliers, working together, all that stuff.

"What a lot of crap! They beat us up, constantly berate us, threaten us, push us, and try to wring us dry. I don't call that teamwork." But they sure look good on paper.

We've seen this same phenomena in hundreds of companies: people giving lip service to change, using all the right words and phrases, signs on all the walls, bells and whistles everywhere. In other words, a lot of talk.

But usually not a lot of change.

THE GATEKEEPERS OF CHANGE

The question is, *Why?* If these processes are so well conceived, why don't they work as promised? What is the problem in turning these ideas into effective action? The answer is *people.*

People are the gatekeepers of change. They have the power to breathe life into a new program or kill it. If they're excited and positive; it's open sesame. If they're not—and that's most of the time—it's *clang!* The gate's slammed shut in your face.

People's resistance to change, says Mike Hammer, is "the most perplexing, annoying, distressing, and confusing part" of reengineering.[7]

The reason that three fourths of reengineering efforts fail, emphasizes leadership consultant Joan Goldsmith, is that "the focus of change is on work processes, new technology . . . and decentralized services rather than on the people who must implement change. Enabling executives, managers, and employees to shift long-held behavior patterns [sacred cows] is an intense and complex task. And most organizations avoid or ignore it."[8]

CHANGE HAS NO NATURAL CONSTITUENCY

Management consultants who deal with companies in transition know that the "people" part of change is critical. And that it is most often overlooked and undervalued.

"The ability and willingness of individual employees to change is the key factor limiting an organization's ability to reinvent itself," says Erika Andersen, the head of Proteus International, an organizational development firm with many Fortune 500 clients. "Change is personal. . . . Forceful leadership can accomplish only so much. The shift from machine-age bureaucracy to flexible, self-managed teams requires that lots of ordinary managers and workers be psychologically prepared. . . ."[9]

Terry Neill, a partner at Andersen Consulting, the number-one U.S. company in computer-systems integration, says, "A new computer system spreads confusion, doubt, and stress. The hardware may work, the software may work, but the system won't work if the people who are supposed to use it don't cooperate."[10]

The head of the change-management division at another major consulting company concurs. "Change is rarely accepted readily. We have installed terrific systems, great strategies, cutting-edge technologies. We've done reengineering and quality programs. But they never seem to live up to expectations.

"Why? Because when you get right down to it, people are the obstacles. The key to the success of any new process, system, or strategy is implementation. And that's about people. People have to execute. They have to support the new system or it will go nowhere. Processes are easy, people are tough. It's been my experience that *people naturally resist change.*"

DINOSAURS DON'T DANCE

Why don't people embrace change? For starters, change is *un*comfortable, *un*predictable, and often seems *un*safe. It's fraught with uncertainty and always looks harder than it is. What if it doesn't work, we ask ourselves. Or, What if I can't learn the new skill, or fit in with this new team in this new place on this new project?

Change brings us face-to-face with the unknown, and that evokes our worst imagined fears: We'll be fired, humiliated, criticized. So we dig in our heels.

People resist change in all kinds of ways. They resist actively, passively, consciously and unconsciously, by sabotage and subterfuge. They resist it rationally, emotionally, and sometimes spiritually.

An internal survey of 1,200 top managers at IBM, taken after the company had already fallen from grace, showed that 40 percent *still didn't accept the need for change.*[11] We don't know where those people have been living, but we know where they're heading: Jurassic Park.

CEO Gerstner has struggled mightily to cut costs, develop new strategies, and improve customer focus. But his toughest battle is with this entrenched patriarchal culture. It's tough to get dinosaurs to dance.

ATTENTION-DEFICIT DISORDER

Management guru Tom Peters stresses that the last 25 years have been about technological advances transforming the workplace. The next 25 are about people catching up with them.

Well, if they're going to catch up, they're going to need some help, and from the looks of things they'll be hard pressed to find it. A Gallup poll reported that 75 percent of American business leaders are not well prepared to manage change.[12]

Hammer says that most reengineering efforts crash in flames, shot down by people's reluctance to go along and by management's—especially top management's—ineptitude and fear.[13]

Another reason: the big boys' love affair with the "magic bullet" approach—chasing one new fad after another without fully committing to any. "I sometimes wonder if the people at the top of most big U.S. corporations are afflicted with attention-deficit disorder," remarks change consultant Barry Spiker.[14]

KISS OF YES

Many organizational theorists argue that if you introduce a clearly delineated change with a convincing rationale and attractive rewards, employees will get on board . . . eventually. Don't worry about pockets of resistance. Fire the troublemakers or make their lives miserable.

We've seen workers fight change for months and years because they didn't understand it, were afraid of it, or didn't see it as being in their self-interest. It's naive to assume that the bulk of the workforce will come around. Even when resistance seems to disappear, most often it's just gone underground and will surface when you least expect it.

"Most dissenters won't stand up and shout at you that they hate what you are doing to them and to their comfortable old ways," says *Fortune* magazine's Ann Fisher. "Instead they will nod and smile and agree with everything you say—and then behave as they always have." Hammer calls this "vicious compliance, or the kiss of yes."[15]

Companies that make wholesale changes without addressing the complex system of thoughts, feelings, and wishes that constitute a human being are going to end up with a lot of heel dragging and silent sabotage. "Unless decision-makers are willing to acknowledge and address the full range of reactions to change, including the ones that are not rational, reengineering is an interesting theory and nothing more," notes Fisher.[16]

FROM RESISTANCE TO READINESS

How can we get our people on board, get them to be positive about change and proactive? This is the most common question asked us by organizations large and small.

It's not magic done with mirrors. And it's not FedEx, delivered overnight. Change is a process that is both exciting and difficult, and resistance to it is natural and should be expected. The key is to turn resistance into what we call *Change-Readiness*.

Change-Readiness is an attitude that is

- *open* and receptive to new ideas;
- *excited* rather than anxious about change;
- *challenged,* not threatened, by transitions;
- *committed* to change as an ongoing process.

Change-Readiness is taking actions to

- *anticipate* and initiate change;
- *challenge* the staus quo;

- *create* instead of react to change;
- *lead* rather than follow (the competition, the customer, and the industry).

Individuals and organizations that are *good* react quickly to change.

Individuals and organizations that are *great* create change.

FIVE STEPS

This book will show you how to coach yourself and your people to be Change Ready so that your organization can respond quickly to the challenges and opportunities of the twenty-first century.

There are five steps in this process:

1. *Rounding up Sacred Cows*
   Challenging your well-worn beliefs, assumptions, and practices and identifying those that have outlived their usefulness
2. *Developing a Change-Ready Environment*
   Creating an environment in which people are more open to innovation and new ideas
3. *Turning Resistance into Readiness*
   Coaching yourself and others to recognize and overcome the four resistances to change
4. *Motivating People to Change*
   Getting people excited about change and motivated to act
5. *Developing the Seven Personal Change-Ready Traits*
   Cultivating the personal characteristics needed to thrive in a changing environment

SACRED-COW HUNTING

In the next chapter we've identified a number of outmoded beliefs and practices to get you started on step one: *the sacred-cow hunt.* Our list of cows is only a beginning, but it will give you some ideas for thinning out your own herd. Happy hunting!

Paper Cow

Two

The Paper Cow

SACRED PROMISE

Welcome to the information age. Remember its promise? *The paperless office.* Know anyone who's got one? Most people's desks look like they've been hit by a paper avalanche. Would you believe that since 1983 shipments of office paper have increased by 51 percent?[1]

Computer technology has given us instant and cheaper access to more and more information. So naturally that's what we think we want. But what do we get? More information than we need and certainly more than we read. We are suffocating in that avalanche of paper, much of which just gets filed . . . *unread.*

And most of those reports, proposals, printouts, projections that take so much time to do end up in the round file, the one under your desk.

INCOMING HERDS

A vice president at a major telecommunications company showed us a study that measured the number of incoming messages received in a given period. On average, people got over *90 hours'* worth of "stuff" to read each week! And only 20 percent of that was electronic. The rest of it was on paper. The same study showed that despite all the advancements in information technology, the amount of paper received today had not been reduced from ten years ago. "The paper flow hasn't been lightened at all. People don't trust the technology. They're printing out their E-mail and filing it," said the vice president.

Ninety hours? That's about 14 hours a day 7 days a week just to read your correspondence. "How do you handle it?" we asked her.

"I've developed a system," she responded. "I have three piles. The first are things I pass on to my staff. The second is urgent stuff that I do right now. The third and biggest pile are things I can take care of later, when I have time."

Knowing no one has the time to catch up, we asked her what she did with that pile. Grinning, she told us, "When it gets too big I just sweep it into the basket! If it's important enough it'll come back again as urgent and then I'll put it into my second pile."

Her strategy isn't atypical. People don't read most of their mail. The plant manager of a major chemical company told us that he *never* reads his. "Hell, if something is important enough, the message will be taped to my door. Then I'll read it."

Rush report. The chief information officer of a Big Five accounting firm told us that the company was spending $600,000 a year on a major bi-monthly report sent out to all partners and clients. A sacred-cow hunt showed that some of its information was unnecessary or could be disseminated in other ways. The cost of the report was reduced to $75,000.

The CIO was pleased with the savings, but he was still troubled by the FedEx bill of $45,000. The report was time sensitive so the company sent it same-day delivery. We asked him whether people read the report the minute they received it. If they didn't, why not send it second-day FedEx and cut costs in half?

He laughed. "Not read these reports the day they get them? Wait until the second day? You obviously don't know this business. Hell, I bet that ninety percent of those things never get read at all."

RED TIME/GREEN TIME

"About forty percent of my day is red time," Chris Brown, a regional sales manager for a super regional bank, told us. *Red time* is Brown's term for the time he spends doing what he calls housekeeping and clerical chores: call reports, monthly forecasts, account information reports, zone plans, expenses, etc. "The rest is green time—time spent with the client, which is what we are paid for. Green time is action time that brings in the green." Like many other managers, Brown complains that excessive paperwork causes his people to spend too much time in back of their desks rather than in front of the client.

A study among several divisions at the bank confirmed his objection. It showed that sales staff were using almost 35 percent of their day on red-time activities.

A paper-cow hunt decreased the red time to 20 percent and resulted not only in an increase in sales, but also in higher morale.

We gave the bank three questions to ask to determine whether paperwork was increasing their red time:

- Does the paper provide *value* to the client in terms of improving quality or service?
- Does the paper improve *productivity* or *cut costs?*
- Does anybody *read* the damn thing and, more important, does anyone *act* on it?

If you don't get a yes to any of these questions, you've got a paper cow in your herd.

Below are some examples of other paper cows. You'll probably notice some that look familiar. In our sacred-cow hunts we usually find that 50 percent of a company's paperwork could be eliminated without the slightest disruption in business.

Starving paper cows. One of the paper cows we identified at a

Fortune 50 high-tech client's cow hunt was a 10-column monthly financial report that had been done as long as anyone could remember. That's a first clue that something is a sacred or paper cow. The longer some practice has been in effect, the more likely it's outdated.

The report took a corps of people a lot of time to prepare, and because it went to the management committee it had to be reviewed and rechecked for accuracy. Also because it went to the management committee, no one wanted to challenge its necessity.

At a sacred-cow hunt one courageous soul suggested that two of the columns were really no longer needed. The information they contained was outdated and now irrelevant. Everyone agreed. So, with more than a little trepidation, the manager sent it out with eight columns. And waited . . .

No response.

Emboldened by the lack of reprimand, two other employees spotted a number of duplications. The manager took a deep breath, and sent it upstairs with six columns, and waited . . .

No response.

"Maybe there's no one out there," said one staffer. "Let's find out!" said another. "Why don't we prepare it but not send it out this month and see what happens?" Everyone agreed.

No response again.

They didn't send it out the following month either. Or the month after. When they finally did release the thing, it had only four columns and was titled "The Quarterly Report."

This time they got a response . . . from the chief operating officer: "Great report. Simple, clear, to the point. Keep up the good work!" And they did. In fact, the COO announced that their new format should be the standard for every other department.

All this led the division to place a cowbell in its offices, to be rung any time someone spotted a sacred cow. They even handed out cowboy hats every month. Operating costs in that division were reduced 18 percent, while morale soared.

Daily trouble. "See this report?" the chairman of a large health-care company asked me, holding up about four thick inches of printout. "With our new computer system, we get this information every day," he explained, beaming.

"We know what is going on in every one of our branches at every level, from daily expenses to the volume of sales. With this kind of detail we can keep tabs on everything and everyone so we can spot a problem before it becomes one. Or we can quickly take advantage of an opportunity."

We were impressed. But in the six weeks we worked with the executive committee and senior management, we never saw anyone read that report or even refer to it. On a hunch, we asked one of the secretaries what she did with the report. "Oh"—she laughed and gestured with a wave of her hand—"we just file it."

Jones signed it. . . . One software manufacturer routinely required its salespeople to get 13 approvals before they sent in bids for government contracts. Everybody had to sign off on it: Engineering, R&D, Manufacturing, Accounting, Marketing, Legal, maybe even Legal's mother-in-law. The process took weeks. And if one person threw it back, the whole process had to start over again.

The sales staff hated the system, not only because of the time involved but because of how helpless they felt. A cow hunt revealed that 7 of 13 staffers never read the paperwork.

Their typical response: "Oh, Jones signed it. He knows about this project; I trust him." And if you asked Jones, he'd probably tell you "Oh, Smith signed it. He knows about this project; I trust him."

What was probably true was that the only one who read the bid was the guy who wrote it. Within three months we got the process down to one signature by giving each of the salespeople responsibility and accountability for their own contracts. Sales increased by 18 percent.

PURCHASE PROBLEMS

Long and tedious approval procedures account for a significant part of the paper avalanche. We have talked with many managers with $500,000 budgets who have to get three sign-offs for a $150 purchase. It costs more to get the approval than it does to buy the needed equipment and supplies. Many managers faced with having to go through this hassle simply elect to forgo the purchase. And the company loses because its equipment doesn't get upgraded.

And what do all these obligatory authorizations say about trust and responsibility in the workplace? What message do they send employees?

Often the need for approvals doesn't even come from the top but from some scared CYA (cover-your-ass) middle manager. During a sacred-cow hunt at Greyhound Financial Corporation, one of the managers brought up the RFPs (requests for purchase). CEO Samuel Eichenfield was shocked. "Why do we have those?" he said. "As of today we don't anymore." The audience cheered.[2]

BURN THE BULLETINS

Another paper problem results from a company's obsessive concern with rules and procedures. Some businesses spend more time focusing on how a decision should be made than on making it. One of the major fast-food outlets had a 900-page rule book that spelled out the specifics of how to handle any problem that might arise. "Oh, that monstrosity," one manager commented. "I use it for a doorstop."

A major retailer compiled a whole library of bulletins spelling out problem-solving procedures. "You'd spend more time looking up the bulletin than it would take to make the damn decision and get on with it. Hell, you need a degree in library science just to find the rule. I think we'd be faster and better if we just burned up all those bulletins," says a store manager.

Forms, files, and folly. When IBM was selling its Lexington operation and the rest of its laser printing, typewriter, and office supplies business to Lexmark, the new company went through drawers and drawers of forms evaluating them for future use. Greg Survant, a manager in printer development, says the information required to justify an engineering change was cut from 58 items to 24.

And then the engineers investigated who had needed all that information in the first place. "You couldn't even find anyone who knew," said Survant. "That's the crazy thing. Nobody even remembered."[3]

ROUTING TO OBLIVION

Almost as bad as the interminable sign-offs is the endless routing that goes on with every memo or report. If you have even a remote connection to the subject or if you happen to be sitting next to someone who does, it gets routed to you.

Many companies have standard routing lists in their software, so after you write something, you just press a button and presto, everyone on the list gets it. No thinking involved.

A friend who is the assistant to the mayor for a major U.S. city received a routed memo from the mayor requesting an immediate response. She panicked. The memo had gotten overlooked at the bottom of her in-box and was now three weeks old. Her mind was racing to come up with a reasonable excuse when it struck her that no one had called to ask why she hadn't responded. So she quickly and quietly trashed it . . . and never heard anything more about the issue.

TIME MISMANAGEMENT

A CFO gave the following rough time allocations for his financial organization:

- About 15 percent on various forms of statutory-compliance reporting (audit, tax sec, ERISA, etc.)
- About 20 percent on ongoing or one-time project analysis that clearly adds substantial value to line organization efforts
- About 65 percent on maintaining, updating, and operating internal financial systems that *add little value if any* to line organization efforts

---

Change-Ready Thinking

If it doesn't
- add value to the customer
- increase productivity
- improve morale
it "moos"!

Three

The Meeting Cow

Are you lonely? Working on your own? Hate making decisions? *Hold a meeting!* You can see people, draw flow charts, feel important, impress your colleagues—all on company time.

Meetings have become the practical alternative to work. People aren't at their desks anymore, no one's answering the phone, no one's doing any actual work because they're all in meetings. Staff meetings, client meetings, goal-setting meetings, "everybody on the same page" meetings, meetings to jump-start the project, meetings to wind down the project, conferences, committees—you get the point. Managers spend 40 to 60 percent of their time sitting around talking to each other.

"It feels like all I do is go to meetings," one insurance executive told us. "The only time I get any real work done is after five, when everyone's gone home."

MARATHON MEETINGS AND COLOSSAL CONFERENCES

Then there are the marathon meetings and conferences held out of the office. The conventional wisdom at these events is "The more information, the better." People are stuck in their seats from 8 A.M. to at least 5 P.M. listening to sales managers, marketing directors, CEOs, COOs, CFOs, and CIOs with all sorts of charts, overheads, and videos. A motivational speaker to pump up the troops is usually part of the dog-and-pony show.

After cocktails and dinner, another speaker. By this time the group is so totally brain-dead that they couldn't distinguish Jack Welch from Raquel.

And that's just the first day. Ten hours later it starts all over again with a schedule that makes Parris Island look like Club Med. By the end, participants' eyes are glazed and their minds numb from all the information, most of which goes in one ear and out the other.

FROM HERE TO ETERNITY

Remember Milton Berle's classic line about committees? "They keep the minutes and lose the hours." One of the reasons that meetings often take so long is that decisions are made by consensus. Consensus is great in theory but in practice it often results in endless meetings, conversations, and committees before everyone gets on board.

Time is the currency of the nineties, and *consensus takes forever.* Long meetings are costly and take employees away from billable and client-servicing activities. These days decisions must be made quickly and decisively. Trying to get everyone on board is a time-consuming luxury many businesses can't afford.

Big Blue in the red. In his scathing book *Big Blues: The Unmasking of IBM, Wall Street Journal* reporter Paul Carroll says that at least one important reason for IBM's fall was its insistence on consensus. Any time an employee "nonconcurred," to use IBM's tortured lingo, the decision got kicked upstairs to yet another meeting.

"Nonconcurrence" was also a problem for Digital Equipment, the nation's second largest computer maker, which is now struggling to reverse the billion-dollar losses of the last few years. Digital called its brand of consensus "matrix management."

Matrix management was a corporate policy that required consensus decision-making. It meant interminable meetings, decision delays while tracking down input from someone in engineering, marketing, sales, or manufacturing. It also meant that Digital could not respond quickly or flexibly to new circumstances in an industry known for overnight changes. Matrix management is good alliteration but bad business practice, according to Digital president Robert B. Palmer, who pronounced the matrix idea dead in 1994.[1]

Organizations that thrive on change find decision by committee to be anathema. In PepsiCo's freewheeling culture a committee is defined as a "dark alley down which ideas are led . . . and then strangled."[2]

MEETING COW

LOWEST COMMON DENOMINATOR

To get out of all those interminably long, synapse-dulling "time wasters," many people will compromise their best ideas to reach quick agreement. And who can blame them? They're already tired and antsy. Getting out of there, even with an uninspired solution, is preferable to a drawn-out struggle to achieve a breakthrough idea. Especially when you've got two more meetings that day.

When priority is on getting back to your desk, not on reaching the best solution, the quality of thinking suffers and you get watered-down potato soup rather than nouvelle cuisine.

Bill Gates's numbering system. Before his astronomic rise, when Bill Gates was just a fledgling computer hacker, he worked with IBM executive James Cannavino to create an operating system for the company's new PC. Apparently, Cannavino was as fond of talk-

ing as he was of meetings, and he would spend a significant part of each encounter making small talk and droning on about IBM's values.

This would drive Gates crazy. He imagined himself telling Cannavino that instead of going on about IBM's great customer service he should just designate it Number 13, and call out the number so Gates would know it was time for the spiel.

"And for every one of those gibberish slogans, we can also get little numbers," Gates would imagine himself saying. "There are a lot of little integers available. We'll just tighten these meetings up. You know, Cannavino, if you want to talk about how you're going to save the U.S. educational system, okay, we've heard that story. That's a good fifteen-minute one. That can be number eleven."[3]

TIME LIMITS AND VERTICAL REQUIREMENTS

Gates isn't the only one who hates nonproductive meetings. Most people identify them as a problem but don't know how to put this sacred cow to pasture.

We asked one of our clients about the effectiveness of its weekly 1½-hour staff meeting. Participants usually came late and spent a lot of time schmoozing in the halls. Most felt restless after about forty-

CONSENSUS COW

five minutes, and everyone admitted that productivity and clarity slipped markedly after this point.

We suggested an obvious solution: forty-five-minute meetings. After serious objection from the manager, who was convinced he'd never get through the full agenda, they tested the idea. It worked fabulously. People came on time, stopped the premeeting chitchat, and kept closer to the agenda. Everyone agreed they got more done in forty-five minutes than in an hour and a half.

Meetings are a lot like the hot air they produce: They'll expand or contract to fill the space available. If you're scheduled for an hour and a half, people will fill up that time. Shorten the meeting and generally the same amount of work gets done.

Vertical Meetings

Companies like Corning Glass, Equitable Life Assurance, and Johnson & Johnson noticed that people got too comfortable in meetings and they were going on too long. So they removed the chairs! Everyone had to stand up. The average time of those *vertical* meetings was cut drastically. So were the number of meetings.

Meeting Meters

The meeting mess has gotten so bleak that someone's actually started an organization to deal with it. At Bernie DeKoven's Institute for Better Meetings in Palo Alto, California, they devote themselves to creating technologies that make meetings more efficient.

Among other things, the institute has developed the software for a "meeting meter" that measures the actual cost of a meeting based on participants' salaries, room and equipment rentals, plus miscellaneous expenses. It looks like a taxi meter and can even make the same clicking noises as the dollars run up. The number crunchers in the backroom love it! An extra option: When a meeting's costs exceed what it figures to produce, a buzzer goes off. Using that device, DeKoven reports some of the shortest meetings in history.

One company used the meter to see how much time people spent *waiting* for everyone to show up. They found that meeting delays increased costs by about 15 percent.

Sometimes the savings are even greater. An international consulting company estimated that its weekly video conference, attended by all partners at all offices, cost $6,500 per minute, or over $1.5 million per month. Needless to say, those meetings are less long winded these days. Says DeKoven, "The 'meeting meter' is a conversation piece. It's a silly device growing out of a serious premise: helping people to start thinking about the value of meetings."[4]

NOTES ON THE BIG SCREEN

Another technique for improving meetings is to use a technographer to type notes on a computer attached to a big screen. By regularly making sure participants agree with the notes, the technographer keeps everyone focused on what has been done, and a sense of collaboration emerges.

DeKoven points to a meeting he conducted for Time Warner and Sega. "Traditionally it would have been a high-anxiety dog-and-pony show." But with everyone watching and commenting on the screen, the adversarial attitude disappeared. And when the meeting ended participants got an immediate printout of what had occurred. They knew right away if they'd just wasted an afternoon.[5]

Change-Ready Thinking

Halve your meeting time and double your productivity.

Four

The Speed Cow

Remember the White Rabbit in *Alice's Adventures in Wonderland*? He was always racing here and there, jabbering nonstop about how late he was. Well, it's the roaring nineties and we've all become White Rabbits, dashing around, trying to do more in less time. *Only this is no fairy tale.*

These days we walk fast, talk fast, drive fast, think fast, even diet fast. Time is at a premium, and most of us are afflicted with hurry sickness.

Yet despite the scrambling, we're always a little behind and forced to play an unrelenting game of catch-up.

SPEED TRAP

The high-speed gear is really a high-speed trap. When you've got the pedal to the metal all the time, you catch the "gottas"—the latest stress disease:

- I gotta make the deadline.
- I gotta prepare for the meeting.
- I gotta make my quota.
- I gotta read this, write that, review something else.
- I gotta check my voice mail, E-mail, real mail.
- I gotta make calls, check overheads, prepare the presentation.
- I gotta fix this, fax that, finish both.
- I gotta pick up the kids, do the shopping, make dinner.

SPEED COW

- I gotta make this traffic light.
- I gotta _____ (You fill it in.)

A lifestyle study of over 5,000 people found that 90 percent were stuck in the speed trap. The other 10 percent were probably lying or working for the government.

HIDDEN COST

Not surprisingly, living in the fast lane produces enormous stress, which eventually affects health and productivity. Stress-related health-insurance claims by white-collar workers soared 700 percent in the eighties. Still, many people seem willing to pay the price.

Disabilities and accidents caused by stress due to speedups have already cost U.S. industry $100 billion a year, says Richard Riordan in his highly acclaimed book *Stress and Strategies for a Lifestyle Management.*[1]

But there are also hidden and more far reaching costs. Stress is residual and builds up during the day. It doesn't suddenly disappear when you walk in the front door and kick off your shoes. You can't work like a lion or lioness, rushing and roaring all day, and suddenly transform yourself into a soft, caring, and sensitive parent or spouse. You're more likely to bite your dog, snap at your kid, and growl at your partner. Stress is not only harmful to your health, it's also bad for your relationships. Is it any wonder the divorce rate runs around 50 percent?

QUALITY NOSEDIVES

And there is an additional twist. The reason we're racing along at this dangerous clip is to increase our productivity and profits. Yet exactly the opposite happens.

One of the most critically important business issues of the last decade is quality. Nothing less than the best is expected and accepted. "Good enough" isn't. Programs like TQM (Total Quality Management) are as popular as Elvis T-shirts at Graceland.

But what happens to quality when you're in a hurry? You make more mistakes . . . dumb ones, careless ones. Racing to get to a meeting, you leave some notes in your office. Pushing to finish a proposal, you write the numbers in the wrong columns. Or you quote from the old price list, forget to write a meeting on your calendar, spell the client's name wrong, or, worse, send some important message to the wrong person. It's not that these tasks take any brainpower. It's just that when you're rushing you get sloppy. And there's no time to double-check your work.

At a rehearsal for a major sales conference, the director of marketing realized that in his rush to get everything done in time, he'd brought the wrong set of slides. Sound familiar? Panicking, he called his secretary and told her to send the right ones no matter the cost. He got them . . . $350 later. These kinds of errors may not seem costly, but they quickly add up.

Beer bust. Small mistakes have a way of producing big ramifications. During a major campaign to reduce costs at a national brewery, an engineer figured out how to cut in half the time it took to brew a batch of beer—a major cost savings. Everyone was excited!

So they hoisted it up the flagpole to see if any of the other departments might shoot it down. None did. The new product got universal head nods. Next step: an expensive promotion campaign. Management saw the chance to outflank the competition in the rough-and-tough beer wars.

Shipments were rushed to market as the huge ad campaign broke. In-store displays touted the beer's quality at an affordable price. People responded initially by buying the stuff in droves. It was only then that the company realized that in its haste to get to market, it forgot to do one simple thing: *taste it!* Had they taken the time to sit down and down a few, maybe they wouldn't have been in such a rush.

Overcooked shrimp and chewy rice. General Mills also moved too fast in its ambitious efforts to establish the first nationwide chain of sit-down Chinese restaurants. China Coast, which first appeared in Indianapolis, bore all the telltale signs of the speed trap. The iced tea was cloudy, pan-fried dumplings arrived without the sauce, the shrimp was overcooked, and the steamed rice was chewy. Even the bill was wrong.[2] "It's a direct result of expanding too fast and having our operations weak," says Joe R. Lee, vice chairman at the Minneapolis-based company, which also owns the Red Lobster and Olive Garden chains. "We expanded China Coast four to five times faster than we'd done with Olive Garden. . . . We were trying to build on our expertise." But moving too fast also means disorganization and sloppy preparation. "We didn't put enough effort into the training," admits Lee.[3]

SERVICE SUFFERS

Whether we admit it or not, we're all in the service business and most of us have two sets of customers: the consumer and the people within our own organization whom we need to sell or satisfy. The way we treat those inside customers influences the way they treat the end user.

There are countless ideas and theories about good service. Consultants make it sound like rocket science, but it's really very simple: Service is about relationships. It's about connecting with human beings—understanding their concerns, challenges, interests, and needs—and offering something of value to assist them.

We were created to be perfect at this, blessed with the right equipment in the right proportions: two eyes, two ears, and *one mouth*.

But when you're in a hurry, it's as if you have nine mouths and no eyes or ears. There's no time to listen and respond. There's no opportunity to clarify, restate, and summarize. Good communication takes time. Building trust takes time. Standing in someone else's shoes takes time.

A hard-driving executive for a national public accounting firm complained to us about how his administrative staff was always making mistakes. "I tell them what to do," he said, "but they never seem to get it right. I'm beginning to think it's intentional. Sometimes I'd rather just do the work myself."

When we interviewed his staff we got another picture. "He's always in a rush," said a secretary. "He throws things at you with almost no explanation. He's impatient and makes you feel his time is too precious to go over tedious directions. Then he expects you to do a perfect job. Well, we're not mind readers. We can't know what he wants. If we make mistakes it's because he hasn't told us what we need to know to do the job."

CREATIVITY AT THE SOURCE

"How many of you do your best thinking and get your most creative ideas at work?" When we ask people in our groups this question, no one ever raises their hand.

Our next question: "In what room in your house do you do your best thinking?" The usual response: the bathroom. Why? No faxes, no phones, no interruptions. No hurrying. Without the time pressure and the interference, the lightbulbs flash and the great ideas just come.

It's hard to think clearly or creatively when you're on the run. There's no time for incubation, contemplation, or even observation. What can you really know of the landscape from a car blasting down the highway at 80 miles an hour? Speed kills:

- Quality
- Service
- Innovation
- You—if you don't watch out

"Slow down! What, are you kidding? I can't afford to slow down. The competition's breathing down my neck." That's the response we get when we suggest easing up on the throttle.

But you'll actually do more and better by learning to slow down when everything around you is speeding up. John Wooden, the great UCLA basketball coach who won an unprecedented 10 national championships, offers this advice: *"Be quick, but don't hurry.* If you hurry you make mistakes."[4]

THE 90 PERCENT SOLUTION

In sports a passionate 90 percent effort is more effective than a panicked 110 percent. And a passionate 90 percent effort will yield 110 percent results.

The rule holds for work, too. The conventional wisdom in selling, for instance, is to make as many calls as you can. Some organizations even evaluate their salespeople based on how many calls they make.

We decided to test that assumption by dividing a group of successful insurance agents into two groups. We told the first group to reduce their calls by 10 percent, while the second was instructed to keep doing business as usual. At the end of three months the group that made fewer calls had more sales—22 percent more.

Why did the 90 percent solution work? The agents told us themselves. They had more time to prepare, they weren't rushed during the call, and they felt more relaxed so they could respond better to the customer's concerns.

We've used variations on this experiment in other situations. We've slowed down production lines in food-processing, steel, and chemical plants all with the same result: decreased waste and downtime; increased productivity and profits.

LESS CAN BE MORE

A stressed-out general manager for a major newspaper told me his system for getting all his work done. He wrote a "to do" list each night and then added two or three things the next morning. "Got to keep raising the bar," he said.

"How's it working?" I asked.

"Lousy!" he replied, "I never finish my list."

I told him about the 90 percent solution and, like most people, he was skeptical but willing to try it. "I'm at the point where I'll try anything," he said.

For the next three weeks he deleted rather than added things from his list. When we next met he told me, "I've noticed three things. First, I'm finishing the list. I expected that because it's shorter. But it still makes me feel better. Second, the quality of my work has really increased because I have more time to spend with the editors. Third, and here's the surprise, not only am I finishing my work but I'm getting to some things I deleted from the list. I'm actually working faster."

No time to think. When a top executive from a high-tech corporation was being shown through Microsoft's offices in Seattle, he spotted somebody with his feet up on his desk, staring dreamily out the window. "If that guy were working for me he'd be out of there in a heartbeat," the exec boasted.

"He's probably doing what we're paying him for," replied the Microsoft manager, *"thinking."*

A full schedule, every minute accounted for, no wasted time—that's the key to success according to the conventional wisdom. But when do you do your thinking? Surely not during all those meetings or when you're putting out fires or sorting through your daily quota of E-mail, voice mail, and faxes.

Check your calendar. The CFO for a major fast-food company told us he'd been embarrassed by a consultant in an unusual way. He was explaining to her how busy he was by showing her his appointment calendar, which had no white space left. Rather than being impressed, she looked at him and asked, "When do you think?"

"I realized," he told me, "that she was right. All I was doing was reacting to what was coming at me—checking the financials for each division, talking to store managers about profitability or investment. I wasn't taking any time to think about how to improve our business or get an edge on the competition. I was like a guy bailing like hell to keep the boat afloat, not realizing he was heading for the rapids."

"Work all day, work all night. Deliver on time, on schedule, and on budget." That was the motto of George Shaheen, the head of Andersen Consulting, whom *Fortune* magazine called the "perpetual motion machine." It's rumored that Shaheen challenged Santa Claus for the most frequent-traveler miles.

"But this dynamic style of management comes out of our hides," says Shaheen. "It's physically demanding." Sometimes, he admits, he needs just to sit in one place and think.

And Shaheen isn't alone. A *Fortune* magazine report found that a majority of effective executives "keep lots and lots of open, unstructured time in their day."[5]

"I schedule unscheduled time," one executive at a manufacturing company told us. "I make sure I have lots of time in my schedule to just wander around the building and talk to people, or I'll take a walk outside, even jump in my car and go for a ride. I need uninterrupted time to think. If I don't I'm just reacting and putting out fires. We won't keep ahead that way."

George Bernard Shaw once said that the average person thinks *once a year* and that his own brilliance came from the fact that he did some thinking *once a week*.

LEARNING TIME

Success doesn't come from how much you *know* but from how well you *learn*. The knowledge base is always changing. Just look at an "old" encyclopedia like my 1960 *World Book*. When I looked up *manufacturing* I found impressive sections on *toolometers* and *automation*. Those words have all but disappeared from the business lexicon. Ever hear anyone talk about the keypunch or the ENIAC?

Acquiring knowledge has become less important than knowing how to find and use the knowledge warehouses. And the ability to learn quickly and well and to *keep* learning throughout life is the key to it all. How can you create a learning organization when everyone's speeding? They may complete a record number of tasks or make an awful lot of telephone calls, but learning—not likely. Learning requires time to reflect, assimilate, and practice. Even the business schools from Harvard to USC are taking this seriously by offering exercises in reflection in their course work.

Research shows that repetitive tasks can be learned and performed quickly but more complex thinking requires the luxury of time. To demonstrate this to fast-lane types, we ask people to read a complex paragraph and answer a series of questions on the material.

Then we do it again with another paragraph, except that this time we impose a tight time limit. Know what happens to learning? It plummets. Less time, less learning.

LEARNING ABOUT YOURSELF

Ever since the publication of Peter Senge's best-selling book *The Fifth Discipline,* cutting-edge managers have started to recognize the importance of self-awareness on the job. Senge's subsequent *Fieldbook* teaches an elaborate series of personal-awareness exercises with names like Dialogue, the Container, and the Ladder of Inference. His point is simple: Changing organizations begins with changing people, and changing people requires personal awareness.

The more you know about yourself, the more you'll understand the ways you limit your effectiveness through self-imposed obstacles, distortions in thinking, and unproductive habits. Information about yourself will also teach you how to make the most of your strengths.

"The most important trait of a good leader is knowing who you are," says George McCracken, CEO of $1.5 billion Silicon Graphics. "You have to do all your homework, but then you have to go with your intuition without letting your mind get in the way." To sharpen his intuition and self-knowledge, McCracken has been meditating daily for decades.[6]

Richard Abdoo, the CEO of Wisconsin Energy, a $1.6 billion utility, sets aside eight hours a week for solitary reflection. He also walks, works in his shop, and rides his Harley. "You have to force yourself to spend some time away from the hustle and bustle of your job," he says. "If you don't spend enough time doing that, you can lose hold of the reins and get into all kinds of trouble."[7]

Mainline companies in all fields like AT&T, PepsiCo, Hoechst Celanese, and Aetna are including various types of introspection training in their management development programs. AT&T devotes roughly one-fifth of its annual executive training budget—$3.5 million—to courses that encourage introspection.[8]

Learning about yourself and your situation is directly related to success, according to the Harvard Business School's John Kotter. "You grab a challenge, act on it, then honestly reflect on why your actions worked or didn't. You learn from it and then move on. That continuous process of lifelong learning helps enormously in a rapidly changing economic environment."[9] You can't learn on the run. You need to get out of the speed trap and give yourself time for discovery.

CALL A TIME-OUT

When things start to get out of control, sports teams call a time-out in order to calm down, gain composure, and think more clearly. Most people do the reverse. They speed up and race around trying to put out fires, usually starting more than they put out.

To help managers slow down, we give them three 10-minute time-out cards with the instruction that all three must be used every day. People take walks down the hall or around the block, listen to music, meditate. Some consolidate their time so they can go for a run.

Ann McGee-Cooper, author of *You Don't Have to Go Home from Work Exhausted,* suggests taking "joy breaks" like calling a loved one, doing a few stretching exercises, or playing a computer game—whatever "floats your boat."[10]

"Fun changes your neurochemistry," says McGee-Cooper. "Most managers think they can't enjoy anything until after their work is done. The trouble is, these days their work is never really done.

"Without any fun in their lives they go into a state of exhaustion and depression. Fun is necessary. It's good for you. It not only helps to get you rejuvenated but it's a right-brain activity that gets creative juices flowing."[11]

Sinking putts and trashy reading. A well-known syndicated columnist told me that when he gets stuck writing, he stops and does something to shift his attention. "I may do some menial task, some trashy reading. It's too bad there are no showers at work; I get some of my best ideas there."

Says a busy broadcast executive, "I'm a golf nut, so when my mind starts to race in all directions I take out my putter, throw a couple of balls on the rug, and practice putting for a couple of minutes. It takes all of my attention to get that damn ball in the cup. That little break relaxes and energizes me."

We also know people who bring their own gym to the office. They'll hit the floor right next to their desks and pop off a few push-ups and abdominal crunches. Some keep barbells in their file cabinets for a quick set of flies or curls.

And of course there are the yoga devotees. They slow down and relax with stretching exercises in the lunchroom or conference room. Any kind of stretching will work as long as it's done slowly, without pressure or speed.

Zen and the art of auto repair. One of the best times to take a break from rushing around is right after work. A bank vice president told us that as soon as she got home she'd go into the kitchen, put on an apron, and *go out to the garage*. That's right, she'd work on her car for about 15 to 20 minutes, cleaning the spark plugs, changing the oil, whatever was needed. It was her meditation.

"I never know if all that tinkering has much effect on the car's performance, but it sure does on mine," she says. "After a few minutes under the hood, I'm more relaxed and calmer. I start becoming more myself instead of that impatient and demanding boss I usually turn into by the end of the day.

"I actually get my best ideas when I'm working on the car. It's a quiet time, and it's easy to reflect on what happened today and what needs to happen tomorrow."

Change-Ready Thinking

Speed kills quality, service, communication, innovation . . . and you.

A passionate 90 percent is more productive than a panicked 110 percent.

Five

The Expert Cow

"The concept is interesting and well formed, but in order to earn better than a 'C,' the idea must be feasible," wrote a Yale University management professor in response to Fred Smith's paper proposing an overnight delivery service. Smith went on to start Federal Express.

"A cookie store is a bad idea. Besides, the market research report says America likes crispy cookies, not soft and chewy cookies like you make," the experts told Debbie Fields, founder of Mrs. Field's Cookies.

"Drill for oil? You mean drill into the ground to try to find oil? You're crazy," people said when Edwin L. Drake came up with the idea in 1859.[1]

So much for the voice of experience. How often do the experts get it wrong? Probably about as often as they get it right.

It's generally assumed that experience is the foundation of wisdom and that experts who've seen and done it all have the special knowledge to lead a company into the future. That might be true in periods of stability, but when environments are in flux, experience can be a major obstacle to change and innovation. If you use yesterday's solutions, strategies, and systems for today's problems you'll be out of business tomorrow. And that's just what experts rely on: the past.

Experts trade in the illusion of knowledge. They think they know the lay of the land, but most of the time they're operating with antiquated maps and charts. They're experts all right, experts in the old paradigms. The fact that they are generally unaware of their limitations can have grave consequences for a company they're hired to help.

EXPERT MISTAKES

Here are some other mistakes the experts made when they relied on the old paradigms to look into the future:

• In 1959 Haloid, a small research firm, offered IBM the sales rights to their "914" paper copier. IBM retained hired gun Arthur D. Little, a major consulting firm, to advise them on the product's potential. After three months of analysis, Little recommended against the acquisition, estimating that the worldwide potential for the plain-paper copier was less than 5,000 units. One of their reasons was the cheap price of carbon paper—how's that for a sacred cow? IBM took the advice and rejected the offer.

Ten years later Haloid—now known as Xerox—was generating over $1 billion in sales annually from their copiers.

• Xerox fell prey to the same type of "expert advice" when its advisers counseled against going into the small-copier business. The Japanese—new to the field—didn't have the benefit of such counsel. They jumped in, and Xerox's share of the copier market fell around 50 percent.

• During the mid-1960s IBM experts, based on their knowledge of existing technology, estimated the worldwide potential for word processors at 6,000 work stations. By 1973 there were 100,000 units in operation and by 1990 there were over 50 million.

• In the mid-1970s Sony engineering executives and market researchers told chairman Akio Morita that they could not sell 10,000 Walkmans because the units did not have recording capability. Morita, one of the great champions of Change-Readiness, ignored their advice and offered to resign if the product was not as successful as he predicted. Within 10 years Sony had sold over 20 million Walkman units.

"I have never had much use for specialists," says Sony founder Masura Ibuka. "They're inclined to argue why you can't do something while our emphasis has always been to make something out of nothing."[2]

BEGINNER'S MIND

The key to keeping ahead in a changing environment is to think not like an expert, but like a beginner.

Beginners ask embarrassing questions. They don't know all the rules and rationales for why things are done. And that's precisely what makes them so valuable. They have open minds and see with the "fresh eyes" of people free of preconceived notions. They notice the obvious, and they don't know that things can't be done. While experts are adept at telling you why something won't work, beginners have the advantage of seeing only possibilities.

Once you've looked at an apple a dozen times, once you've named it an "apple," then the next time you look at it, you're not as likely to see its roundness, its texture, its very "appleness." You've lost the beginner's mind.

The same is true with anything you do. What stands out at the beginning fades to the background with experience. Think of your commute to work every morning. When you first started it, you probably noticed everything—the sights, the sounds, and even the smells. Now it's second nature and you hardly pay attention. You no longer see what's there. You take it for granted.

OUTSIDERS TO THE RESCUE

When IBM, Kodak, ConAgra, GM, Compaq, Allied Signal, Tenneco, Mellon Bank, Goodyear, and Wang needed a new CEO they didn't study their list of succession candidates. They were looking for an outsider, someone who had the advantage of a beginner's mind-set. In fact, almost one third of all the Fortune 500 companies that hired new CEOs in the first nine months of 1993 went outside the organization. That's the highest number in almost 50 years.

These companies understood that when you hire someone from within the organization, you're hiring the past. Insiders, born and bred within the corporate culture, are anything but beginners. They are generally working off the old assumptions and business practices they know so well and have a vested stake in continuing to work that way. After all, those are the things that got them to the top. Though they may preach change, they are usually reluctant to break up the corporate ship. Even former IBM CEO John Akers said, "The only effective agent of change is somebody who doesn't come with all the history and trappings of the enterprise."[3]

You'll find outsiders behind most corporate turnarounds. CEO George Fisher successfully reversed Kodak's slide and posted earnings of $452 million during the first nine months of 1993. Fisher came from Motorola—not exactly the film business. Jack Smith, who scripted GM's $11 billion turnaround, came from the company's European division, not the MoTown Towers. Same with Paul Allaire, who has been revolutionizing Xerox culture. And Jack Welch, who transformed GE, was plucked from plastics, the company's young iconoclastic division.

What is it about outsiders that make them better at change? "One answer," says Harvard Business School professor John Kotter, "is the intuitive ability to continually view problems in fresh ways and to identify ineffective operating practices and traditions."[4] When outsiders see a sacred cow they have no compunctions about putting it out to pasture.

Rookies. "If you are designing something new that is higher priced with lots of features you give it to the rookies," says Kozo

Ohsone, senior managing director of Sony's audio group that developed the Walkman and Discman CD.[5]

Sony looks for people who are *neyaka:* optimistic, open minded, and wide ranging in their interests. The company thinks the best results come from people who have moved around among product groups and like to try their hand at technologies they haven't formally studied.

Changing jobs. Workers develop routines when they do the same job for a while. They lose their edge, falling into habits not just in what they do but in how they think. Habits turn into routines. Routines into ruts. And when people get into ruts, they tend to furnish them—they buy a rug, a couch, or a television set for the office. When that happens innovation ceases and productivity and profits fall way off.

Keystone Ski Resort is known for its great service, but executive vice president John Rutter figured he could make it even better by injecting a beginner's touch into top management. He had his top managers switch jobs. The ski-operations manager took over retail, the head of the ski school took over snowmaking and lift maintenance, and so on.

The result? Chaos. What did you expect? But not in the way you think. It was a positive, creative chaos, a shaking up of the old ways.

The new managers at Keystone brought fresh eyes to their assignments. They saw *problems* that had been covered up inadvertently and *opportunities* that were passing them by.

Since they weren't "experienced," they were forced to rely on their staff for day-to-day operations, and they discovered that their people could handle the new level of responsibility. Great ideas began to emerge from employees who used to just follow orders. And everyone liked the shake-up because empowering people increases morale.

Rutter found that changing jobs widened their perspective, giving them a sense of the larger picture. Gordon Briner, a former pro ski racer who was the head of Keystone's ski school and retail and rental operation, was one of the first of Rutter's top managers to change jobs. His growth was so positive that he got promoted to head of operations at the Breckenridge ski area, one of Keystone's partners.

ASK "STUPID" QUESTIONS

At a tire manufacturing plant, a young man from purchasing happened to walk by the operation that was wrapping tires in paper and foil for shipping. He asked a naive question: "How come we wrap the tires?"

"To prevent the whitewalls from getting scuffed and dirty," said the plant manager, barely hiding his disdain. Maybe the question wasn't so stupid. How many people drive cars with whitewalls? Only about 3 to 5 percent of manufactured tires have stripes. And how thick are those whitewalls? About the width of your fingernail. And the rubber is scuff proof.

Forty years ago, when whitewalls were all the rage, the striping was thick and bold. It was easily roughed up, so there was good reason to wrap the tires. But not anymore. Yet nobody thought to question the practice until an outsider—whose weekly salary wouldn't buy an hour of an expensive consultant's time—happened by. Someone listened to him, and the company saved $22 million.

A major clothing company was manufacturing most of its garments in the Southeast, then shipping them to the company's distribution center on the West Coast, the sight of its corporate headquarters.

Until a neophyte "cow hunter" asked an embarrassing question: "Why are we shipping our garments from the Southeast to the West when most of our major markets are in the East?" Six-figure savings resulted from that question.

John Calley, the CEO of United Artists, started out in the mail room at NBC. Hard work won him a promotion to a nighttime clerical job in which he assisted the people in charge of television scenery.

One day he noticed that scenery was being sent down the warehouse elevator on one dolly and then transferred to another because the first dolly was too big for the elevator in the RCA building. Calley sent a memo to his supervisor pointing this out and suggesting that the company build one dolly that would fit into both elevators.

"Your cat could have figured out that what they were doing was insane," recalls Calley, "but no one thought of it before. The change was made immediately and the savings amounted to several hundreds of thousands of dollars a year."[6]

UNEXPECTED CURES

Expertise does not guarantee success in even a highly scientific field like medicine. In his groundbreaking book on tuberculosis, *The Forgotten Plague,* Frank Ryan notes that almost every significant advance against the disease was made by individuals working in related fields, not specifically in tuberculosis research. In fact, those most *resistant to these new ideas* were the physicians doing mainstream research, the experts once referred to as "TB-popes."

Ryan points out that cures often lie in unexpected places where only beginners might bother to look. For example, isoniazid, a "new" wonder drug for tuberculosis, was actually disovered in Prague by two chemistry graduate students who were not searching for a medical therapy but only looking to satisfy a requirement for their degrees. The year of the discovery: 1912.

A FRESH GAME PLAN

You may not be a beginner, but you can learn how to think like one. Take real estate agent Michael Young, for instance. He was his company's most successful agent in northern California but he couldn't make the leap from selling houses in the $100,000-to-$200,000 range to those around $500,000 and up.

"I don't get it," he said. "I'm using the same prospecting strategies, making calls in the evening to people at home, giving them advice and telling them about the market, and I'm in the same marketplace. But it's not working."

"Think like a beginner, forget your old strategies, start fresh," we advised him. "Look at the business like you're a novice. What can you do to break into this market?"

Instead of competing with other brokers, Young spotted an untapped opportunity in the high-end market. He discovered that many listings expire before the house is sold. So he developed a strategy for buying old listings and sharing commissions. The technique brought in so much business that he formed the Michael Young Company in San Francisco. Now brokers call him unsolicited.

Want to know something? We're all in the same position as Young. You may think your market is the same as it was last year. But it's not. Everything is changing: people's life- and work styles, their jobs, their expectations, their attitudes, their family situations—everything. And technological advances have only accelerated the situation.

With business in a perpetual state of flux, we need to keep reinventing our game plan every six months. To do that we have to look at things through fresh eyes.

BEGINNER'S PRACTICE

One way to practice a beginner's mind-set is to take a simple object like a saucer and imagine you've never seen it before. Now, without any preconceived notions about the object, write down as many uses for it as you can. It's amazing what people come up with. Suggested applications: paperweight, doorstop, sunshade, paper-clip dispenser, hat.

Try it yourself right now. Pick up an object like a pencil and with a beginner's mind think of five uses for it.

Often when I go for a run or a bike ride I pretend it's the first time I'm out on the trail. I'm always amazed at how this perspective enables me to be aware of things I hadn't noticed before: a hawk's nest, a sweet fragrance, the sound of the wind sweeping across the valley.

RESTARTING YOUR JOB

Reengineering, the hot new management tool that aims at redesigning core processes, is essentially based on the beginner's-mind premise. One of its main tools is a blank sheet of paper. It starts at the beginning with such basic questions as, How do the customers want to deal with us? and, What would the company look like if it were created today?

You can restart your business today by asking yourself that last question. What rules and strategies would you use if you were starting fresh? Write down what you know about your goals, the competition, the industry, the customer . . . everything. Include current conditions as well as anything you know or can intuit about the future. Then develop a game plan based on what you've written. Notice what sacred cows keep creeping back.

Change-Ready Thinking

Think like a beginner, not an expert.

Be smart: Ask stupid questions.

Six

The Cash Cow

Been down to the mailbox lately for your Sears catalog? Know anyone who receives fewer than four catalogs a day, mostly from companies they've never heard of, for products they don't want?

Well, these people aren't getting any thick mailings from Sears. The company that practically started the mail-order business and was its leader for years has gone belly-up. Its catalog is available only in the reference room of the local library.

What happened? On the surface Sears had it made. More and more people with less and less time were buying through the mail. But while many new competitors came out with slick formats, targeting specific markets with state-of-the-art products, Sears stuck stubbornly to its old formula—that Webster's dictionary of a catalog selling the same old products, with the same tired format.

And when everyone from Patagonia to Victoria's Secret to NordicTrack was doing all they could to make buying easier—800 numbers, 24-hour service, next-day delivery to your door—Sears didn't even have a toll-free number and you had to go to their warehouse to pick up your order. Playing by the old rules while the game had

CASH COW

changed, the once highly profitable catalog business of Sears became a cash cow whose milk ran out.

CASH COWS GIVE SOUR MILK

Sears is not alone. Many other giants have milked their cash cows dry or run them into the ground. Years ago if you had news that had to get there fast or you really needed to make an impression, the telegram was not *an* option. It was the *only* option. Those undersized yellow forms with their pasted-on phrases were conversation stoppers. They caused more than a few hearts to fibrillate wildly. And that was before the message was read.

Western Union created an industry and made a fortune delivering telegrams. Today, clowns and mimes deliver telegrams to children on their birthdays. When you need to send information fast, you fax it.

Western Union kept milking its cash cow while the telecommunications industry was surging beyond it. Once the leader that defined the industry, it got left behind with a bucketful of sour milk.

Punched out. Everyone knows that IBM made a similar mistake by pushing its mainframe computer long after the PC had eclipsed it in popularity. It cost Big Blue billions. But few remember how years before, IBM nearly forced itself into early retirement with the same mildewed thinking.

Founder Thomas Watson had made the company successful with punch-card technology. When the computer was first developed, Watson tried to keep milking his cash cow by insisting on selling the punch card as an accessory to the new invention. He gave strict orders to his sales force not to sell a computer if it compromised a *single* punch-card order. If it hadn't been for a serendipitous antitrust suit that forced the company out of the punch-card business, they might have continued to rest on their laurels all the way to Chapter 11.

DON'T MESS WITH SUCCESS

Many companies, small entrepreneurs and major corporations alike, get blinded by success. Having found the winning formula, they're apt to keep riding the gravy train. It's perfectly understandable. You've put in all that time and effort discovering what works. Why not reap the rewards for a while? Besides, the winning formula is a sure thing. It's kept your earnings healthy and your shareholders happy. Why take a risk on something new and upset the apple cart?

This kind of thinking made perfect sense in the former USSR and was extremely popular in the Middle Ages—static situations in which tomorrow looked disturbingly like today. But it won't work in a fluid, fickle, fluctuating environment, where change is as constant as a Washington scandal and the apple cart leans precariously over the edge.

In the disk-drive business, for instance, smaller-sized units have typically been introduced by hungrier challengers rather than the reigning leaders who were too busy reaping profits from their previous products. Seagate Technology, the king of 5.25-inch drives, found itself usurped when start-up Connor Peripherals spearheaded the switch to 3.5-inch drives.[1]

"Whom the gods wish to destroy they send 40 years of success," goes the old proverb. And so it is with cash cows. They create blindness toward the future and dullness in the ways we think.

"No currently working business theory will be valid 10 years hence," claims Peter Drucker. "The years ahead will be years of rapid changes—in technology, in markets . . . in consumer behavior, in finance, in political and geographic realities, in economic and trade policies. . . . Almost every large organization will have to rethink its business theory."[2]

BREAK IT BEFORE IT'S BROKE

In a changing marketplace, you can't rest on your laurels. Things are moving so quickly that by the time a new product is introduced, its successor is generally being developed in someone's garage across town, across the country, or across the globe. Our rule of thumb: If a product or an idea has been out in the marketplace for a year, without changes, it's already outdated.

If you don't think it's broke and you don't fix it, you soon won't have anything worth fixing and you *will* go broke.

COMPLACENCY BREEDS FAILURE

It's not just companies that rest on their laurels. Once they're making big bucks, many people tend to get complacent. They stop attending to the basics, lose their hustle, and go on automatic pilot. One salesman told us that when he was just starting out he did a lot of prospecting for new clients and would "prepare, prepare, prepare" for every sales call.

"I'd be up at the crack of dawn calling prospective clients. And before every call I'd review the account, the competition, the market, everything. Then I'd rehearse my presentation and have my answers ready.

"But when I got to six figures I got lazy and stopped doing those things. I figured I could succeed without the extra effort. I stopped preparing and started taking shortcuts. I gave up prospecting and relied on the accounts I already had. All of a sudden my numbers were way down and I didn't know why. At first I thought it was just bad luck or timing. Now I realize I forgot to do what got me there. I have to get back to thinking like a beginner."

Bond's fatal mistake. The same thing happened to Australian Alan Bond at the America's Cup. In 1983 when the Aussies challenged the United States, America had held the cup for 134 years, the most remarkable winning streak in the history of modern sport. To break it, Bond questioned every aspect of boat design, from the keel to the halyards.

From this no-holds-barred approach Bond developed an innovative and revolutionary double-keel design that gave the Aussies a distinct advantage. The result was a major upset: Bond's boat, *Australia III*, beat the U.S. entry in four straight races.

But in preparing for the rematch Bond made a fatal mistake. Forgoing the innovative approach that had developed his winning boat, Bond rested on his laurels and used essentially the same design. He didn't even make the finals.

Rest on your laurels and rest assured they will collapse.

NICHES TURN TO RUTS

Conventional wisdom says the way to succeed is to find your special niche and own the market. Nothing beats that kind of competitve advantage in the short run. But niches quickly turn to ruts, and if you stay in them too long the rut turns into a grave.

Look at some of the great American institutions. Greyhound had its niche. They were king of the road. They *were* the bus business. Remember: "Take the bus and leave the driving to us." Know anyone who has lately?

PIGEONHOLING

Greyhound is a classic victim of niche thinking or "pigeonholing." The company's fatal mistake was in thinking it was in the bus business. So narrow was its vision that the company could not respond quickly to the trend away from bus travel to cars, planes, and light rail. Had they realized that they were really in the transportation or people-moving business, they could have jumped into other vehicles.

Niche thinking has victimized many other institutions that we grew up with, like the telegram, the Pullman car, and the corner drugstore.

And don't forget those dual carbs, the heart of Detroit's high-powered speed machines that roared through quiet residential streets scaring little children and senior citizens. Seen any of those lately? Not unless they're on your '57 Merc or some other antique. The fuel-injection system made them extinct.

Ma Bell is dead. We're not saying there's no value in owning a cash cow or niche. It's a sweet deal, provided you constantly keep your eyes and ears open to the future and are willing to reinvent your company when the time is right.

Look at what AT&T and the Baby Bells are doing. What business would you say they're in? If you answered the phone business, you either work for MCI or you've been living in a cave in darkest Peru.

Forced out of their rut by the FCC, these previously soft-bellied monopolies are inventing a new industry every day. They've widened their niche from phone calls to telecommunications—merging with satellite, entertainment, education, and computer companies to build the information superhighway. The range of possibilities before them is almost limitless. In fact, you could say their cash cow is beginning to give what looks a lot like heavy cream.

Wouldn't this kind of reinvention have been a natural for Western Union if they'd been willing to give up their safe, comfortable niche? A Change-Ready organization like AT&T knows that you can't fly like an eagle if you're viewing the world from a pigeonhole.

A shopping center on skates. Professional sports is another industry moving out of its rut. Not that long ago, a sports stadium was a place you went to watch a ball game, have a hot dog and a beer, and let off a little steam.

Now sports is almost incidental to these arenas. The Toronto Superdome is like a giant mall with a first-class hotel, restaurants, and dozens of retail stores. You can watch the ball game from your hotel room or trendy restaurant, maybe even from the checkout line in one of the stores.

To call Chicago's spanking new Comiskey Park a stadium is a misnomer. There are 85 private suites accessible by elevator, with catering and concierge services. They also have a two-level club restaurant designed to accommodate even the busiest executive. It includes private phone booths, faxes, and much more. And a few days a week they even play ball there.

Many sports facilities now view themselves as entertainment companies. This affects what they do and how they serve the fan or, we should say, consumer. Richard Evans, CEO of Madison Square Garden, which owns the New York Knicks and Rangers, defines his business as producing live entertainment and putting people in seats to view it. With this in mind, his company presents 420 *non*sports events a year.

Even losers are winners. It doesn't even matter if your team wins or loses. Sports franchises have so broadened their game that if they can't win on the field, they can at the retail counter. Big money comes from snappy logos and cool colors. You don't have to go to the ballpark to see the logo. It's on hats, T-shirts, jackets—practically everything you wear except a tuxedo.

The new NFL team in Charlotte, North Carolina, started cranking out snarling Panthers T-shirts right after they got the franchise, printing 120,000 in the first 26 hours. They sold them about as fast as they could make them. And their first game was still more than two years away.[3]

The hockey team with the second largest clothing sales is a relatively new franchise, the San Jose Sharks. And now there's Anaheim's Mighty Ducks owned by—who else?—Disney, with a Disney-type logo that may soon be outselling Mickey Mouse.

KEEPING THE MILK FLOWING

Other examples of companies that have broadened their niches to keep their cash cows giving sweet milk:

- Hallmark is no longer exclusively in the greeting-card business. Redefining themselves as a provider of products to enhance human relationships, they sell gifts, gift wrapping, stationery, computerized greetings, and party paraphernalia.
- Many supermarkets have undergone a metamorphosis from food stores to megamarkets. One Kroger emporium apprentices chefs from a nearby culinary school to whip up delicacies for customers. While they wait they can also have a cappuccino at the espresso bar or take advantage of the in-store post office, fax machine, parcel-shipping center, or two-story bank with its own commercial loan department. There's also a mall-style food court that includes a Japanese restaurant and sushi bar.[4]
- Zoos are widening their cages by holding corporate meetings, weddings, cocktail parties, banquets, and conventions right on the premises. Think of enjoying a power lunch next to the tiger cage or making a deal while watching a seal.
- Cities are broadening their boundaries. San Diego has opened gift shops selling not only souvenir T-shirts but also such surplus city

property as parking meters, fire-fighter boots, hydrants, and signs like the one for a former "clothing optional beach."[5]

• Magazines are moving out of publishing and into information and entertainment. "We have to redefine our publications and think of them not as publishing but as a resource," says John Beni, senior vice president and general manager of *Variety.*[6] Many business magazines, including *Fortune* and *Success,* conduct seminars and sell training videos.

• Canadian banks are no longer just bankers. Since deregulation they are in the financial-services industry, controlling much of Canada's securities, trust, and mutual-fund industries. And last year they got the right to underwrite insurance. Next step: selling it.[7]

Sloane's super human service station. While speaking at the International Car Wash Association I met Devin Sloane, who owned a car wash but wasn't in the car-wash business. Recognizing that car washing had become a rut, especially in southern California, Sloan decided to broaden his niche.

"I realized that I was really in the auto-service business," he told me, "so I added some gas pumps and eventually a Jiffy Lube to service cars more completely."

But he wasn't finished yet. He installed an automobile-accessories shop and even began selling and installing car phones. And since people were waiting, Sloan realized he could service them, not just their cars. His "human service station" now has a deli, yogurt bar, and a small grocery-convenience store.

Stay tuned for the next installment: Sloane's bought the adjoining acre lot. And none of this would have happened if he'd stayed in his comfortable car-wash niche.

USING SUCCESS AS A CATAPULT

PepsiCo is an example of a company with successful "cash cow" brands in both soft drinks and chips that doesn't milk them dry.

"Some might argue that we should not tamper with these brands in either image or substance," says chairman Wayne Calloway. "We don't agree. We know that in a fast-paced world, today's popular brand could be tomorrow's trivia question."[8]

Case in point: their Doritos brand, the country's biggest-selling snack food. Sales and overall volume are up and the chips have been gaining in market share. Why fix what isn't broke, right? Wrong!

Pepsi is spending $50 million to jazz up the corn chip. Echoing Calloway's thinking, Brock Leach, vice president of brand marketing at PepsiCo's Frito-Lay division, says, "We aren't trying to correct a problem, but to *accelerate the growth* of our biggest brand. We're trying to make it harder for other companies to compete against us."[9]

Change-Ready organizations like Pepsi use success as a springboard to catapult them to even greater heights.

EATING YOUR OWN LUNCH

Tough competitors eat the competition's lunch. Change-Ready competitors eat their own lunch before someone else does. In other words, you've got to cannibalize your own products to stay ahead.

Hewlett-Packard knows this. It dominated the laser-printer business throughout the eighties, but that didn't stop it from developing and selling ink-jet printers, which are less expensive. Now the company sells more ink-jets than lasers.

Manufacturers of sporting equipment don't leave well enough alone, either. In skiing, for instance, every season sees innovation and redesign in ski materials, bindings, and boot structure. Even the poles are rethought with form and function in mind.

Some of this redesigning is just gimickry, of course. How many features can you put on a 12-inch sneaker? But the overall impact is better and safer equipment for the consumer and higher profits for the manufacturer.

To widen your own niche, do a careful analysis of your company's competitive advantage and core competencies and ask how those same skills could be applied in a broader context. A company that sells mortgages, for example, might naturally extend itself into general financial services.

Redefine what you do in the most general of terms. If you sell lampshades, think of yourself as being in the lighting business. If you make pencils, you're in communications. A broader definition gives you new ideas about how you can expand into other areas, moving you from carburetors to fuel systems, from sports stadiums to entertainment centers, from car washes to human service stations.

Another way to get out of your sandbox is to look at what you do from the customers' angle. Don't describe yourself based on the product you sell or the service you provide. Define yourself by the customers' perception of what they are buying. That takes you from telegrams to instant communication, from buses to travel, from food markets to convenience shopping.

NEVER BE SATISFIED

When asked by a reporter if he was satisfied with his accomplishments, five-time batting champion and future Hall of Famer Tony Gwynn replied, "No. I'm happy and proud of what I have done. But I'm not satisfied. The minute you're satisfied with where you are, you aren't there anymore."

Not bad advice for players in any game.

Change-Ready Thinking

Keep milking your cash cows and they'll run dry.

Broaden your niche before it turns into a rut.

Break it before it's broke.

Seven

The Competitive Cow

LEAPFROGGING AND COPYCATS

Remember Rose Ruiz? She was the woman who came in first in the New York City Marathon several years ago. Until it was discovered that her speed wasn't a result of great training or her superlight Nikes, but the New York City subway system. Although she got disqualified we think Rosie was on to something.

Don't get us wrong. We're not saying you should cheat or do anything illegal. We *are* saying don't play by conventional rules, change them. Tilt the playing field in your favor. Whether you're in software, hardware, or underwear, head-to-head competition won't get you where you want to go. Every time you improve your product or service, your competition will copy and eventually "one-up" you.

You can't outcompete the competition. If you come out with a

3-year 30,000-mile warranty they'll leapfrog you with 5 years and 50,000 miles. If you've got free checking and quarterly statements they'll put the customer's photo on the check and send out a monthly accounting. If you're open 24 hours they'll stay open 25. And on and on.

The problem with competing on a level playing field is that no one ever really gets the edge. You might get ahead for a minute or two, but that's only temporary. Like the cola wars between Coke and Pepsi, you'll be locked in a battle in which you can't gain a clear advantage.

Ultimately the only thing you'll get from head-to-head competition is a headache. The only way to take a real lead is to change the way you play the game. The level playing field is a sacred cow. To gain competitive advantage, we need to rethink the rules of the game and tilt the field in our direction.

COMPETITIVE COW

Of course, even if you change the rules to gain an advantage, the competition will eventually catch up with you. The trick is to tilt the field continually so that when your opposition is pulling even you're changing the game again.

TILTING ATHLETES WIN GOLD

As a sports psychologist working with many Olympic athletes and teams, I noticed that many of the big breakthroughs came when athletes challenged the old "rules":

• Dick Fosbury led with his head when everyone else was jumping feetfirst and won the high-jump gold medal in 1968 at Mexico City. Now the ridiculed "Fosbury flop" is the standard for world-class high-jumpers.

• Sonja Henie introduced ballet to figure skating. While the competition was doing figure eights, she "pirouetted and arabesqued" her way to a gold medal in the 1932 Olympics at Lake Placid.

• Stein Eriksen made quick, tight little turns with his shoulders forward and his skis together while everyone else was making wide, round turns with their skis apart for balance. His technique, the experts said, defied all the rules, including gravity. But it won him a gold and a bronze at the 1952 winter games in Oslo.

• Bill Walsh: Other professional football coaches used the run to set up the pass, but 49er coach Walsh turned convention on its head: He used short passes to set up the run. And he passed to people who traditionally never caught the ball—tight ends, running backs, even tackles. Walsh's strategy brought him three Super Bowl championships.

• Jean Vuarnet: Most downhillers raced with woolly, wind-catching sweaters but Vuarnet poured his body into a sleek one-piece stretch suit. And while the other guys recklessly swooped down the slopes, their down jackets whipping in the breeze like luffing sails, Vuarnet crouched as low as possible, skimming over the course in an "egg" position at the Squaw Valley Olympics. You guessed it: He won the gold medal.

Vuarnet also broke the rules in another area. He developed a whole new concept in sunglasses, combining fashion with function. As with his skiing style, he went beyond conventional approaches to earn another kind of gold.

RULE #10

Ever since the first caveman started selling clubs, the first and only rule in retail has been location, location, location. So where did the king of retail, Sam Walton, open up his first big warehouse store? Bentonville, Arkansas, whose total population couldn't fill up one of those megamalls.

Walton had 10 rules of success, most of which revolve around giving great service, top-quality products, and treating your people right. But it's his 10th rule that sets him apart from his competitors. Walton called it the most important one: *Break the rules.*

If all of your competitors are doing it one way, Mr. Sam used to say, "do it exactly the opposite," and that's where you'll get the edge.

More dough. Throughout the eighties, Domino's was the king of pizza, with over 90 percent of the growth in that market. The reason? They gave the rules, not the pizza, an extra flip. While their competitors were doing everything to get you into their restaurants, Domino's went the other way.

They realized that convenience was as important as crust. Since working families have no time to cook, they brought the restaurant to the customers. And they did it in less than 30 minutes.

Motel mogul. "Don't bother with little motels. You'll lose your shirt." That's conventional wisdom in the motel business. The formula for success has always been to build facilities with at least 100 rooms and only around big cities, so you can charge high rates.

At least that *was* the formula before Gary Tharaldson came along. Tharaldson became the largest motel developer in the country by changing the game. He builds small, family-oriented motels in small towns where no other motelier dares to go.

And he dominates the market by owning franchises that are in motel chains. In Topeka, for example, he owns the Comfort Inn,

Days Inn, and Fairfield Inn. The advantages of this contrarian strategy are that instead of building a bigger motel, he can construct two smaller ones—a Comfort Inn and a Fairfield Inn, say—and benefit from two different market niches and two national reservation systems.[1]

Court coach. Call most lawyers on the phone and you can hear the "clock" ticking. Every sentence, every silence, every cough, is costing plenty. Barbara Shea is a lawyer who measures her success the opposite way: by how *few* rather than how many hours she bills.

Shea teaches nonlawyers how to handle much of their legal work themselves. They get the benefits of hiring a lawyer but can save on a myriad of details they can do themselves. Shea's three-year-old service is called Court Coach. Although she reviews every document and gives legal advice, much of the time-consuming drudgery like photocopying or filing court papers is done by the client.

When Robert Matulonis retained Shea to help him in a fee dispute, the case had been dragging on for two years. After she reviewed the situation and gave him advice, Matulonis drafted most of the correspondence and filed the court order. Shea oversaw his efforts. When the case was settled, Matulonis estimated he saved about $5,000 using his Court Coach.[2]

Services like Shea's give lawyers a chance to compete with lower-priced paralegal services and legal how-to books, which have been proliferating due to growing legal fees.

"More and more entrepreneurial lawyers are going to see there is a huge market in serving people who can't pay for soup-to-nuts representation and don't need it," says S. Determan, chairwoman of the American Bar Association's committee on alternative legal services.[3]

Swiss sneakers. Have you seen the latest in athletic footwear: running shoes with lights, sneakers cushioned with liquid, pumps to increase traction? Soon they'll invent a shoe that'll run and jump for you. And they're all being hyped by His Airness, the Shaq, Grandma Johnson, and other seven-foot NBA stars with seven-figure endorsement contracts from Nike and Reebok, two companies who own the store.

The teenage market for these shoes is as fast moving and shifty as Michael Jordan running downcourt. By the time a company has worked out the bugs in one model, it's releasing another with some new innovation. The average life span for a model is about four months.

Realizing he couldn't compete on a level playing field with these megabuck giants, Steve Nichols changed the game. He bought K-Swiss sneaker company and decided to offer basic, "classic"—read "boring"—sneakers to the other market: mature weekend athletes and tennis enthusiasts.

Further changing the rules, Nichols said no to retailers who asked for the usual discounts and hype promotions so typical of the industry. "Impossible," everyone said. "Those big guys will swallow you whole and spit you out for lunch."

But Nichols persisted, and soon K-Swiss was the number-three tennis sneaker, winning quality awards from retailers. Nichols is now moving K-Swiss into "classic" versions of hiking and mountain footwear, the fastest-growing segment of the shoe market. And he's going to Europe, where the company expects runaway growth in the next few years.

Nichols already has one big fan in Europe. On his last visit to the U.S. Pope John Paul II bought a pair. The pope may start a fashion trend. Can you imagine thousands of gentle old priests walking around their churches, tennis sneakers under their robes? Nichols's shoes may be basic and boring, but his strategy is bold. It's turned around K-Swiss revenues from only $20 million in 1986 to $150 million in 1993.[4]

No Barbies, thank you. Pleasant Rowland, a writer of primary-school reading books, had the same realization as Nichols: You can't compete head to head with giants. You need to go around them. And you go outside the lines.

While shopping for dolls with her nieces, all she could find were Barbies or Barbie look-alikes. There were astronauts, doctors, ballerinas, and businesswomen, it was true, and they came in different skin colors and ethnicities, but they were still Barbies with the pinupgirl looks and the vacant stares. Rowland figured she could create an alternative that would give young girls a different kind of role model and a history lesson at the same time. She created the Pleasant Company to make dolls that taught kids about American history, family values, and self-reliance.

Each of her dolls represents a different era in American history. Samantha Parkington fights for women's suffrage, Addy Walker escapes from slavery, Kirsten Larson builds a life on the frontier. And each comes with accurate replicas of clothes, furniture, and memorabilia such as the June 6, 1944, *Chicago Daily Tribune* headlined ALLIES INVADE FRANCE made for Molly McIntire, the 1940s doll.

The dolls even have their own series of novels in which the heroines go on adventures and deal with moral dilemmas. Felicity Merriman, a Colonial girl, has to decide whether to go to a tea party at the governor's house while her father fights King George III's tea tax— a little different from Barbie trying to figure out which pair of heels goes best with her chiffon dress.

Another way Pleasant Company changed the game: They sell their dolls through mail order. They cost more than Barbie, too, but Rowland gambled that parents would pay more for a doll that was both fun and educational. Pleasant's sales aren't anything near Mattel's billion-dollar Barbie, but at a little over $100 million we'd say her heroines are doing heroically.[5]

Venice goes native. Towering atriums, dizzying glass elevators with outdoor views, elaborate lobbies with dazzling marble and brass, artwork that looks like it came from a heist of the Louvre. Sounds like an Arabian prince's pleasure palace. Not really. It's just the big hotel chains' answer to the question of how to keep their rooms occupied. The trend in the eighties was to build them lavishly, like Hyatt's Hawaiian Resort on the big island where you take a boat to your room. It's Venice gone native.

William Kimpton didn't have the capital to compete with that, but he had a "Fosburian" idea that gave him an advantage. Forgetting the lavish lobbies and fabulous fountains, he started buying small, older buildings in downtown San Francisco at bargain prices and developing an intimate, European-style atmosphere in each.

No banquet facilities and seventh-floor swimming pools that most people never used. "We check you in, carry your bags to your room, and make sure it's quiet," Kimpton says. "We sell sleep."[6]

And rather than offering typically mediocre eateries off the lobby, Kimpton has linked his small hotels to critically acclaimed restaurants featuring celebrity chefs. Some of his B&D (bed and dinner) combinations include Wolfgang Puck's Postrio in the Prescott Hotel and Masa's, the internationally known French restaurant at the Vintage Court Hotel.

Kimpton's company operates 18 hotels and 212 restaurants. In San Francisco alone it controls over 2,000 rooms—more than any other hotelier except Hyatt, which owns four hotels.

Change-Ready Thinking

Tilt the playing field in your direction.

Don't play by someone else's rules. Make your own.

Head-to-head competition will give you a headache.

Eight

The Customer Cow

Recently I went out to buy a new car, but I got talked out of it—*by the salesperson!* What I was looking for was a reliable four-wheel-drive vehicle stable enough to handle the tortuous ocean road to my house, and I'd narrowed the choice down to two makes of cars.

When the salesperson at the dealership heard what I needed, he walked me over to a formidable-looking 4-x-4, which he proceeded to drive *backward* six steps off a concrete platform. A neat trick for a monster truck competition, maybe, but not exactly the kind of demonstration that would impress me. I was especially suspicious of the car's extrahigh tires and elevated suspension. It didn't look too stable on curves. Did this guy know something I didn't?

Not exactly. When we tried it out on a country road, it rocked and rolled so much that I didn't need an airbag; I needed an airsickness bag.

Realizing that I was experiencing a failure to communicate, or, more precisely, a failure to get my communication heard, I retreated to the next dealership. Here things seemed much better. Right off, I relaxed and settled down because the salesperson smiled and nodded his head at all the right moments.

He's paying attention, I thought, although I got a little suspicious when a few minutes after telling him I lived off a winding road in Muir Beach he asked me if I was from San Rafael.

Then he took me for a test drive on the freeway—which has about

CUSTOMER COW

as many curves as a ruler—all the while rambling on about how the car was loaded with extras like lumbar-support seats, CD player, and tilt steering wheel.

The coup de grace? He cornered me in his office and whispered, "Look, you're probably a lot like me and want to save a buck. I can give you *the deal of the year* if you buy now because they have a sales contest on."

Great! Here's a guy who hadn't listened to a thing I said, wasted my time, and ignored my needs, and he expected me to help him win a sales contest. Who trains these guys, the Don Rickles Institute for Sensitivity Training?

Okay, you say, it's not news that you need to listen to the customer. We all know that in a competitive marketplace, customers are not only kings but dictators. They don't want to choose from what you have to offer. They want to tell you what they want, when they want it, how they want it, and at what price they want it. And they expect to get it, either from you or from someone else.

And you'd better smile when you give it to them.

CUSTOMER PEDDLER

Satisfying the customer isn't rocket science and it's certainly not innovative. It's been a hallmark of successful business throughout the ages.

In Russia and Eastern Europe, poor agrarian villages had customer peddlers, men who traveled to the markets, buying supplies for those who worked such long hours farming that they had no time to shop. Eastern European immigrants to the United States continued this custom. Customer peddlers could be found in every ethnic neighborhood where people working two or three jobs couldn't get to the market. And they didn't just stick to the big cities. They roamed the country from the mountain regions of West Virginia, Kentucky, and Tennessee to isolated areas of Montana and Wyoming.

These humble entrepreneurs had their priorities in order. In the term *customer peddler,* the *customer* comes first. To survive they had to listen. Bring someone a pound of potatoes when they asked for tomatoes and you'd soon be on the bread line.

CUSTOMER SATISFACTION—HO HUM—SO WHAT'S NEW?

But in this business environment, *satisfy the customer* is a sacred cow. Even most car dealers are doing that. Sales managers and store managers everywhere are imploring their people to put the customer first. But they're all playing catch-up. In the new world of commerce, *satisfying* is only the beginning.

"We decided 'satisfaction' was just business as usual," says Skip LeFauve, CEO of Saturn Automobiles, which boasts one of the highest customer-approval rates in the industry.[1]

They believe in delighting the customer and they do so in many ways, from cheering people when they take delivery on their new car to giant barbecues at the Tennessee factory for anyone who's ever bought a Saturn.

At Northstar Ski Resort they also believe in delighting the customer. When management noticed tired skiers waiting in the cold at bus stops for transportation back to their condos, they began serving free hot chocolate. And anyone arriving after the parking lot is full gets a free lift ticket for another day.

Surprise, surprise. I finally did buy a 4-x-4, but from another dealership. When I called to schedule a 5,000-mile service, here's what I heard: "Wednesday morning, eight-thirty A.M., and we'll pick it up at your house and drop off a loaner."

"Pick it up!" I couldn't believe it.

That meant I didn't have to drive to the dealer, stand on line for 30 minutes, and arrange for a ride to work. And then do it all over again at the end of the day. I figured I'd save close to two hours, not to mention all the hassles. All this for a modest rental fee.

I was so delighted with the service that I called the general manager who had instituted the policy. He was new on the job and he told me, "I've been trying to get the edge by focusing on value—the quality of our cars, superior service, and good prices.

"But what I realized is that so are the other dealers. Everyone's doing and saying the same thing, and as a result no one really has an edge.

"So I started putting myself in my customers' shoes. What would make a difference to them? One morning I wandered into the service bay. It was like a loony bin. People were rushing around, talking impatiently on their car phones, sending and receiving faxes. Tempers were short and it was only eight in the morning.

"It hit me that maybe I could do something about the mess and make it easy for my guys too. I started out offering economy loaners at our cost. Then we upgraded to more expensive models because everyone enjoys driving a luxurious new car. We got the idea of salespeople delivering cars at day's end, and it's not coincidental that they carry the customer's leasing information along with the car keys."

My dealer made it so easy to service my car that when it came time to buy another I didn't even look anywhere else. Maybe I would have saved a few bucks shopping around, but here I had a ready-made relationship.

Other customers must feel the same way because my dealership has become the largest on the West Coast. And now everyone is copying their ideas. Chevrolet even has a customer-enthusiasm officer responsible for better serving the needs of its buyers.

Unlike his competition, my dealer understood that time and convenience were as precious to me as getting the job done well. He didn't only give people what they wanted, he gave them something they didn't expect.

So don't satisfy customers; everyone does that. Surprise them. Give them something they don't expect.

GAMBLING ON MARKET RESEARCH

"Surprise them" sounds good, but how do you do it? The usual solution: market research. In fact, in 1992, American companies forked over a record $3.5 billion to the 50 biggest research firms to learn more about their customers.[2] But according to a *Fortune* magazine report, "measured by the luck companies have had introducing new products, they wasted a bundle." An executive for the Center for Strategic Research in Cambridge pulled no punches: *"Most of what is done right now is so poor as probably to be fraudulent."*

The problem is that traditional research methods are not effective in a rapidly changing environment. Surveys, for example, generate an average response of 20 percent.[3] People just don't have the time or interest to answer them. Those who do represent too small or atypical a sample to base any thoughtful decision on.

"They [surveys] also don't provide enough rich information to yield a close understanding of the customer," says Forum Corp's Jennifer Brotman. "It's important to get the voice of customers, to capture their words, in order to really understand what they want."[4]

HENRY FONDA AND POLITICALLY CORRECT FOCUS GROUPS

Focus groups are seen as the answer to this problem. They have real advantages over question-and-answer surveys because they are relatively inexpensive, easy to do, and yield a richer tapestry of information. But unless you do thousands of them, the sample of opinion is far too small to be statistically significant. And they are prone to bias. Sometimes what you get is the *Twelve Angry Men* syndrome in which one persuasive person—like Henry Fonda in the film classic of the same name—turns the others to his way of thinking.

It's not uncommon for focus-group members to disguise their responses out of fear that they may be politically incorrect or socially unacceptable. Without controlling for this, the research may be horribly skewed.

HUNCH RESEARCH

Says media maven Barry Diller, who pushed Fox broadcasting when surveys showed the public wasn't interested in another network, "We become slaves to demographics, to market research, to focus groups. We produce what the numbers tell us to produce. And gradually, in this dizzying chase, our senses lose feeling and our instincts dim, corroded with safe action."[5]

One of the things we frequently advise open-mouthed executives to do is to trust their hunches as much as their focus groups.

Guilt-free pigging out. When focus groups indicated that advertisements for potato chips made with canola oil should stress how they were good for you, Jeffrey Jury was skeptical.[6] As director of marketing of Intermountain, a manufacturer of canola vegetable oil, he suspected that "healthy potato chip" was an oxymoron, like "army intelligence" or "giant shrimp."

What customers liked most about canola-made chips, Jury intuited, was that they felt less guilty about eating them. This was a sentiment they were reluctant to voice directly in focus groups.[7] Based on his hunch, Intermountain conducted more in-depth research and discovered that Jury's intuition was correct. The company changed the product slogan from "Choose to be healthy" to "A taste you can feel good about," and the chips have been a healthy hit with the CFO ever since.

Same story at Outback Steakhouse. Market research showed that people were changing their diets and eating less red meat. "But we saw them lining up to get into steakhouses," says CEO Chris Sullivan. He followed his gut feelings and today runs a fast-growing chain of 117 Australian-motif beef joints.[8]

Don't forget Chrysler, which rode the minivan to success despite research showing that people recoiled from such a strange-looking vehicle. And all those fast-food joints who followed their researchers into oblivion with products like McDonald's McLean, KFC's skinless fried chicken, and Pizza Hut's low-cal pies.

WALK THEIR WALK

To surprise your customers, you've got to go beyond conventional research to the customer's experience. That means you've got to walk their walk. Here's an example of what we mean.

The president of a $100 million vacation time-sharing company brought us in to help with two problems. Only 10 percent of prospective buyers who came to view the real estate actually bought any, and the turnover rate of the sales staff was huge, costing the company $5 million annually to hire and train new personnel.

"We've tried everything to up our conversion rate and keep our salespeople," he told us. "We have a great training program, terrific incentives, and terrific leads. You name it, we've done it, but nothing seems to be working."

"Let's go for a walk," I said, and took his arm. "Let's be customers."

Waiting outside the hotel for the bus to come and take us to view the property, we got a first taste of the customer's experience—a sour one. All of the prospective buyers were couples. Most appeared a little nervous. They didn't know what to expect, where they were going, and what they were going to see. They had all agreed to spend two hours listening to a real estate spiel in return for a handsome prize. That was it.

When the little Napoleon who was driving the bus jumped out and ordered them to line up, a low murmur spread through the crowd. When he refused to let anyone board until he had called everyone's name from the roster, the grumbling got louder. People seemed to be wondering how they had let themselves get into this for a lousy door prize they probably would never use. On the way over, a VCR blared but no one paid it any mind.

When the bus stopped everyone exited a bit too quickly, and we were all ushered into a large room filled with round tables with big numbers on them. Each couple had to line up again. Everyone got a number and was told to go to their corresponding table. *Told,* not asked, requested, or implored.

After watching a surprisingly entertaining video presentation, each couple was assigned to a salesperson who drove them off to walk through a few of the models. When you got back, the sales pitch started. A time-share cost $12,000. I forgot how much time that bought because I was thinking about how I had to decide right there and then whether I was in or out of the deal. They wanted me to plunk down the whole 12 grand and sign on the dotted line.

When I naively told them I needed to think it over, that I wasn't prepared to buy on the spur of the moment, I got what I believe is called the bum's rush. I could really feel the pressure mounting and when I continued to resist, my salesperson called in his boss. This wasn't your good cop–bad cop routine. The new guy pressured me even more.

When it was clear I wasn't buying, the salesperson got downright nasty. He slammed down his books and called me stupid for passing up the chance of a lifetime. Later, others told me they had been treated the same way.

Afterward, the president was incredulous. "It's amazing we get anyone to buy with a sales approach like that," he said. "I don't know, we developed our sales procedures based on industry practice, and most of the feedback we've gotten has been from people who've bought property. I haven't felt so hustled since I went to buy a car. We're trying to sell a Cadillac like it was a used car."

I could only agree: "I felt like a cow being herded around, and not a very sacred one at that."

STAND IN THEIR SHOES

Direct firsthand experience is the best way to understand your customers. Get to know them as people, not statistics. Learn to think like they think, feel what they feel. After you've walked their walk, stand in their shoes. Be a customer.

"I look in my closet, and if I need it, I design it," declares Donna Karan, who heads a quarter-billion-dollar fashion empire. A hardworking wife, mother, and business professional, Karan is similar in some respects to the women for whom she designs.

Her clothes are cut generously because she knows that most women, like herself, are not built like Twiggy. And before a design goes into production you can bet she's tried it on and modified it until it's right.[9]

Practically moving in with them. The next best thing to being the customer is to live with them. No, you don't have to marry them; just move in. That's practically what 3M's medical and surgical products division does. All 750 employees, production-line workers as well as senior execs, meet face to face with doctors and nurses at three area hospitals. They don scrubs and go into operating rooms to watch their products in action.

"We get to feel the pulse of our customers. We see their problems and frustrations up close," says Gary Borgstadt of 3M.[10] One of their customers, Valerie Smidt of Sioux Valley Hospital, describes the situation as positive for everyone: "The 3M people give us pointers on how to better utilize some items and we, in turn, suggest how to make some of their products more user-friendly."[11]

Hanging with them. Black & Decker takes it a step further. To gather information for a new line of tools, they found 50 typical "do it yourself" customers—male homeowners aged 25 to 54 who owned more than six tools—and sent their marketing executives to hang out with them *in their own homes and workshops.*

For months the execs watched how these folks used (or misused) the tools. They talked to them about what they liked and why, how the tools felt in their hands, and even noticed how they cleaned up their workspaces. They even tagged along on shopping trips to monitor what they bought and for how much.

Some of the products that resulted from this "hanging with your friends" research included a cordless drill that didn't run out of power before the job was completed, a mini vacuum attachment for sanders and circular saws that sucks up sawdust, and a unique safety mechanism that stops blades from spinning immediately after the saw is turned off.

The company also noticed that "do it yourselfers" love to talk about their projects and tools. So they provided customers with a toll-free hot line to keep the dialogue going. Great for customers and even better for them. They've got a continual source of input for research and development.

Such close contact with its customers allowed B&D to avoid creating new tools that were simply novelties with little added value. These kinds of faddish products (have you checked the latest new buckle on your ski boots lately?) are really promotional gimmicks with limited staying power.

The bottom line: Black & Decker's new product line called Quantum turned out to be one of the darlings of the 1994 National Hardware Show, winning the prestigious Retailers Choice Award. The company expected to gross $30 to $40 million in sales in 1994.

"OUT OF THE BOX" SURPRISES

Another way to surprise your customers and get the edge on your competition is to go beyond selling to helping your customers address long-standing problems and concerns. You may not see yourself in the consulting business, but showing customers that you're interested in their welfare and will help them win their game is an important step in winning yours. Long-term relationships are cemented by going "out of the box" to provide needed assistance. Here are some examples:

Tech Talk Tools

A large software company whose major clients were CIOs of Fortune 1000 companies recognized that one of their customers' thorniest and generally overlooked jobs was not software acquisition but sales. That's right, the CIOs had to sell their recommendations to financial officers and heads of marketing and manufacturing. Sell? The idea was foreign to these "tekkies" who sometimes didn't speak the same language as other staff. They used jargon and "technospeak" that no one but another CIO could understand. As a result, some of their smartest software choices often got nixed.

So we designed a users' meeting for CIOs that focused not on software or technical issues, the usual agenda items at such gatherings, but on teaching people how to make presentations, develop listening skills, and communicate in language understandable to individuals who thought a hard drive was going from Chicago to Des Moines.

Attendance at that conference was three times the industry norm.

Helping to Keep Customers

Did you ever get one of those envelopes—from companies like Val-Pak—full of discount coupons from local retailers? They're great for getting consumers into the store. But what about getting them to come back a second and third time?

I once received one of those envelopes, which included a half-price coupon from a new dry cleaner and a two-for-one dinner at an Italian restaurant. I decided to try both of them. Although I told the cleaner "No starch," the shirts I got back were so stiff they could have walked home by themselves. I brought them back and gave them another try, with no better outcome. Result: one lost customer.

I gave my son and his girlfriend the two-for-one coupon, which they showed when they went in. Big mistake. The hostess seated them next to the kitchen. Okay, maybe all the other tables were reserved, but when the waiter told them the coupon didn't cover the regular specials, they knew they were second-class patrons. They ordered something with a long name that was short on taste and were told that wine, although clearly indicated on the coupon, wasn't part of the deal. Result: two lost customers.

Realizing that local retailers like these are often so rushed and financially squeezed that they don't have the time or the inclination to give the kind of service that would keep new customers coming back, one resourceful Val-Pak saleswoman in Minneapolis went out of the box to exceed her customers' expectations. She offered them a training library of books and tapes on how to give superior service, motivate staff, and deal with coupon customers. Another sales rep took it one step further by educating herself on service issues and offering seminars for local retailers. Results from both of these efforts: many new customers.

Sizzler's Seniors

Sizzler's restaurants feed a lot of senior citizens, who are one of their target markets. One Sizzler's local manager put two and two together to delight his older patrons. He knew that many seniors could no longer drive. He also knew they still needed to eat, and though many lived alone most didn't necessarily like to eat alone. So he started a van service to the nearby senior housing complex. The response was so great he should have rented a bus.

He didn't stop there, though. He began offering late afternoon—translation: slow time in the restaurant—lectures for seniors on topics that were of specific interest to them. He even got the speakers to donate their services. After the talk, it was time to eat and schmooze, so guess where they ate and schmoozed?

These senior afternoons were so successful that the group began holding support groups at the Sizzler's on other afternoons. And after those meetings, more food. The story goes on. The manager began offering afternoon bus trips to shows and excursions to nearby gambling casinos. Not only did he get paid for the trips but he supplied box lunches from guess where? And when the trip was over, well, it was time for dinner.

Return on Investment

To get new customers, banks offer many traditional "in the box" incentives. One-stop banking, Saturday service, 24-hour loan approvals—these inducements are indelibly recorded on the back shelves of our minds like bad dreams. One enterprising banker took another approach. Recognizing that his principal customers—businesses with up to $10 million in sales—often lacked human-resource personnel and money for training, he offered three hours with a training consultant to any new company that opened an account.

Another bank executive hired me to give a speech on sacred cows to a local chamber of commerce luncheon. He gained visibility by welcoming participants, and after the speech he gave them an evaluation form. Guess what was at the very top of the paper? A space for their names and addresses.

Now he had 250 people with whom to discuss the concepts and tools from my program. "The total cost of the luncheon was about $20k," he told me. "But for that I got instant rapport and an immediate relationship with two hundred and fifty people. I'll bet I made that back in three months. That's a return on investment I'll take anytime."

Food for Thought

A frustration for many companies that sell their products through supermarkets is getting their promotional displays on the floor in high-visibility locations. There are just too many products and too many promotions in a limited space. Companies offer all kinds of incentives above and below board to curry favor with store managers, but nothing succeeds like a personal relationship.

Knowing that a major frustration for these managers is hiring, training, and keeping employees, one major food company took a different tack. They began offering local seminars on employee relations, creating goodwill by helping out with a tricky problem.

Naturally their local sales reps and brokers attended, giving them a chance to form more personal relationships with the managers.

Other examples of "out of the box" surprises:

- Owners of Lexus automobiles in Germany receive a free bottle of that year's Beaujolais *before any other Germans can purchase it.*[12]
- Lexus owners also receive a reminder to make the seasonal clock change from daylight saving time with an elegant—and correctly set—Lexus clock.[13]
- Several mortgage brokers who rely on realtor referrals send tip sheets—bimonthly sales and presentation tips—to agents to help them develop great listing presentations.
- The *Utne Reader,* a bimonthly general-interest magazine, assists in the formation of subscriber discussion groups called Utne Neighborhood Salons. These gray-matter gatherings boast 20,000 dues-paying members.[14]
- Cal Comp, a manufacturer of printers and plotters for architects, recognized that their clients had virtually no training in marketing and selling. In fact, many architects look down on sales even though it is a critical part of their job. So several members of the sales staff developed a training course for reluctant architects, and attendance is booming.
- Japan's largest cosmetics concern, Shiseido, has a credit card with a 20-page monthly newsletter, a magazine with a circulation of 400,000 for Shiseido users, and a discount club to which 10 million Japanese women belong.[15] By becoming a source of information and a financial partner, the company has become more than a purveyor of products.

Change-Ready Thinking

Don't follow customers; lead them.

Don't satisfy customers; surprise them.

Don't be market driven; be a market driver.

Nine

The Low Price Cow

NO MORE HAND CALCULATORS

Question: If there are two brands of peanut butter with identical ingredients and one sells for $2 while the other goes for $2.35, which would you choose? No-brainer, right? You'd take the lower-priced jar and head for the checkout.

Don't be so hasty. Millions of Americans no longer think that way. Low price is still important, of course. That's what Wal-Mart and Costco are all about, but price is no longer king. Value is.

These days consumers want and expect more than just "inexpensive." They want the right features, service, convenience, and quality. The days of using price as your main sales strategy are over. A study conducted by Grey Advertising found that consumers are less likely to compare prices than in the past.

"We're learning that people want more for their dollar. It isn't about lowering prices," claims Larry Flax of California Pizza Kitchen, who believes customers equate "getting your money's worth" with larger portions. "If I took a quarter off the pasta, it wouldn't make a difference."[1]

"Americans have become very purposeful shoppers. They are reengineering just as corporate America is doing," says Barbara

LOW PRICE COW

Feigin, executive vice president at Grey. Feigin's name for these new, informed buying patterns: "precision shopping." "We think it will be here for a long time, if not forever," she predicts.[2]

Customers aren't chasing the "one-day" bargain sales the way they used to. Instead they are flocking to stores they believe have EDLPs—everyday low prices—and sticking with them. The shopping experience is a lot less effort and a lot more enjoyable when you just assume everything in the place is a good deal. No more mental gymnastics or handheld calculators in the shopping aisles. They're going to stores where they know they can get a good deal.

LOSS LEADERS LOSE

The conventional wisdom has always been that loss leaders get people into the store. But offering one really great deal doesn't work anymore. "Everyone has tried [that strategy] with no significant success, in terms of getting the customer into the store," says Rick Fiedelman, a partner in Deloitte & Touche, the accounting and consulting firm. "Except," notes Feidelman, "for coming in the door, buying the loss leader, and walking out the door."[3] Another problem with the loss-leader strategy is that once people pay a low price for something, they feel cheated when the price goes back to normal. And they go elsewhere.

Fast-food wars. Even the fast-food chains are realizing that low price no longer produces a competitive advantage.

"Now everybody has ninety-nine-cent and two-ninety-nine offerings. You drive by most fast-food places and the whole building is for sale," says Allan Hickok, a restaurant analyst with Piper Jaffray in Minneapolis.

"Value is not price point; it is the whole experience. In fast food we'll start to see a sorting out of who really is and isn't offering value," he says.[4] It's the same story in the $11 billion-a-year pizza business, where the eight major chains, fatigued by a long, costly, and bruising discount war, are moving beyond their low-price strategies.

"The great dough wars ended up with the customers getting all the dough and the companies not getting any," says Malcom N. Knapp, president of a New York–based food-service consulting firm. "All of these huge pies, low prices, and two-for-one deals drove traffic but didn't do much for profits."[5]

Fix your flat for free. At Direct Tire Sales, it's not rock-bottom prices but valuable extras that keep customers flocking in. The Massachusetts-based retailer loans cars to customers, picks up the cab fare if you need a ride home, and fixes flats gratis.

All this plus a customer lounge that more closely resembles a hotel lobby with cappucino, croissants, and *Cosmopolitan* for your waiting pleasure. Sure, these extras cost the company money—the fifteen rental cars are $500 a month alone—but you've got to spend money to make it. And Direct is certainly making it.

Explains owner Barry Steinberg, "People call in and say, 'Is it true that I can get a free ride when I bring my car in to have the brakes changed?' We've put price on the back burner."[6]

Loyalty to price? We know a mortgage broker with the same idea. He gives customers value by offering them more than low rates. To refinance homeowners he offers financial advice on how to invest the money they save on their new mortgage. To his growing realtor network, he sends a monthly mailing with tips on how to increase sales and gain the competitive edge.

"It's not about price, it's about building relationships," he says. "If you only sell price someone will always be there to undercut you. And the customer's loyalty will be to price, not to you.

"Once you've created a relationship, your customers will tell you if they've found a lower price somewhere else. Then you've got a chance to match it. All because you've made the extra effort to listen to them and respond to their needs."

A family legacy. As a boy I used to buy clothing at Robert Hall, a budget men's store with its own line of low-priced suits and coats. I remember the cinder-block walls and dim lighting. The place was singularly unattractive and the selection limited, but the price was right. I always hoped no one saw me go in the place.

Robert Hall went under sometime back but not without leaving a legacy. The father of George Zimmer, CEO, of the Men's Warehouse, worked for that clothing chain. Zimmer's company also sells clothes at 20 to 30 percent below retail. But that's where the resemblance ends. Go into any of his stores and George "guarantees" you'll find an attentive sales staff that will call you fifteen days after you buy anything to make sure you're satisfied. He offers a wide selection of name brands, and free pressing and alterations for the life of the garment.

You may find it hard to believe, but one of Robert Hall's main competitors for low-priced menswear in the old days was Barney's. Apparently, though, old man Barney learned that when you're selling price *there's always someone who will sell cheaper.* He flipped his strategy around, and now Barney's is one of the most successful high-price, high-quality, and high-tone retail chains around.

Change-Ready Thinking

Sell cheap and that's what people will think of you.

Loss leaders lose.

Customers look for price *and* value *and* service *and* quality *and* convenience. And you'd better give it to them or someone else will.

Ten

The Quick-Reactor Cow

Have you ever watched how surfers catch the big waves offshore? They don't choose the wave that's right on top of them. It's coming too fast and furious. There's no way they can react in time, and if they try, they'll end up flailing in the backwash or eating sand. Even if they could catch it, there'd be no room to maneuver. Some other dude who started paddling well in advance of the wave is already riding its crest.

The first rule in surfing is to look "outside," toward the horizon, to find your wave and start paddling long before it approaches you. Good surfers don't wait for the swells. They anticipate them and act before they arrive.

Today's marketplace is a turbulent ocean, and we're all surfers struggling in a sea of change. Huge waves are breaking on us, barreling in at breakneck speed. To keep ahead we've got to think like a surfer focusing on the horizon. We have to start moving before the change hits.

Reacting—even quickly—doesn't work. It's a sacred-cow belief that quick response to change is possible. Experience shows that rapid responders are forced into a catch-up game. Even if they manage to pull even, the competition is already onto the next wave while they're left struggling to catch their breath. You can't *re*act anymore; you've got to *pro*act.

QUICK-REACTOR COW

DON'T LISTEN TO THE CUSTOMER

The first step in keeping ahead of the change wave is to start with your customers. But don't listen to them. Listening will only tell you what consumers want or need *now,* not what they're going to want next year. And many companies have found that by the time they've got their "new" product to market, customers are looking for something else.

"It is hard to be a market leader if you do no more than listen to your customer," write Gary Hamel and C. K. Prahalad in the *Harvard Business Review.*[1]

Go back a decade. How many of us were asking for cellular phones, compact-disk players, home fax machines, or electronic whiteboards?

One Detroit automaker recently introduced a new compact car. The company had conducted extensive market research and began its product-development efforts in the late 1980s. Four years later, it introduced the perfect car to compete with its Japanese competitors' models, which were already three years old. The company was following its customers, all right. But its customers were following more imaginative competitors.[2]

CRYSTAL-BALL GAZERS

To differentiate yourself from the competition, you have to lead the customer. That's what Change-Ready companies do. Toshiba runs a lifestyle research institute to preview customers' future psychographics. Sony spends considerable dollars on exploring "human science." Mazda has formed a subsidiary company under the control of the director of R&D, whose role is to develop new products based on lifestyle information.

Some companies utilize their customers' imagination to "pre-view" the future. Yamaha maintains a "listening post" in London to gain insights into as-yet-unarticulated preferences and ideas. Loaded with cutting-edge electronic wizardry, the facility invites top musicians from Europe to experiment with musical equipment that one day may be in every recording studio. The feedback they get allows them to refine their technology and anticipate future products and markets.

Yamaha's approach is brilliant. It not only allows the company to apply the observations and critiques of its most demanding and sophisticated customers, but it also brings them the latest technology and challenges them to imagine ways of utilizing it.

Toyota has done something similar. They give potential buyers a chance to design their dream cars using the same computerized tools their engineers work with in the lab. The company gets insight into product possibilities that may be outside the realm of their designers' imaginations.

"Companies that succeed in educating customers to what is possible develop both marketers with technological imagination and technologists with marketing imagination," say Hamel and Prahalad.[3]

"PRE-VIEWING"

But you don't have to be a futurist or a scientist to "pre-view" the customer. You don't have to set up elaborate laboratories or listening posts. Educated guesses and informed hunches have yielded incredible returns too. Remember Steve Jobs and Steve Wozniak?

To stay in front of the wave of change you need to think about three things:

- Demographic, sociographic, and psychographic trends of your customers
- Emerging social and cultural directions
- Advances in technology

Banking Futures. At one of our programs, we asked bank presidents and CEOs to "pre-view" what banking would look like in five years using our three areas. Here's what they said: "People will have even less time to take care of their personal business than they do now so they'll do their banking from home. And, of course, they'll expect loan approvals in minutes, not weeks, without having to fill out forms. The whole process will be done through a computer database almost as fast you can press the buttons.

"We'll be selling a whole range of investment products, maybe even insurance, by then. But people won't want to be sold. They'll want to make their own choices and at their convenience. We'll probably have an investment channel that outlines the range of products with rationales for buying them. Then they'll be able to purchase them then and there or click on their screen for more information. The bank of today is going to become a dinosaur in five years. We won't need buildings. It'll all be done through computers, phone lines, and interactive networks."

Concluded one, "We need to start thinking that way and either partner with some high-tech firms or hire them, so we can change our game before we don't have one to change."

HOME SHOPPING, LITERALLY

To get people thinking creatively about the future, we jog their minds with a game called Let Your Fingers Do the Walking. Teams of five are given three random pages from the classified phone book. Their task is to conceptualize a business combining one entry from each of the three pages. For instance, one team combined a jewelry store, golf-ball manufacturer, and personalized nameplate company into a business that made personalized, jeweled golf balls. Another combined a pet shop, dating service, and seller of religious articles into a dating service for pets of your own religion. We didn't say these odd companies made sense or that you'd want to invest in them. The purpose of the game is only to shed the confines of conventional reasoning and encourage "out of the box" thinking. Once people loosen up, we have them focus on their own industry. We challenged a group of Prudential Realty franchisees to combine real estate, the phone company, and home shopping. "But this isn't a game," we told them, "this is your life." They came up with the following look into the future: In five years consumers won't be going *out* to look at houses anymore. They'll choose a neighborhood they like and a price range they can afford from a database of multiple listings or an interactive television channel. They'll press a couple of buttons and see the house from the outside, front and back; then from the inside, room by room. They might even get a look at the neighborhood, schools, and shopping malls. "With virtual reality they'll be able to *try* before they buy," joked one of the agents.

"But what would they need us for?" one realtor asked. Programs like these always generate unanswerable questions like, How do you create trusting relationships by computer? or What will be the role of the real estate agent, or car or insurance salesperson in the future?

No one had a good answer but they all agreed on one thing: It will be different than it is now.

Smell-o-vision. Some other kinds of interesting questions were raised when we conducted the "pre-viewing" exercise with sales staff and executives from Pet, Inc., a giant food company. All agreed that in the future people would buy foods in the same manner that they will buy everything else—from home.

But what about impulse buying and browsing the supermarket aisles waiting for something to grab you? And what about special sales?

"There'll probably be videos of whole aisles," said one sales manager to a sea of nodding heads, "so you could actually browse from home. And there would be ads at the bottom of the screen for special sales and new products."

"There'll probably even be smell-o-vision," joked another. "Wherever you stop the screen, you'll get a whiff of the product in front of you." How about touch-o-vision so you can squeeze the fruit?

Pitchforks to Star Wars. "You're talking Star Wars and my people are fighting with pitchforks," said one of the real estate executives. "Virtual reality! Half of them can't even program their VCR." And he wasn't exaggerating. A survey done by the National Association of Realtors found that over 80 percent of real estate agents were computer illiterate.

The exec's response is typical. The "pre-viewed" future can be so far removed from current reality that people totally reject it.

To combat this resistance, we help them move into the future incrementally. Small steps build confidence. Before you know it, you've walked a longer distance than you ever thought possible. For some of the realtors, small steps meant simply getting a beeper or using voice mail. We even suggest playing video games with your kids to learn the basics of interactive technology.

HIT THE ROAD

"Remember those previewing exercises where we came up with the in-home interactive multi-listing service?" asked one of the realtors at our six-month follow-up meeting. "Well, the future isn't as far away as we thought. They're already doing it in Dallas!"

The truth about the future is that anything you can imagine for to-morrow might already be happening today. A few months after the Pet, Inc., program we heard that a company in Canada was already testing something similar in a small city outside Quebec. They didn't have smell-o-vision or touch-o-vision yet, but maybe that's just around the corner. In a world changing this fast, you never know when fantasy and reality will meet.

And like the wave, once change hits it'll be going too fast to keep up. "If you want to be one of the first into a new territory," says futurist Joel Barker, author of *Future Edge,* "you cannot wait for large amounts of evidence. Poring over numbers can't help you see what is ahead."[4]

So move before the wave. If you don't you'll end up flailing in its backwash.

Change-Ready Thinking

Good companies react quickly to change; *great* companies create the change.

Move before the wave; change before you have to.

Eleven

The No-Mistakes Cow

THE PERILS OF PERFECTION

"Get it right the first time." It's not only the credo of the quality movement, it's the downtown gospel for anyone struggling to meet quota or make budget. No one wants to make mistakes. They cost you profits and time. They make you look stupid. You could lose dollars, face, clients, even your job. Besides, you don't get gold stars for having the wrong answer—that's not how life works.

But this "no-mistakes" ethic designed to improve work practices, products, and services does more harm than good. It fosters an atmosphere of caution that makes people afraid to take a risk or gamble on the brilliant idea. When people get cautious, innovation, creativity, and originality go out the window, and the possibility of gaining an edge on the competition goes right along with them.

In an aggressively competitive environment, you can't afford *not* to experiment, and mistakes are a natural by-product. They may be costly, but they're not nearly as expensive as an organization where none are permitted.

"The moment you let avoiding failure become your motivator, you're down the path of inactivity," notes Coca-Cola CEO Roberto Goizueta. "You can stumble only if you're moving."[1]

Bill Gates goes out of his way to hire people who've made mistakes. "It shows that they take risks," he says. "The way people deal with things that go wrong is an indicator of how they deal with change."[2]

NO-MISTAKES COW

DECISIONS, DECISIONS, DECISIONS

People who are afraid of making mistakes are petrified of making decisions. That means more meetings, memos, approvals, and endless analysis. By the time you reach certainty—and you rarely do—half the information you've collected is outdated. And that great opportunity has gone south on the wings of a less cautious competitor.

"The problem when the personal price for experimentation is high," say management consultants Gary Hamel and C. K. Prahalad, is that "managers retreat to the safety of 'test it to death,' 'do only what the customer asks for' conservatism.

"In an environment where managers seldom get punished for *not trying* but for trying and coming up short, few will be brave enough to step up to the plate."[3] And not getting up to bat means no home runs or singles. It means you've forfeited the game.

Test, test, test. This "no-mistakes" ethic pervaded every department and division at a huge packaged-goods manufacturer. Their advertising followed a static formula that everyone was afraid to challenge. You had to show the package in the first five seconds, demonstrate the product, and use their spokesperson. Try to be creative under those constraints. And if the advertising didn't work, the marketing manager could shrug it off because she'd followed instructions.

To avoid errors they researched every idea to death. They always used the same test markets so the whole world knew when and where they were testing something. The competition would do everything it could—blitz advertising, sampling, special displays—to skew the results. And if they saw a good idea they'd snatch it up and get it to market before the company could respond.

YESTERDAY'S LUNCH

Striving to avoid mistakes leads to rehashing old ideas. When you can't afford to be wrong, you rely on what worked in the past. But yesterday's thinking produces ideas, solutions, and products as fresh and appetizing as yesterday's lunch.

Swiss watchmakers were so busy perfecting the quality of their watches, refining their intricate movements, that they failed to see that quartz and digital technology had made their fine timepieces obsolete. Manufacturers of mainframe computers kept upgrading their tepid product when the marketplace was heating up with the convenience and ease of the PC.

Complacency is what is produced in a no-mistakes environment. Employees check their creativity at the door. They lose the sense of excitement that is so critical to peak performance. The fire goes out, and with it the joy and fun of new ideas, experimentation and possibility.

Complacency also produces the very thing that a mistakes-phobic environment is trying to avoid: mistakes. Lack of concentration is a consequence of doing the same old, same old. It leads to a dulling of the senses, and that ultimately generates errors in thinking and judgment.

ONE PLUS ONE EQUALS FOUR

When failure is not penalized, people are more willing to experiment, to look for innovative new solutions, products, processes, and ways to surprise the customer. They're more open to learning and less scared about change. Morale is much better because fear is minimized.

In organizations where failure is punished, the opposite happens. People play not to lose. They look over their shoulders and protect their flanks. Managers become cops, making certain everyone follows the rules and punishing those who screw up.

A director we worked with at a West Coast bank had been put on a time-sensitive special project by one of the vice presidents. When he missed the delivery date on a critical report, he was removed from the project.

"I'm done at the bank," he told us. "Once you screw up you're history. I'm no longer promotable." We assured him he was exaggerating, but it turned out he was right. The bank began to underutilize him and eight months later they let him go. He'd been tainted by this one failure to deliver the goods.

In some companies 1 plus 1 equals 4. One mistake, one time, equals *for*ever.

WATERGATE AND OTHER COVER-UPS

When failures are seen as catastrophic, employees go to great lengths to hide them and to avoid being seen as responsible for anything that goes wrong. Mistakes are like tumors: Catch them early and they can be cured; wait too long and they spread like cancer.

Covering up mistakes is less likely to happen when you aren't severely chastised for making them. Organizations that are tolerant of human fallibility minimize the need to create smokescreens and other diversions.

Refusing to admit a problem has turned many bottom lines bright red. And created difficulties far greater than the original problem.

Look at what happened in one of the country's most infamous cover-ups: Watergate. Initial denials led to ensuing cover-ups, exacerbating the problem, and eventually to the resignation of the President of the United States. Had the error been admitted early, political devastation might have been avoided.

It takes courage to admit mistakes even in a forgiving environment, but when someone, especially the boss, acknowledges error, it gives everyone down the line permission to own up. When Intel finally acknowledged that its Pentium chip had a problem and agreed to fix it "no questions asked," their stock price actually increased.

BLAME-GO-ROUND

After years of successfully wooing working women with stylish, well-made clothing, Liz Claiborne, Inc., had a run in its stock-ings. Earnings in 1993 plunged lower than Madonna's neckline.

Retailers say top managers were slow to admit that their new designs were unpopular. Claiborne's people, of course, pointed the finger right back, saying that the retailers didn't know how to sell the merchandise. Said a former Claiborne executive, "If the product didn't sell it was always someone else's fault. The buyers didn't show it right, or it wasn't delivered the right way. They didn't allow themselves to think that, maybe, they just weren't listening to the customer."[4]

What happened at Liz's place is typical of the "no-mistakes" workplace. If you can't hide or deny the problem, sharpen your fingernails and start pointing.

Wherever we consult with companies who are having a tough time with change, it's always someone else who's the problem. Top management blames middle-level employees. Middle managers blame the boss. And everyone blames the workers, who swear up and down that it's their supervisor's fault. Another version: Marketing blames Manufacturing, Design blames Engineering, and everyone blames Sales for practically giving away the merchandise. Anyone with a finger is pointing it . . . except at themselves.

In a "no-mistakes" environment avoiding fault becomes more important than solving problems, and that's a surefire way to avoid being successful.

DON'T LOOK DOWN

Worrying about making mistakes actually causes you to make more of them. The golfer worried about hitting the ball into the lake thinks, Don't hit it into the lake. And where does the ball go? Right into the drink. And what happens when you tell yourself "Don't worry" before a pressure situation? You worry more.

Thinking about what you don't want to do focuses you exactly on what you don't want to happen. That's why when someone tells you not to think of a pink elephant, the first image in your mind is a blushing mastodon. You've programmed yourself.

Ever give an important presentation and the client in the front row is scowling at you like you've just lost his luggage and insulted his wife? "Don't look at him," you tell yourself. But where do your eyes keep wandering?

When acrophobic people in our ski clinics rode the chairlifts, we always told them, "Don't look down." But that never worked. Fear grabs your attention like few other things. Even though we prefaced our instruction with "Don't!" they only heard "down," and that's just where they looked.

So we changed our strategy and began giving them something positive on which to focus. "Look out at the mountains," we suggested. "Check out those skiers on the adjoining slope." "Aren't those clouds beautiful?" Anything to get them not to look south.

The same strategy applies at work. Instead of thinking about the terrible mistakes that *could* happen, think of what you *want* to happen. Instead of *not* looking at that gruff client in the front row, look at the smiling face across from him.

DOUBLE YOUR FAILURE RATE

No matter how much effort you put into something, no matter how well you prepare, *you will make mistakes.* Fallibility is human. It's how we learn.

Nobody learns to walk without falling, to ski without a few head-plants, to surf without wiping out. No writer, salesperson, senator, or suitor escapes rejection. Who learns a language faster, a person who studies endlessly before attempting a conversation or a person who jumps right in undaunted by making a lot of errors?

Says former IBM chairman Tom Watson, "If you want to succeed, double your failure rate."

FAILURE TO LEARN FROM FAILURE

Many people tell you to forget your mistakes, to put the failure behind you and keep moving forward. That's like a golfer who slices one, shakes it off, and then slices another . . . and another. Although moving on stops you from getting down on yourself, if you don't stop long enough to learn from the mistake, you'll keep repeating it. That's a lot of double bogeys.

When mistakes are seen as a part of the learning process they can help you to rethink, reconceptualize, and restrategize. Going back to the drawing board usually results in a more well conceived solution. But only if you go back to the drawing board and learn from where you went wrong.

"Failure is not a crime," said Citicorp chairman Walter Wriston. *"Failure to learn from failure is."* [5]

Charles Garfield, who worked on NASA's initial moon shot, said that it was off target 80 percent of the time. But it kept making adjustments until it ended up on target.

FAILING FIRST

Many fabulous successes didn't do it right *the first time.* They failed first. Football coaches Bill Walsh, Tom Landry, and Chuck Knoll were responsible for winning 9 of 15 Super Bowls from 1974 to 1990, but they also had the *worst* first-season records of any coaches in National Football League history.

San Francisco 49er coach George Seifert, who has the highest winning percentage of any NFL coach in his first six years, was fired from his first head coaching job at Cornell after a two-year record of 3 wins and 15 losses. After they took over the Dallas Cowboys, the first-year record of Jimmy Johnson and Jerry Jones was something like 1 and 15. Three years later they won the Super Bowl.

The list of fabulous early failures in business includes such incredibly successful companies as L.L. Bean and Fidelity's Select Leisure Fund. *Sports Illustrated,* one of Time Life's most profitable magazines, *lost money* for its first *11 years!*

As head of the new products division at Johnson & Johnson, Jim Burke failed miserably in his first stabs at innovation. But instead of reprimanding him, his boss, General Johnson, congratulated him for taking risks and making tough decisions. Burke went on to become the CEO and a director of J&J.

And don't forget this: If everyone did it right the first time, we'd live in a world without Post-its on your desk, sugar substitutes in your coffee, the Walkman in your ear, and Scotchgard on your clothes and furniture. All were the by-products of human error.

WHEN SUCCESS MEANS FAILURE

In fact, a perfect record is not always a sign of success, but one of failure. Doing it right every time may mean you aren't trying anything new, challenging the status quo, or learning.

Batting a thousand might mean you're playing in a league far below your ability and not challenging yourself. Said one executive, "If you aren't making mistakes you aren't doing anything worth a damn."

THE RIGHT KIND OF MISTAKES

We're not saying you should try and make mistakes or that you should feel good when you do. We're not suggesting you should leap headlong into the abyss without thinking or carrying a strong rope.

The mistakes essential for success aren't the sloppy, careless ones that come from being ill prepared or confused. They're the kind of errors that come from trying something new, from marching into uncharted territory or taking calculated risks. It's impossible to get it right every time when you're innovating and everything around you is in a constant state of flux.

Change-Ready Thinking

Don't penalize mistakes; reward good tries.

The biggest mistake: not learning from mistakes.

If you're not making mistakes you're not trying anything new.

Twelve

The Downsizing Cow

READING THE OBITS

"It's depressing to read the business section," a Bank of America vice president told us recently, "you never know when you'll read about your own funeral. It's scary."

He's right. "Obituaries" run right next to earnings on the front page. With all the downsizing going on it's rare that a week goes by without big companies merging, restructuring, downsizing, rightsizing, or streamlining. Whatever the word, the result is the same: Millions have gotten their pink slips as American business goes on a drastic weight-loss program to rid itself of excess fat.

In fact, the American Management Association's surveys show that one in four companies planned a major downsizing last year (1995), the highest level in eight years.[1]

If you think you can run for cover and wait it out until the business climate improves, think again. Restructuring is no longer a one-time phenomenon but a well-entrenched management option. Many companies are on their second or third go-around.[2]

"Downsizing is not the child of recession," says Eric Greenberg,

DOWNSIZING COW

director of AMA management studies. "If you think of it as a one-time extraordinary event in a company that is having difficulty in the marketplace, you aren't seeing it accurately. Instead, it has become an ongoing corporate activity without regard to the economy's current performance or market conditions."[3]

LEANER AND MEANER DOESN'T MEAN GREENER

Downsizing is supposed to create a leaner and meaner company—in other words, a more profitable one. But does it? The results are now in, and they won't make the number crunchers happy.

Leaner and meaner doesn't usually mean greener. Many companies have rightsized only to find that they're doing no better than when they carried around all that fat.

A survey of 531 large companies conducted by the Wyatt Co., a consulting firm, indicates that restructuring alone is not a panacea. Only 46 percent (who restructured) saw a rise in earnings within two fiscal years. And less than 34 percent realized an increase in productivity from the layoffs. Strange as it may seem, more than half of the companies *refilled* the positions they had eliminated within a year of the downsizing.[4]

Unless you're using early retirement inducements to downsize, laying off workers usually reduces labor costs, at least initially. But these savings "are significantly reduced by a decrease in survivors' productivity and morale," says Joel Brockner, a management professor at Columbia's business school.[5]

OFF WITH THEIR HEADS

"Companies still think that all they need to do is cut heads. But that won't yield what they're looking for. Downsizing requires more planning and thought in order to be effective," concludes John J. Parkington, Wyatt's director of research and development in San Francisco.[6]

Cutting back has become an automatic response, a no-brainer

strategy, to eliminate corporate red ink. It's the "in" thing to do. But it is not always the right thing.

Consulting with companies who are restructuring, we sometimes get the feeling that more than a few CEOs are caught in a macho competition over who's got the biggest sword. To these hatchet men ruthlessness is seen as a virtue, a sign of true leadership that demonstrates they're not afraid to make the hard choices.

The way many of these hatchet people have downsized is downright stupid. They order a 10 percent personnel cut across the board in every department. So departments and divisions that are profitable and contributing get axed along with those sacred cows that have long outlived their usefulness. That's cutting the muscle of an organization along with the fat. And if you want to keep ahead these days you need that muscle, those people who are Change-Ready and can lead the organization.

What message does this send the rest of the organization? Why kill yourself trying to contribute when they'll lop off your head whether you are any good or not?

Now the survivors have to take up the slack doing the jobs of those who were cut, in addition to their own. The result is that everyone is running, racing, and rushing, trying to do more with less. People working at this fever pitch, as we have discussed, make more mistakes, don't think as clearly, and certainly not creatively. The result is that quality, service, and innovation suffer, and sooner or later—probably sooner—so does the bottom line. And then it's time for another cut.

PENNY WISE AND DOLLAR FOOLISH

Another area that is often meat for the cutter's ax are the so-called non-essentials like marketing, advertising, R&D, HR (human resources), and IS (information systems). Cutting these back may save some bucks up front, but it can cripple the company's growth in the long run. Most successful corporations focus on leaping forward, aggressively developing new products and services.

3M, for example, has long operated on the policy that 70 percent of its sales five years down the road will come from products that do not yet exist.[7] For them R&D is the key to the future. Cutting back would be penny wise and pound foolish.

Gillette lives by this rule: Increase spending in "growth drivers" like plant equipment, R&D, and advertising at least as fast as revenues go up.[8] They innovate constantly to stay ahead of the competition.

The National Science Board warns that U.S. industry is spending too little on R&D. A decade ago there was only one Japanese company among the top 10 patent recipients. Today over half are Japanese, including the top three. GE, the former U.S. leader, fell from first to sixth.[9] Peter Drucker reports that while in Japan he was told by a senior executive at the principal Mitsubishi think tank, "In another twenty years the entire Mitsubishi Group will be organized around this research institute."[10] The Japanese might think to downsize, but never at the expense of those units that feed innovation and sales.

HUMAN COSTS

A major cost of downsizing usually missed in the accountants' cost-benefit equation is the effect on those left behind. Not only is morale devastated, but anxiety can reach epic proportions. People start looking over their shoulders, calling headhunters, and working on their résumés instead of the task in front of them.

"Most managements don't have as firm a hand on the human aspects of restructuring as they do on finance and technology," observes public opinion guru Daniel Yankelovich, who surveyed high-level execs on the topic.[11]

A manager who survived the onslaught at a large California bank told us, "I couldn't get to sleep for months after the layoffs began. I interpreted every signal from my boss as a sign that I was next. The pressure was unbearable."

A scared worker is not a productive one and certainly not an innovative one. Fear causes them to play it safe, to keep their heads down and not try anything new or risky. They just do what is required; no more, no less. And this is exactly the opposite of what is needed to get or keep ahead today.

SURVIVOR SICKNESS

When AT&T slashed managerial jobs for the first time in 1986, stress-related illnesses—from insomnia to high blood pressure—soared. Of 250 managers studied, nearly half had more marital strains after the cutbacks, reported the *Wall Street Journal*.[12] "Survivor sickness" is what David Noer, vice president of the Center for Creative Leadership, calls it. He estimates that 75 percent of Fortune 500 companies have been infected by it.[13]

Downsizing survivors go through the kind of psychic numbing associated with traumas like plane crashes. They often feel guilty for their good fortune and wonder why they have made the cut while their friends and compatriots have not, says Noer. They don't feel worthier, just luckier. And they know that Lady Luck might be out to lunch tomorrow.

It seems almost immoral to take joy in work under these circumstances, and many become morose, worrying and fretting as they struggle with intensified workloads. Many get very resentful toward management. Disgruntled employees will often resort to damaging office computers, stealing property, or even flattening the tires on company cars.

Peller Marion, an early pioneer in outplacement and executive development and author of *Crisis Proof Your Career*, has seen the aftermath of those "Monday massacres." "Senior management gets frightened," she says. "Communication is censored or on a 'need to know' basis. When unexpected situations arise, paranoia sets in.

"In most corporate cultures the emotional dimension of work is left at home. There are very few feelings allowed in the workplace. During restructuring, many people feel anxious, trapped, and stymied, and not free to talk about it.

"Companies consider survivors to be the lucky ones. 'Why do *they* need help?' is the prevailing attitude. In fact, they need assistance badly to work through their negative feelings, recommit to the organization, and come out the other end," says Marion.[14]

Pain and suffering. When Jostens Learning, which creates software for more than 9,500 schools, downsized to cope with revenue losses from school spending cuts, the effect was devastating. Despite attempts at helping employees to adjust, productivity slumped like a night watchman at 5 A.M. People were "mentally checked out," walking around with a glazed look, observed Eduard Schwan, a senior software engineer. "People distanced themselves from each other and from upper management."[15]

An internal survey found that 37 percent of employees were looking for other jobs, and a higher than usual number of people were quitting. In the months that followed the layoff, 16 staffers quit the product-development section, which had already lost 26 percent of its staff of 463. Normal turnover is 10 to 15 employees a year. Productivity dropped off too, especially in the two months immediately following the change.[16]

Adam Zak, an executive recruiter in Chicago, recalls working with a manager who had gone through several rounds of firing subordinates: "He was smoking, had lost weight, had trouble looking me in the eye, was extremely nervous. It seemed to me that a few months of telling people they were out the door had gone a long way in destroying his personality."[17]

THE WRONG QUESTION

"A great many companies are asking the wrong question," says Eric Greenberg. "They are asking, What is the irreducible core that we need to turn on the lights in the morning and lock up the doors at night and still continue to do business? The right question is, How can we change the way we do business so that the people we have are better able to contribute to organizational success?

"What companies have been doing is firing their customers," he says. "People who lose their jobs are not spending their money and not driving the industrial machine."[18]

Most companies are cutting the muscle—the people—and leaving the fat—the outdated processes. Not a very healthy diet. If you're going to cut, start by rounding up the sacred cows, not the cow hunters. Cut cows first. In other words, cut the fat, not the muscle.

A second look. Even when cutbacks seem like the obvious way out of trouble, a second look can spare everyone a lot of grief. When Sister Carol Keehan took over as president of Providence Hospital in Washington, D.C., she thought the auditor's report showing a 21 percent loss was a typographical error. Instead of taking the conventional route of slashing employees and services, she embarked on the road less traveled. She went to the staff and assured them that no one would be fired except as a last resort. Then she solicited their advice on how to turn the situation around.

The result was expanded services, not cutbacks. She opened the Center for Life, a care facility for poor prenatal women. She bought three vans to drive into Washington to pick them up, and she spent the entire advertising budget on upgrading facilities to the level of the city's affluent hospitals.

Instituting prudent management techniques like bulk buying of everything from supplies to insurance and fund-raising drives to raise monies, Sister Carol turned the bleak situation into a beacon of success. She didn't take the cheap solution, but instead reinvented and reorganized, building on the strengths of the organization: its staff and its higher vision.[19]

Fueling up. When a national auto-parts chain was losing money, the CEO wanted a 10 percent across-the-board personnel cut. The VP of sales, a little leery about the potential fallout of such a massacre, both to morale and to productivity, offered another solution: "Let's offer our people a choice. We can either do the ten percent downsizing or everyone can take a ten percent salary cut."

The workers agreed to the pay cut. But one regional manager raised the ante. "We'll take the cut in pay," he said, "but if we produce a profit next year can we not only get our salary back but a bonus as well?" The group in the room cheered. Their spirits soared at this suggestion. After a little huddling, the deal was sealed.

It was like a different company. With phones ringing and faxes flying, the store managers were constantly talking to each other about what was working and what wasn't. They shared new ideas and exchanged stories about the sacred cows they were slaughtering. They had teams visiting other retailers, like Nordstrom, to learn about service.

That next year they had a record profit. Everyone got a bonus. And the CEO learned a valuable lesson.

"INSTEAD OF" POLICY

Downsizing is a worn-out and inexpedient policy for solving corporate financial woes. We call it an "instead of" policy. It's done *instead* of reenvisioning company goals, *instead* of anticipating customers' needs, *instead* of finding more efficient and cheaper ways to provide goods and service, *instead* of offering a superior product, *instead* of reinventing the company.

Sister Carol's reinvention tactics are the alternative. Businesses need to move away from bottom-line solutions to top-line approaches that emphasize growth and expansion.

Change-Ready Thinking

Cut the fat (cows) before you cut the muscle (people).

Downsizing costs: morale, motivation, innovation.

Thirteen

The Technocow

When 25-year-old Joel Mack went hunting for a job he didn't look in the want ads. He didn't call a headhunter or a career counselor. Instead he put his résumé *on-line.* Within days he generated 75 responses and 30 job offers without ever having left his home.[1]

Whether it's telecommuting or teleconferencing, virtual teams or virtual offices, home shopping or hoteling, the technological revolution is changing American life- and work styles. With all this fascination with and reliance on techno-advances, it's easy to believe that technology is the magic bullet that can solve any problem.

If your sales are down two years in a row, if your profits have been squeezed like the Florida citrus crop, don't lose one more night of sleep. Invest in a new telecom system. Get a covey of computers for the accounting department. Everyone lives happily ever after. Right? Wrong.

For years companies have worshiped at the altar of new technology, believing in the techno-solution. Yet for all the billions that have been spent on technology in the last decade, an MIT study at the prestigious Sloan Institute reveals no corresponding increase in productivity. In fact, U.S. productivity has dropped from an average of 2.4 percent in the 1950s to 1.3 percent in the eighties.

TECHNOMANIA

One reason is "technomania," the tendency to see the latest U-mail, E-mail or A-Z mail as a new toy to be played with. Wowed by all the bells and whistles, people forget about what really matters: the end use and the end user.

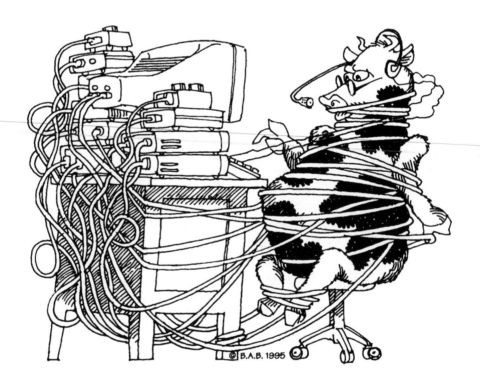

TECHNOCOW

On a recent trip to Chicago, I called the movie-information hot line. The recording included not only what was playing, where it was playing, who was in it, and who directed it, but sound bites from each film. After slogging through all that extraneous information I was told that for show times I had to call *another* number. I rented a video that night.

"It's important to step back from an industry that is full of people announcing new widgets every day—faster widgets, more widgets," says IBM CEO Lou Gertsner. "I mean, it's staggering. What I'm hearing from our customers is that there is an excess of technology out there. The real pressure is how do I use this stuff to achieve something important for my business? Do I really need this piece of software all over my company?"[2]

OFFICE COW

Not long ago the status symbol at work was the corner office with your name on the door and a Bigelow on the floor. No more. The big office suite littered with art and antiques and its own bathroom has been replaced by . . . *no office* at all. We don't mean no job; we mean literally no office.

With all the new technology, people can stay in touch from anywhere. And with everyone spending so much time on the road, there's a lot of money tied up in spaces that are more empty than full. Since real estate represents about 25 percent of the assets of a Fortune 500 company, that's a chunk of change.

Occupancy costs aren't that important when you're on a steep growth curve, but in this globally competitive environment, you have to look under every rock for savings, and that includes the cost of housing your business, says Bruce Russell, Kodak's director of corporate real estate.[3]

AT&T now has about 8,000 people, mostly in sales, working in offices that are little more than cubicles with phones and laptop hookups. The result: fewer lounge lizards and 20 percent more time with customers—probably the ones with offices. Managers are reporting increases of up to 45 percent in productivity from this new arrangement.[4]

For every dollar spent implementing these virtual offices AT&T saves two in occupancy costs. (But will it be reflected in our phone bills?) They also have another 20,000 white-collar workers who telecommute at least part of each week, and hope to add 10,000 more by the end of the year.[5] Not to be left out of this money-saving trend,

OFFICE COW

IBM estimates it will cut occupancy costs by *$500 million* over the next five to seven years.[6]

With the increases in technology, this trend is happening everywhere. In fact, over 43 million people, or 33 percent of the workforce, are right now working at least part time from a home office. Five years ago the number was 24 million—that's an increase of 83 percent! It's predicted that this trend will keep on increasing by 15 percent each year and reach 56 million by 1997.[7]

VIRTUAL ISOLATION

Before you start converting your kitchen table into a computer carrel you need to ask: How do you create teamwork when your people are in twenty different locations connected only by modem? One of the biggest problems with the "no-office" office is the loss of personal, one-to-one contact.

"Few employees spend eight to ten hours a day tied to their desks. Many spend a few minutes talking with and learning from colleagues. The advice shared at the watercooler or the tip shared over an impromptu lunch is a benefit to workers that often isn't measured when companies talk about the advantages of the virtual office,"[8] writes syndicated columnist Julianne Malveaux.

"A lot of the communication and learning that employees do is not technically through doing their jobs but through simply talking with colleagues," says John Tower, a managing director for real estate giant Edward S. Gordon. "If you're cut off, you can't have that kind of informal communication and learning. How then do you transmit corporate culture and how do you motivate people who are working at home or out of their cars?"[9]

There's a lot of truth to the old adage "Out of sight, out of mind." While you're working in your virtual office people forget about you. And a new business lead that needs immediate attention is passed on to someone else. Working at home, you might miss hearing about a possible job opening or a new client opportunity.

LOSING TOUCH

Technology in general can separate people from each other even while appearing to bring them closer together. As powerful as electronic communications can be, they can't replace the "up close and personal" experience that comes with direct contact. You lose the nuances of body language and facial expressions that are vital to good communication.

"Our team is spread out all over the country, so we meet regularly, once a week, by videoconferencing," a Procter & Gamble product manager told us. "The problem is that we only have a limited time to speak at these meetings. They're pretty rushed. Everybody is anxious to have their say, to be heard. They're great for sharing information, but limited for doing anything creative like brainstorming or exploring new ideas or innovative strategies. I miss the old meetings around the coffee wagon and the watercooler. They might not have been as efficient, but I think we came up with much better and more creative ideas that way."

High-tech communication like videoconferencing or E-mail is great for bringing people up to speed and swapping text and documents, but it's not very good if you want to brainstorm or develop innovative strategies, products, or services. With the time pressure to get things done there's no chance to stop and think, to mull over an idea, or get feedback on that "out of the box" inspiration you've been percolating for the last week.

PRECONFERENCE JITTERS

A senior manager at CSX, a large freight company, sees another problem. "We do a lot of videoconferencing because our people are spread out in different locations," he told us. "But before we start, no one's thinking about the agenda. They're all in the bathroom, combing their hair, straightening their ties, worrying about how they look. It sometimes feels like a movie set. It wouldn't surprise me if one day they bring in a makeup artist.

"Videoconferencing's better than teleconferencing because you can see who you're talking to. But it's far less effective than actually being there. What's missing are the little things, the asides, the reactions on people's faces when someone is making a point, the body language. All the stuff that engineers like me aren't supposed to notice. There are a lot of things going on at a meeting that you just can't pick up on the video."

"IN THE HALLS"

At major conferences and conventions where we regularly speak, meeting planners tell us that despite the useful information being presented, the real value is what happens outside the sessions and in the halls when people get together, network, and share information, leads, and ideas.

"One of the most important purposes of our big conferences and conventions is networking," says Ken Jenny, senior vice president at Prudential Real Estate. "We found that referrals increase dramatically when our agents make face-to-face connections with each other. Personal contact increases trust. It's much easier to call someone you *know* than a strange voice on the other end of a phone or a database."[10]

McDonald's means meetings. Some companies still believe in the power of the face-to-face sit-down. It's not that they're technophobic, only that they realize the singular benefits of personal connecting. McDonald's, no stranger to cutting-edge technology—they pioneered point-of-sale computing—has no E-mail system at its headquarters. And no company brings its people together as often and from so far.

Says Bob Kwan, managing director of Singapore operations, "We constantly get together by region as well as discipline, such as purchasing, construction, and accounting. We share successes and failures, and we work together to cut costs."[11]

A typical month's meetings for him includes a store managers' meeting in Sydney, a worldwide comunications conference in Chicago, and a European purchasing-board meeting in London.

ROAD-WEARY WARRIORS

"This travel stuff is getting old," a road-warrior executive told us on a late-night flight. "I'm tired of airports and not seeing my kids grow up. But we're starting to do a lot more videoconferencing, so I'm going to be spending more time at home."

Don't believe it. Advances in telecommunications won't reduce your company's travel budget or get you more at-home time. In fact, they will do just the opposite.

" 'Travel substitution' is shorthand for the hope that ever more capable telecommunications technologies—videoconferencing among them—will allow us to substitute electrons and videoscreens for air miles and in-the-flesh meetings," writes Paul Saffo, a research fellow at the Institute of the Future.[12] But, says Saffo, although videoconferencing is indeed catching on, it will mean *more*, not less, business travel. "Relationships are the essence of business life, and people who become acquainted by wire will inevitably want to meet in person."[13]

Historically, advances in technology have always led to more travel, not less, and likewise better transportation has usually led to advances in telecommunications. The railroads, for example, strung the first telegraph wires along their rights of way. And direct-dial telephone service spurred commercial aviation by making it possible to do business with companies in another part of the country.

It's interesting that air miles traveled and volume of long-distance calls both have risen steadily and in concert with each other. With the invention of air and car phones it's even possible to travel and call simultaneously.

INFORMATION GREED

In an on-line world where a universe of facts is instantaneously available with the push of a few buttons, people collect data the way I collected stamps as a child: the more the merrier.

But, writes Professor Gary Loveman of the Harvard Business School, "In most cases [managers] know the work was done previously with less information, for example, decisions at staff meetings were made with less elaborate analysis."[14] The problem is that most executives and managers don't know how much information is enough. "There is a strong implication," writes Loveman, "that more information and more analysis is always better. . . . It is quite possible that the introduction of cheap computing in an organization can lead to huge overinvestments in costly information generation and processing that, at the end of the day, has scarcely had any impact on business results."[15]

High-tech is vitally important these days. But technology alone won't do the job. High-tech needs to be combined with high-touch. And new technology has to be carefully chosen and set up in the right way. Without these safeguards, technology is just another sacred cow that will cost you as much as it saves.

Change-Ready Thinking

High-tech needs high-touch.

Fourteen

The Team Cow

"BUREAUCRAZY"

It wasn't all that many years ago when the only team you found in corporate America was the company's softball squad. Work functions were delineated by departments. R&D designed a product, then "flipped it over the wall" to Engineering, then over various walls to Manufacturing, Accounting, Marketing, and finally to Sales. God forbid there was a problem, because you'd have to start all over again.

Everyone worked in their own silo, a nice, neat, hermetically sealed environment more suited to a lab than a business setting. And because the walls that separated departments were so high, it took an impossibly long time to get product to market. To streamline the "bureaucrazy" someone came up with the idea of sledgehammering the walls of those silos. Cross-functional teams, a concept that came out of the English coal mines in the thirties, have now taken hold in business like an eel on a rubber glove.

A survey of Fortune 1000 companies showed that a whopping 68 percent use self-managed or high-performance teams.[1] Whether ser-

TEAM COW

vice companies like FedEx or manufacturers like Boeing, it doesn't matter; the team approach is omnipresent. And product-to-market speed plus productivity are up dramatically.

PUT DOWN YOUR POM-POMS

But before you strain your triceps raising your pom-poms, you might want to take another look at this high-flying phenomenon. Has the team concept, once the solution to a herd of sacred "silo" cows, become a herd animal itself?

The answer is yes and no. Teams, according to the latest research, work better in theory than in reality, and they are not the panacea they were once thought to be. You might say they're an up and coming sacred cow.

"Teams are the Ferraris of work design," says management professor Edward Lawler, who oversaw a study at USC's Center for Effective Organizations. "They're high performance, but high maintenance and expensive."[2]

"Teamwork isn't simple," says someone who should know—Pat Riley, who coached the Los Angeles Lakers to four world championships in nine years. "In fact, it can be a frustrating, elusive commodity. . . . Teamwork doesn't appear magically just because someone mouths the words. It doesn't thrive just because of the presence of talent or ambition. It doesn't flourish simply because a team has tasted success."[3]

TEAM TROUBLES

"Just because you put a group of people in a room doesn't mean they're a team," cautions Laura Hotzler, a senior manager at consulting giant Deloitte & Touche.[4]

Here are some typical team troubles:

They're Overused

Not every function requires a team. "You don't use teams with insurance salesmen and long-haul truckers," emphasizes Henry Sims, a management professor and author of *Business without Bosses.*[5]

Too often management reaches for the team solution the way a flu sufferer goes for the tissues. Teams have become a knee-jerk reaction to any problem. Automatic "teaming" is fraught with peril. Team burnout is now being encountered in many organizations.

"I'm playing in too many leagues and I can't keep up with all the players or my responsibilities," complained one manager with five team assignments at a gas and electric company. "I'm completely teamed out."

"Sure this quality program is important," said a supervisor for a ready-to-wear manufacturer. "But it means being on another team and that means more meetings. Hell, I haven't got time to make my other meetings as it is."

Some basic questions to ask before creating a team:

- Does the job require a high level of employee interaction?
- Will teams be too costly or take too long to get the task completed?
- Will teams unduly complicate rather than simplify the job?
- Is it overkill to use a team for this project? Can individuals do the job more easily and effectively?

Mismatches—The Wrong Kinds of Teams Are Created

There are many different kinds of teams. Some are better suited for a specific task than others. Here are five types:

- Problem Solving Teams: They address a specific problem and then disband.
- Work Teams: As the name implies, they do the actual labor. They're down on the floor producing the product.
- Virtual Teams: They don't sit down in a room together but communicate via telephone and computers.

- Quality Circles: They meet intermittently to air problems and upgrade procedures.
- Management Teams: They coordinate management functions, such as sales and R&D.[6]

What happens when the wrong kind of team is chosen? Virtual teams are great for overseeing processes and communicating important information, but they're a poor choice when you need to brainstorm new products or services.

Quality circles are suited for fashioning incremental improvements, but they'll be absolutely wrong for rapid or major organizational shifts. Without a clear sense of what kind of team each situation demands, the group is set up to fail.

Not Everyone Is Suited to Team Play

Some individuals are lone wolves or rugged individualists. The aggressive "fire in the belly" sales guy who loves being where the action is might try to dominate meetings. The "techie" who only enjoys talking to her computer might clam up in meetings or sit there playing videogames. Forcing them into groups can negate their productivity as well as that of the team. The "one bad apple" theory applies to teams.

Individual Initiative Can Be Stifled

Too many meetings and too little action—problems endemic to teams—can squash motivation and dynamism. Since the group, not the individual, is held accountable, some members can sit back on their duffs with a degree of impunity. Decisions are sometimes delayed and actions postponed as all members wait for the slow and cautious to get on board.

It's easier for an employee to hide laziness or sloppy work inside the team. Highly ambitious people may also feel that the team structure blocks their advancement. Their response may be to stop extending themselves. We know of teams in which members reduced their output because others in the group were not working as hard as they were. We've also come across teams in which one or two members were responsible for the group's effort while others sat back and played spectator. The sense of unfairness and the ensuing resentment eventually demotivated the achievers.

Poor Support

Without the tools, support, and training, teams are doomed to fail. Yet many teams are sent out to do a job with inadequate background information, poor access to relevant data, a bare-bones budget, and a substandard communication system. When they come back without results, who takes the heat? You guessed it, even though their problems originated at setup.

Unclear on the Concept

Everyone's been on at least one team whose first and sometimes only job was to figure out the reason for its existence. Successful teams have clear and attainable goals, a definitive time frame, and a method for evaluating their results. Cosmetic teaming that gives the appearance of taking action is a waste of time and money.

Operating in a Vacuum

When teams are introduced in combination with other organizational changes, they work. When they're introduced as an isolated practice, they fail. "My gut feeling is that most are introduced in isolation," says Paul Osterman, a professor at MIT's Sloan School of Management.[7]

At Boeing, where work teams are commonly used in most areas of production, the company found that communication among different groups was poor. So poor that one of the teams had designed the passengers' oxygen system to be installed in the same place another had placed the gasper, the fresh-air vent for each seat.

To combat the problem, the company created airplane-integration teams with access to personnel at all levels of the organization. These special groups of 12 to 15 people moved information back and forth among various crews. They found the problem and got the wing and cockpit teams to fix it, avoiding costly modifications at manufacture.

Boeing's solution points in the right direction. Teams should be structured within a well-conceived master plan. This plan should harmonize functions and outline specific links of communication, both between team members and with other teams. Ad hoc, or casually initiated, teams often find themselves out on a limb or operating at cross purposes with other groups.

Says McKinsey's Frank Ostroff, a consultant in the firm's organization-performance group, "Executives know what teams can do. But they need a picture that links the high-performance team to the whole organization and multiplies the gain."[8]

Personality Problems

How're you going to get two people who've been career-long rivals to buddy up? What about employees who've been avoiding each other at the watercooler for years? Group dynamics are not something you can ignore. Staffers on multilevel teams are often intimidated by managers and reluctant to open their mouths. When you create teams, you're bringing together everyone's history: how they operated in their original "team," their family of origin, and every group they've been in since.

Some people live for conflict. Others live to avoid it. Some people are emotional and expressive; others are rational and reserved. You've got extroverts and introverts. Many teams fail because management is not prepared to troubleshoot on this issue. You can forget the team concept if you don't manage the players and the way they fit (or don't) into the group.

Mouseland feuds. The most successful team in the entertainment industry since Rodgers and Hammerstein ran aground not because of poor performance, but because of personality clashes. Michael Eisner and Jeffrey Katzenberg were the dynamic duo responsible for raising Disney's revenues from $1.4 billion a year to more than $8.5 billion in less than ten years. Katzenberg ran the studios; Eisner, the larger operation. Despite their immense individual talents and business savvy, personality conflicts destroyed their partnership.

Writes Ken Auletta in *The New Yorker*, "This Hollywood tale is another reminder that intangibles often matter more than tangibles like profit and loss or business strategy or so-called synergies. Jeffrey Katzenberg left a big job for reasons having more to do with psychology and personal chemistry than with performance."[9]

DIFFERENT TONGUES

Companies are melting pots peopled by individuals from different cultures who bring their distinct languages and values to the workplace. Employees from different departments in the organization also bring their own particular perspectives and even their own lingo. People from Marketing and people from Manufacturing will take different views of the same problem.

Team members also "speak in many tongues." Marketing talks "sales-talk," Manufacturing talks "production-talk," Engineering talks "design-talk." These differences of language and perspective can work for or against you. Utilizing a team's diverse experience, expertise, and viewpoints enables it to be creative and effective. It produces a synergy where the result equals more than the sum of the parts.

On the other hand, diverse perspectives not handled properly will separate people, producing conflict, petty jealousies, and lack of flexibility.

TEAM TACTICS

Here are some rules for creating synergy and getting more out of a team:

• Clarify at the outset the importance of the perspective each player brings to the table.

- Treat everyone with respect. Make sure each person has an opportunity to contribute. Don't forget that the introvert from R&D or the easily intimidated junior staffer have something unique to contribute. Encourage their participation.
- Value everyone's contribution regardless of how it might appear at first blush. A waste of time? Not at all. The seeds of brilliance may be contained in a notion that at first looks ridiculous. Or the idea may stimulate someone else to come up with an inspired solution. Sometimes a little spit and polish will turn a dull thought into a gem. Look for what's right in an idea before you look for what's wrong. That challenges all participants to move out of fault-finding mode into an inclusive way of thinking.
- Build bridges of understanding. Be open to contrasting points of view. Don't dismiss differences of opinion, beliefs, values, or ideas. Conflict often leads to creativity. Use opposing perspectives to create a larger framework.
- Target the ideas, not the person. Keep things safe by discussing ideas, not people. Statements like "Leave it to an accountant to come up with that," though delivered in jest, can have a dampening effect on risk-taking. Creative thinking can only blossom in an accepting environment where there is no possibility of personal attack or reference. Put up a sign if necessary: NO PERSONALIZING ALLOWED.
- Managers should model behavior. Team members look to the leader for clues on the appropriate actions and attitudes. If the manager respects others, listens well, demonstrates open-mindedness, and acts with honesty, people will follow suit. (More on this in Chapter 17, "Building the Change-Ready Environment.")
- Confront noncontributing or obstructionist team members, but do it without blame or hostility.

THE LIFE CYCLE OF THE TEAM

Teams have a life of their own. Just like people, they go through stages of growth and development. Newly formed teams function differently from fully developed teams, and what they need from their leaders also changes with time. To maximize a team's contribution, it's important for managers to understand how groups evolve and change. It's not a good idea to use a new team to do a job that requires a great deal of trust among members. Neither does it make sense to use a mature team to do a job that will be micromanaged from above.

There are five phases of team development.

Orientation

In the early stage, members ask themselves questions like: "How do I fit in?" "What are the rules and expectations?" "Can I trust these people?" "How are decisions made?" "Is it safe to say what I think?" This is the stage when people are hesitant and tentative. Leaders need to be very directive, establishing the team's mission, objectives, rules, and climate. They need to motivate the players, get them excited about the project, and model standards of participation.

Conflict

Phase two is usually a period of conflict and dissatisfaction as members come to know each other. There are often power struggles and testing of leaders. This is a critical stage when the team can fall apart or the mission can get sabotaged. It's often a period of frustration when members get confused about what is expected and how they are to go about their jobs. Leaders must consistently restate goals, manage conflicts, reassure team members, and respond to challenges without defensiveness.

Harmony

In phase three natural leaders emerge, and respect, trust, and cooperation begin to surface. Members become increasingly concerned about maintaining harmony, and differences tend to be hidden as the team develops cohesiveness. In this stage, the group starts to run itself and formal leaders need to pull back from their active roles and redirect the group only when it gets off track or when important differences aren't being aired. Facilitation, not direction, defines the manager's role.

Maturity

The mature group is one that functions smoothly toward accomplishing well-defined tasks that everyone agrees on. Members feel a sense of cohesiveness and commitment to each other and the team's goals. A strong group identity and a confidence in the group's ability to meet its mandate emerge. Leaders should move to a largely supportive role in this period, allowing members to plan and accomplish the work as well as resolve problems.

Dotage

The final phase is the phasing-out stage, when the team has become a sacred cow. It has outlived its purpose and usefulness. Members have fallen into familiar roles and habits, and the team is too darn comfortable to be dynamic and creative. The role of the leader is to plan a celebration dinner and disband the group.

Teams are one sacred cow that shouldn't be "pasture-ized." Get smarter about how to use them and they'll turn into lead bulls.

Change-Ready Thinking

Throwing a group of people into a room doesn't make them a team.

Don't use teams for jobs that individuals can do better.

Build bridges between teams.

Fifteen

The Work-till-You-Drop Cow

"The secret of my success isn't some fancy strategy. I just work harder than anyone else."

The speaker was the first of five on a "superstar" panel of mortgage brokers who had closed over $30 million in loans in the past year. Her typical workday ran from 7 A.M. to around 2 A.M. and consisted of sending out weekly update sheets to real estate brokers, composing ads, creating referral lists, attending open houses, going to real estate functions, shaking a lot of hands, and schmoozing endlessly.

The next three superstars—also "marathoners"—almost lip-synched her words. Most of the audience took notes, nodded in agreement, and mentally laced up their running shoes.

Great success strategy, I thought, if your idea of success is *not* to have a personal life and to burn out in five years.

13 MONTHS A YEAR

Remember technology's promise of more leisure time? All the new hardware was supposed to give workers less to do and more time to play.

Know anyone who's playing?

Despite the techno-revolution, the downsizing epidemic has left survivors with expanded job descriptions and fewer resources. Typical is the U.S. Bank of Washington (state), which was created in a 1988 merger. The human resources department was shrunk from 70 people to six, yet was still expected to provide the same level of services. "People thought the heavier workload [everyone working late into the evening and weekends] after the merger was going to be

WORK-TILL-YOU-DROP COW

temporary," says Robert Kakiuchi, vice president of human resources. "Instead it's becoming the new norm."[1]

The average American today is working 20 percent more hours than he or she did only five years ago. That's a whole day a week. Fifty-seven percent are routinely at their desks from 50 to 65 hours a week.[2] Many reports are even saying that white-collar Americans are approaching the Japanese tradition of 12-hour workdays and work-filled evenings. In fact, says Harvard economist Juliet Schor in her book *The Overworked American,* people are working the equivalent of *13 months* each year compared to two decades ago.[3]

And it's not only white-collar workers. At GM's Flint, Michigan, plant, workers went on strike partly to protest mandatory overtime that sometimes resulted in 66-hour workweeks. And workers for Allegheny Ludlum Corp's steel plants went on strike after some workers were required to work as much as *174 hours in two weeks!*[4] Vacation? You've got to be kidding. For most people that's a long weekend. And those who do take vacations have a fax in their golf bag or a phone in their backpack.

WORKING MOTHER—A REDUNDANCY

Six million single mothers leave their kids to go to work. That's double what it was 20 years ago. And working mothers average about *44 hours* a week working and *31* on family responsibilities.[5] Is it any wonder that many people consider the term *working mother* a redundancy?

FIRST NEED AND THEN GREED

Economic necessity isn't the only reason people are working until they drop. Many take second jobs to earn discretionary income. "First it's need and then it's greed," says Sylvia Johnson, who sells full time at JCPenney and then works another 20 hours a week doing data entry at a computer firm. "My husband and I have a comfortable home and three cars. But I guess you always feel like you want something more as a reward for all the hard work you've done."[6]

AMERICANS WORK TOO HARD

That's what many Europeans think. The desire to keep hours short is an obsession in Germany, where the average week for factory workers is 30 hours and falling. In America it's 38 and rising. And in Germany workers are guaranteed *by law* a minimum of five weeks vacation.[7] "Germans put leisure first and work second," says Angie Clark, a German-born merchandising manager at JCPenney. "In America, it's the other way around."[8]

When Thursday night shopping was introduced in Germany retail workers went on strike and managers found it difficult to get sales staff to cover the extra hours. "Logically speaking, why should anyone want to buy a bicycle at eight-thirty P.M.?" asked Andreas Drauschke, a department store worker in Berlin.[9] Germans just can't fathom the American fixation with keeping the store open all hours. In their country it is illegal—that's right, *illegal*—for people to work at other jobs during holidays, a time that "is strictly for recovering."[10]

LESS MENTAL MUSCLE

The cost of working marathon days is premature breakdown. Any engine that is constantly running will burn out. Even Arnold Schwarzenegger, the Terminator, a five-time Mr. Universe, advised against working the same muscle groups two days in a row. They need rest to recuperate.

It's the same story with the mind. Overwork your "mental muscles" and you'll lose your sharpness. You won't concentrate as well, and you'll make more errors. Your creativity will suffer, and you'll feel physically, mentally, and spiritually depleted.

Seventy-five percent of respondents in a 1991 Gallup poll said their personal lives suffered because of their ever-increasing work schedules.[11]

CHEATING

A further risk to corporations pushing people too hard for too long is cheating. When people are "overtasked," when they have to do too much and are expected to meet unrealistically high goals, they are much more likely to cheat to make their numbers look good, says Michael Josephson, president of the Josephson Institute on Research.

Josephson believes that the scandal at Sears auto-repair shops in the early nineties, where customers were charged for services not rendered, was a result of the demand that repair-shop managers meet turbocharged sales targets.[12]

LESS IS MORE

It's better to pack it in when you're tired and come back early in the morning. You'll work faster when you're fresh and think more creatively. And your mood and attitude will be far better. Studies show that when the workday has been shortened, efficiency and productivity increase. At the turn of the century, when factory workers put in long hours, shrinking the workday from 10 to 8 hours a day significantly increased productivity. And cutting the 40-hour workweek by up to 5 hours in the U.S. and Britain has led to less absenteeism, less turnover, less personal business on company time, and lower costs.[13]

Half a day. During the summer of 1992, New York Life gave its employees Friday afternoons off. The work that was not done was made up during the rest of the week, the CEO reported.[14] A major publishing house adopted the same half-day Friday schedule during the summer. The stated purpose was to improve morale, but the surprise was that most people found they got as much done on those half days as they did on a whole day. "I just paid attention to what had to be done," one editor told us. "I eliminated all the little stuff that didn't really need attention. It made me realize how much time I waste and that helped me be more productive during the rest of the week."

COOLING DOWN THE SWEATSHOP

Some companies are breaking out of the sweatshop mentality and experimenting with new work schedules. At a Xerox plant, employees were given the freedom to choose their own starting times and to compress their workweeks. Managers panicked! But 10 months into the experiment, employees were completing their tasks without missing a beat. Absenteeism decreased by a third, and teamwork, morale, and customer satisfaction improved. Follow-up interviews found that employees felt they had more control over work.[15]

An employee survey at Chicago's Harris Bank revealed that people weren't looking for reduced hours but more flexibility in their work schedules. Harris responded with a sweeping new alternative allowing more personal control. In the bank's credit-card division for example, four employees created a schedule that combined eleven- and four-hour workdays. By splitting responsibility for the evening hours, which no one wanted, each worker fashioned a workweek that was best for her. The result: increased coverage of early evening hours—prime time for collection—and motivated, productive employees.[16]

"What we're seeing is that if you allow people to have control over their schedule, productivity shoots way up," says Karen Leibold, Stride Rite's director of work family programs whose Sperry Top-Sider division uses flex schedules.[17] And group product manager Joe Hearn reports he was "constantly astounded at the creativity employees bring to bear to make nontraditional arrangements work."[18]

"The workforce today is screaming for flexibility," says Robert Lambert, executive vice president for Carter Hawley Stores. "If you can help employees meet their outside responsibilities, you're going to have a more productive, more turned on, and more energized workforce. Flexibility is a business tool."[19]

FOUR DAYS A WEEK

About one-quarter of large companies in the United States now offer, or require, a four-day schedule, according to a *Wall Street Journal* report. That is double the number offered five years ago, making this the fastest-growing alternative work schedule that companies are using nationwide.[20]

The idea has caught on in Europe, where Volkswagen A.-G. recently gave its workers a four-day week. Many Europeans see it as the answer to unemployment woes.

"The four-day workweek can create two million jobs without sacrificing competitiveness," says Pierre Larrouturou, a French consultant with considerable clout. His plan calls for a 33-hour week and a 5 percent cut in salaries across the board.[21]

The four-day workweek reduces absenteeism, too. The extra day off gives people personal time for doctors' appointments, car repairs, and other obligations, so the need to miss work is eliminated.[22]

My own office has been closed Fridays for the past three years. The staff gets the same amount of work done in four days as they used to in five, and the office is a much happier place. Customer service has improved, people aren't burning out, and they have time for a more balanced life. My one concern was losing accessibility, since the common wisdom is "always stay in touch." Then I realized that people generally get voice mail and call back the next day, so closing on Fridays didn't make that much of a difference.

Unexpectedly, the four-day workweek has served as a marketing tool. It gets clients' attention, and I am always asked how it's working. And people assume that you *must* be successful to work only four days.

Vocational vacations. Even Bobby Knight, the brilliant and hard-driving University of Indiana basketball coach, says, "I see these coaches who say that coaching is their vocation, their avocation, and their vacation. I don't think I'd enjoy that.

"Coaching isn't that complicated," says Knight, who devotes his free time during the basketball season to fishing and hunting. He's more likely to be reading a military history book than a scouting report.[23]

ALL HOOKED UP AND NOPLACE TO GO

The long vacation in which you leisurely unwind over several weeks in a remote corner of the world is dead. It's been replaced by the mini holiday and the four-day weekend. And the way things are going, both of those will be replaced by the virtual vacation in which you never leave your desk—all hooked up and noplace to go.

Accept no substitutes. These ersatz alternatives cannot replace the real thing. When you're working marathon days, you need *significant* downtime. All the research shows that the key to handling stress is in the recovery period that follows it. Without extended relaxation, the body breaks down.

Do something that is as far from work as possible, both mentally and physically. Go to a place that hasn't got any phones or faxes. Stay out of touch. Whitewater raft trips, mountain-biking excursions, fishing on a secluded river; the idea is to get your mind off the office by doing something completely different. And don't bring the phone with you.

We've heard of a group of insurance executives who went fishing on the Salmon River and brought a satellite dish so they could communicate with their New York office. That's missing the point. Hell, that's missing the fish. Recovery time can't be fudged. Your body will know the difference the moment you hear your boss's voice coming out of the earpiece.

I come back from these out-of-touch vacations totally refreshed, excited about work again, and seeing things more clearly than when I left. And something else: All those odds and ends you were worrying about are still there waiting for you, or another person has taken care of them.

WORKING HALF TIME (ALMOST)

Incidentally, the last speaker on that superstar panel we mentioned at the top of the chapter was Duffy Gilligan, a loan officer for Mortgage Choice in Chapel Hill, North Carolina.[24] Well, Duffy surprised everyone. "My strategy," he said, "is to give a full *seventy-five percent effort!*"

I thought maybe he was kidding or that I'd misheard him, but then he continued, "I work about six hours a day five days a week. If you believe that you have to work all those hours, you'll fill up the time. My priority is to be with my son as much as possible. So I get down to essentials real fast. Most agents spend their day beating the bushes marketing for loan prospects. They call on real estate agents, doctors, and dentists, go to open houses and other local 'do's.' I go direct to my ultimate client—the person that wants the loan—give them great service, and tell them that if they like my service to give out some of my cards.

"I know that sounds simplistic, but our business isn't that complicated. We just make it hard. If you think it's necessary to jump through all those hoops you'll go out and buy hoops and practice jumping. You may even succeed. But at what cost? What I've done is to challenge whether we really need those hoops. I'm not good at jumping through them anyway."

That's Duffy. But we have to agree with him. You can work harder or work easier and probably accomplish the same both ways. Your choice.

Change-Ready Thinking

Overwork doesn't work.

Sixteen

Cow Hunting

HUNTING

In the previous section we discussed some typical sacred cows, but there are many more cattle grazing on our profits, productivity, and patience. Sacred cows roam hallways, offices, and conference rooms in corporate America. They can be found in every store and warehouse in small-town USA. To round them up and put them out to pasture, you need to be a cow hunter, continuously on the lookout for outmoded beliefs and practices.

IBM's new CFO Jerome York has all the instincts of a great hunter. York helped turn Chrysler around by shaving off $4 billion in excess fat, and he has plans to save $5 billion a year at Big Blue. That's a lot of cows, partner! Since going to IBM, he's challenged a culture "locked in decades of diehard habits" and reexamined the basic assumptions and procedures of almost everything the company does.

"There's a lot of waste in this company," York emphasizes. "We're going to find it and root it out. . . . IBM is living way over its head."[1]

No cow is too sacred for York to challenge. He is working to change IBM's once renowned but now outmoded management style of time-sapping consensus decision-making. And he is attacking such cherished IBM perks as employee country clubs and fetes.

Take a look at some of what the silver-haired former auto executive did in his first year:

- Whittled down IBM's "air force" from 13 to 7 jets
- Replaced phone-book-sized instruction manuals with electronic instructions—*saving $50 million* in printing costs

THE COW HUNT

- Eliminated the rental of an entire hotel floor (across from the company's Madison Avenue offices), used for introducing new products—*saving $1 million*
- Cut "Golden Circle" conferences for IBM's top salespeople from 11 to 4. No more five-star resort locations, either
- Axed the annual Christmas party for the press at New York's Plaza Hotel—*saving $10,000*[2]

York's "challenge everything" attitude is what it takes to be a successful cow hunter, but you don't have to be a high-level executive to spot sacred cows. The best hunters are often the workers in the trenches or the beginners who haven't been indoctrinated into the culture of the workplace and don't know all the rules and rationales. York is actually a high-tech neophyte himself, which explains why he brings such a fresh perspective to the job. (See Chapter Five, "The Expert Cow.")

SACRED-COW HUNTS

It helps if the company's top executives are hunters, but how do you get people in all levels of the organization involved in spotting sacred cows? Our answer is the sacred-cow hunt, a technique we use not only to recognize antiquated ideas but to get employees psychologically ready for change.

We don't know whether it's because people enjoy tumbling an icon or just delight in the heady feeling of challenging the status quo, but once we lay out the ground rules, people get swept up in cow hunts and become genuinely excited about the idea of change. In fact, some employees get downright gleeful about putting cows out to pasture.

For this reason, cow hunts are a great first step in getting employees ready for major organizational shifts. Hunts not only identify herds of sacred cattle, they are also motivational tools that get everyone on board. And people have a great time participating in them.

NO-BULL CAMPAIGNS

Tractor Supply Stores finds cow hunting so productive and exhilarating that it issues cowbells to employees. Every time a sacred cow is identified, those bossy bells get rung and the din can be heard echoing down the halls. Employees who spot the bygone bovines are heralded and toasted. Awards are given for the best cow of the month, and cow images and accessories are conspicuously displayed around the offices.

Cow hunts at Merck Pharmaceutical's 59 plants have been so successful that the company has been conducting *monthly sacred-cow barbecues.*

But Williams Pipe Line Company, a petroleum products pipeline from Tulsa, Oklahoma, wins the award for cow hunting hands down. They're already into their second "no-bull contest." If you identify a

sacred cow in your department, they used to give you a free lunch—hamburgers, of course. In "part deux" they've upped the ante. Now you get a $10 gift certificate if your idea is "irresistabull." And if your suggestion is "udderly" wonderful you get a $50 certificate or a "porta-bull" propane gas grill. You even get to go to a luncheon with all the district managers of operations.

"Help us corral worn out and broken down procedures that take more time and money than they're worth. We're loadin' 'em up and movin' 'em out to make room for a herd of productive prime beef," says a poster from the "No Bull, Part Deux" campaign.

Results have exceeded all expectations, according to Steven Ball, senior vice president. In the first round, the company received 533 ideas for eliminating sacred cows. Seventy percent were implemented at a cost of about $41 an idea. Not bad when you consider that several of the suggestions, like streamlining auditing procedures, each saved more than $15,000, the cost of the whole campaign. And the program isn't just "profitabull," it's great for morale. Over 85 percent of employees contributed ideas in round one.

"This kind of program is far superior to the suggestion box it replaced," says Ball. "You know what you get with a suggestion box? Cigarette butts and coffee cups. Our sacred-cow contest has worked so well that two of our people haven't paid for lunch in a couple of months!"

AN ORGANIZATION OF HUNTERS

Getting employees ready to change and ridding the organization of antiquated theories and practices are the immediate goals of the cow hunt. But the overriding and most important objective is to *create an organization of hunters.*

A company where people do their jobs while keeping an eye peeled for outmoded ideas and processes is a creative, powerful, Change-Ready organization able to reinvent itself before the need is pressing. The best hunters are often the people who are closest to the customer and the production process. Who would know better about redundant, counterproductive, or unnecessary work than those who sell the product, deliver the services, fill out the forms, and work the line?

Yet most companies have such poor mechanisms for getting worker input and *responding* to it that the incentive for innovation at the staff level is dismal. When businesses run cow hunts, employees understand someone's listening. They feel they are an important part of the team and can influence what happens on the job. Hunts are a human-resource asset that creates a sense of empowerment, they boost morale, develop teamwork, and increase motivation. Not a bad benefits package.

"I've noticed that everyone has a much greater interest in work since we've started the cow hunts. People are more involved. They feel their opinions and ideas matter," reports John Rutter, executive vice president at Ralston Resorts, which runs Keystone, Breckenridge, and Arapahoe Basin ski resorts. "Everyone feels more committed and there is a sense of closeness and teamwork that wasn't there before."

HUNTING IN POSSES

Although there is nothing wrong with solo hunting, we've found that searching for sacred cows in teams is more fun and productive. The more diverse the team, the better. We often bring together employees from different parts of the organization who rarely see each other, let alone see eye to eye. A typical cow-hunting team might include line workers, support staff, sales people, number crunchers, engineers, human-resources people, and *customers.*

The range of opinion resulting from this diversity creates new perspectives that could never have developed with a more homogeneous group. And someone from another department may have the needed distance to spot some of the more invisible cows.

CUSTOMER HUNTERS

Customers make great hunters because they come with a different set of priorities and point of view. Including them insures that your hunt is not done in a vacuum, isolated from the real concerns of the marketplace. Since end users ultimately determine your company's success or failure, their views are especially valuable.

ROUNDING 'EM UP—COWS IN PLAIN SIGHT

Some cows are obvious. They're just standing out in the open range chewing their cud. With a little direction, everyone recognizes them and agrees they should be eliminated.

That's what happened at Ameritech where auditors, a group not usually considered daring and reckless, and often blamed for creating cows in the first place, turned out to be great hunters. They generated 25 cows in 15 minutes!

INVISIBLE COWS

Many sacred cows are not so transparent. They're usually too woven into the fabric of an organization's assumptions and practices to be noticed. Or they're so automatic as to be imperceptible. Invisible cows are hidden by a variety of obstacles, including one of our favorite syllogisms: "If it's still around it must work; and it must work if it's still around."

One of these hidden cows was an activity report I had to fill out when I was a trainee at a major advertising agency. Developed by my manager who'd been in the company so long he'd grown roots, the purpose of the thing, he told us, was to teach us organizational skills like how to prioritize. He also used it as a weekly status check to see what we were doing.

The report consisted of writing down everything we had to do and rating it "A," "B," or "C" in terms of importance. There were also separate columns for "action to be taken" and "time expended." We all did our "ABC"s religiously.

At one point, the agency was making several important business presentations and a few of us had to race around getting everything ready. At the end of this hectic two-week period, several of the trainees noted that we hadn't had time to do our "ABC"s. "And I didn't miss them at all," one quipped. "Not only didn't I miss them," said another, "but I got more done without them and I didn't forget anything, either. The 'ABC's rate a 'D' on my priority list."

At that moment we all realized that we were spending as much time on that activity report as we were on getting two "real" jobs done. Someone pointed out that if we just did the "A"s on our list, the "B"s and "C"s would either take care of themselves or eventually become "A"s. Even listing the "A"s wasn't really necessary because they were obvious and immediate. So, armed to the teeth with rationales, we stormed the boss's castle and, over his objections, got him to kill that cow.

WHAT YOU DON'T KNOW CAN HURT YOU

Invisible cows are especially dangerous because they give birth to entire herds. When you don't know something exists, it can (and will) take on a life of its own. Before you know it, the printout that wasn't anything more than an old relic from another time requires a special meeting to discuss it and numerous reports to analyze it. It's not just sacred cows that eat up your productivity, it's all those little calves, like corollary practices and procedures, they've borne that create the bigger problem.

PRIMING THE PUMP

When people are having trouble getting started on the hunt it's necessary "to prime the pump." At any discussion about work, someone's always objecting to something: the weekly status meeting that's a waste of time, reports that never get read, time sheets that are simply filed away. Instead of ignoring such complaints we use their energy to get people going.

Complaints are often the spotting of sacred cows in disguise. When several people agree that something is a waste of time, doesn't work, or is redundant . . . *listen to them.* They're probably on to something.

At a program for PB&Z, an energy company, employees were having trouble getting into the spirit of the hunt. Everyone was holding back and we thought we had a real disaster on our hands. But in the hallway it was a different story. People were alive with complaints and criticisms. To harness their energy, we initiated a "Pee on PB&Z" exercise, a bitch session in which everyone had a chance to complain. The response was tumultuous and turned the whole program around.

Out of that session alone we identified more than 30 cows, including triplicate forms, inventory duplications, and suggestion boxes that were mockingly called "dead letter boxes" because no one ever got a response.

Giving people permission and encouragement to complain generates a hunting spirit. Have them complete sentences like:

- This job would be great if I didn't have to . . .
- What a pain it is to . . .
- No one reads this . . . so why am I doing it?
- It's a waste of time to . . .
- I could be much more productive if I didn't have to . . .
- We could save a lot of money if we stopped . . .

CHALLENGING ASSUMPTIONS

A detective seeking evidence follows every possible lead and assumes that everyone is a suspect. Cow hunters are no different. They challenge everything they're doing. Try this method for identifying invisible cows: Write down the basic assumptions you make about your customer, competition, product, or service. Examples: "Price is most important to the customer." "They won't pay extra for service." "The competition doesn't have the technology to develop a better product." "We can outproduce our competitors."

Then do a reality check to determine if these are (still) true. Sometimes they're not. A national coupon mailer company assumed that retailers would pay extra for top-quality printing. The national sales manager's rationale: since coupons were the first contact retailers made with customers, business owners would want them to be of the highest quality.

"We sell quality," he said. "We have the best design department. Our six color presses and superior printing technology allow us to offer more colors and better printing than our competition. And we use top-of-the-line paper. Retailers who use our service are assured of a top-quality product they can be proud of."

A reality check done with retailers exposed a cow. While their assumption had been true in the past when the other guys had been offering "schlock" coupons, most retailers agreed that the current difference in quality and design was minor. Customers couldn't tell the difference.

Quality and design were still important, but even more significant were factors like the ability to target specific audiences, cost per thousand, and the maintenance of up-to-date mailing lists.

BRANDING 'EM

Another way to identify cows is to keep a daily log of *every*thing you do in an average week. The *every* is emphasized because there is a natural tendency to focus only on the essential tasks of your job. But even those "taken-for-granted" support activities such as making up daily schedules, going through the mail, reviewing expenses, revising budgets, attending meetings, and returning phone calls are just as likely to contain a few sacred cows. And they add up, costing time and money.

Once you've listed all your activities, the next step is to evaluate or *brand* them. Are they bulls or sacred cows? Do they help you respond quickly and effectively to change and new opportunities?

Here are some questions that will help you evaluate each activity. Because cows come in all shapes and sizes, every question won't fit every circumstance. Choose those that fit your situation, and keep in mind: *Nothing is sacred. Question everything!*

1. Why are you doing it? What is the rationale? On a scale of 1 to 5 (1 = definite no; 5 = definite yes) ask yourself, Does this activity

- *add **value** to the product or the customer?*
- *improve **quality?***

- *improve* **service,** *make you more responsive to the customer?*
- *improve* **productivity,** *cut costs directly?*
- *improve* **communication?**
- *increase employee* **motivation** *or morale?*
- *encourage* **innovation?**
- *speed up* **decision-making?**

If the activity doesn't score at least a 4 on one of these factors it moos, and you've probably got a holy heifer that needs "pasture-izing."

2. What if it didn't exist? Imagine what would happen if you just plain stopped attending that meeting, or writing that report. What would be the <u>real</u> consequences to the company—both positive and negative? Are those consequences worth the price of continuing the practice? The "real" is underscored because people tend to "catastrophize" about changing the status quo.

Our experience is that many cows can be eliminated without making any difference to the organization's effectiveness. Rarely a week goes by that we don't hear from managers how they inadvertently stopped doing something *important* and no one noticed.

Sometimes people get so personally invested in a business practice that they fight its elimination. It's hard on the ego to acknowledge that your beautifully crafted monthly report not only doesn't get read, it gets tossed . . . in the round file. And the fact that most managers read less than half their mail isn't much solace. That's why it's good to remember that getting rid of a sacred cow will free up time, energy, and resources so you can tackle more valuable work.

When the "Cow" Is Feeding You

"That report you want to get rid of is a major part of my job," an anxious manager informed us at one cow hunt. "Eliminate it and you eliminate me."

Her anxiety is understandable. Many people are afraid to herd a cow to pasture because they fear losing influence, power, or even their job. They offer all sorts of rationalizations to keep that cow well fed and content.

While it's always easier to round up cows in someone else's field, when they're standing in yours the situation looks quite different. That's why hunters need positive motivation for pasture-izing their own cows. Without it they're likely to hide them behind a tree or some other obstacle. (See Chapter Nineteen, "Motivating People to Change.")

Change-Ready organizations motivate hunters by rewarding them *especially* for finding cows in their own fields.

A health-claims administrator at a large paper-manufacturing plant acted as an intermediary between employees, human resources, and the insurance company. She realized that her job was essentially a sacred cow that could be eliminated by having workers enter claim information into a computer connected to the insurance company's system. Her solution decreased the time it took to get a claim paid from three weeks to about four days! This was a great idea that was roundly applauded by all the managers in human resources.

But others nervously withheld acclamation, waiting to see what "reward" would go to this brave cow hunter for essentially eliminating her own job. She got a promotion! Think of the message that sent out to the rest of the company.

3. Is it already being done by someone else? A cow hunt at a major retailer revealed that the same task was being performed by three different departments! When a shipment was delivered, the receiving department compared the packing slip with the actual shipment to see if it matched the purchase order. The goods were then sent upstairs to the department that ordered them. The department buyer or stock clerk would check the shipment again and update the inventory of in-stock merchandise. The accounting department also checked the invoice against the purchase order and the goods actually received to see that everything matched.

You would be shocked at how much duplication cow hunts uncover (or maybe you wouldn't). In fact, some companies intentionally duplicate their practices. In a cow hunt for a shoe manufacturer, one manager told the group that duplication was necessary to avoid mistakes. With two departments doing the same task, they'd always be sure to get it right. His rationalization sounded like wasted effort to the other cow hunters, who pointed out that if you don't trust your people to do their jobs right, then something is wrong. And not with your people.

One cause of duplication is that many companies are still organized around functions, each department having a view of its own operations but not the whole picture. If you produce widgets, for example, your design department focuses on the design function, Marketing concentrates on marketing, and no one sees the whole process from start to finish. In this structure there are no safeguards against duplication of effort.

The cow hunt, with it cross-functional teams and healthy irreverence, provides the overview needed to identify duplications and repetitions.

4. How and when did this practice come into being, and who started it? At one time or another most sacred cows made sense. There was a good reason for their existence. But with the passage of time and changes in circumstance, that rationale no longer exists. The problem is, no one's noticed.

When Bismarck was Prussian ambassador at the court of Alexander II in 1860, he asked the czar why a certain sentry was on duty in an isolated area of the palace lawn.

The czar asked his aide-de-camp. The aide-de-camp didn't know. So he asked the officer in command, who didn't know, and so on down the chain of command. Finally, the commanding general was summoned and the question put to him.

The answer: "I beg leave to inform Your Majesty that it is in accordance with ancient custom."

"What was the origin of the custom?" asked the czar.

"I do not recollect at present," responded the general sheepishly.

"Investigate and report the result," ordered Alexander.

The investigation took three days. In the end it was found that the sentry was posted by an order put on the books *80 years before,* by Catherine the Great.

It seems that after a long, hard Russian winter, she had looked out her window and seen the first spring flower thrusting through the frozen soil. She ordered a sentry to stand guard and prevent anyone from picking that blossom.

Eighty years later, the sentry remained, a memorial to a single flower and to an unchallenged custom that had become sacred without anyone realizing it.

Similar memorials are commonplace in most organizations that have been in existence for any length of time. Doing the archaeology—digging up the whys and wherefores of a particular practice—can illuminate whether the original rationale still makes sense.

Kicking Tires and Cows

Remember the story about the tire company that wrapped its tires to prevent the whitewalls from getting scuffed in shipping? Only no one was buying whitewalls anymore.

Asking how the practice originated revealed the sacred cow. The process was over 40 years old, having been started when 75 percent of all tires were whitewalls. Buying patterns had changed but nobody had questioned the operation. They just took it for granted, focusing instead on how to wrap the tires faster and cheaper.

Check Your Inheritance

When we ask the question about how a practice got started, we usually get a puzzled look accompanied by enough head scratching to suggest psoriasis. "Actually, I don't know," admitted a manager at a sporting-goods company. He was referring to a suspected sacred cow: a lengthy report that required inventory data, forecasting, and future purchasing requirements.

"I've been in this job for seven years and we've always done it that way [a telltale sign it's a sacred cow]. I guess," he laughed, "this procedure, along with many others, was part of my inheritance when I took over the job."

One of our rules about inheritances is that if you or your department has been following a process or procedure for two years it's probably outmoded. So check your inheritance. It's probably not as valuable as it once was.

5. Can another person, department, or company do it faster, better, or more easily? A cow hunt for an underwear manufacturer revealed that to buy almost anything, with the possible exception of paper clips, a requisition had to be filled out and sent to the purchasing agent. After reviewing the order, the PA would send out requests for bids. Then she'd analyze them and choose the lowest bidder. Sounds good on paper, but . . .

"By the time we got what we wanted we didn't need it anymore," joked one vice president. "Going through channels meant we lost the benefit of talking to our suppliers, who usually have good ideas about how to improve quality and streamline the operation. Now when we want something we buy it ourselves. We include our suppliers in the manufacturing cycle and get them involved in planning. We might pay a little more up front but it's worth it. It's faster and we get what we want, when we want it."

Interview-itis. Same story happened at a packaging company, only this time it was Personnel, not Purchasing, that was slowing things down. When a department wanted to hire staff it would notify Personnel, who would run an ad in the paper or contact a headhunter, then conduct the initial screening process. Final applicants were interviewed by the department head who made the request.

"Took a long time," a sales manager told me, "and we didn't always end up with the right people. It's hard to tell someone else what you want in a person. Sometimes someone can come in with the 'wrong' qualifications yet you just know they'll do a great job, so you hire them. I got one of my best salespeople that way. He was a cartoonist, with no sales experience, and he was older than we wanted. But he was really motivated and was terrific with people. He's brought in two of our biggest accounts and he would never have passed through Personnel's screening."

Now every division in that company hires its own people—from start to finish. And in many instances, it's not the manager who does the hiring but the work team itself, which has the power to hire *and* fire.

MAKING MACS

It is not enough to ask which one of your departments might do a job better; ask whether anyone in the company should do the job at all. Many businesses have discovered that outside specialists can often do it faster, better, and more cheaply than they can. Combined with just-in-time delivery, "outsourcing" cuts down on inventory and eliminates overhead so you save money on storage, wages, training, and fringe benefits—all Excedrin headaches.

A recent study at MIT's Sloan School of Management reported: "To insure their competitiveness, companies are emphasizing their core competencies and strategically outsourcing everything else."[3]

Apple Computer outsources 70 percent of its manufacturing costs: design is done by Frogdesign, printers are manufactured by Tokyo Electric, much of marketing is handled by Regis McKenna. Apple focuses its own resources on operating systems and supporting software, two core competencies that give their products a unique look and feel.[4]

One of the sacred cows that nearly destroyed IBM was the assumption that it alone should provide its customers with soup to nuts. The result was a lot of low-margin products that the company really didn't need to sell.

CFO York, who came from Chrysler, where 70 percent of manufacturing costs are contracted out, says, "You can't manufacture every nut and bolt that goes into your hardware, because somebody can do that better than you can."[5]

STARVE YOUR COWS

When the cow isn't all fat, pasture-izing may not be the best choice. Instead, keep the part of the cow that has value and eliminate the rest. In other words, starve your cow. Put it on a restricted diet or cut down on the frequency of meals!

Examples:

Cow hunters at Hewlett-Packard turned a monthly 10-column financial report into a four-column quarterly summary sheet.

Managers at AT&T decided that a particular monthly strategy meeting had limited value. Instead of eliminating it altogether, they cut it back to once a quarter.

Another streamlining technique is to starve the cow and measure the consequences at specific points down the road.

Engineers at a high-tech company agreed that their weekly ninety-minute staff meeting was too long. They thought they could accomplish the same work in about half the time. The vice president objected. He was concerned that they'd rush through delicate decisions and important issues would be given short shrift. Or no shrift at all. Under pressure, he agreed to try it for a month. Turned out the engineers were right. At last check it's still a 45-minute meeting.

Streamlining with built-in reevaluations provides a safeguard against poor decisions taken in the heat of the cow hunt and allows for quick correction should it be necessary. It may also placate skeptical and cautious vice presidents.

LOCKING HORNS

But what happens if you can't reach agreement? Your manager wants a particular monthly progress report, but you find it a waste of time that takes you away from more important, income-producing efforts. We often find that one person's sacred cow is another's prized bull.

The sales staff for a pharmaceutical company that marketed to doctors thought their call reports took too much time. One salesman actually clocked how long it took each day to fill out the report: "One and a half calls," he concluded. "I could be seeing one and a half more docs every day or three more every two days if I didn't have to fill out that damned report. It's really cutting into my productivity."

Management, however, insisted it needed the report for planning and FDA requirements. Who was right? By looking at the needs of each group we came to a solution that pleased both. The company distributed handheld computers, which allowed each person to complete a short interactive checklist after each call. That provided the needed data and cut report time by two-thirds. So everyone got what they needed. And the sales force felt that someone was listening.

There are many ways to skin a cow.

SELLING THE BOSS

One of the sacred cows identified by a financial-service organization were RFTs (requests for travel). Any expense over $100 had to be approved by the department head and division vice president, as well as by the accounting and travel departments. And this was at a company where some managers had responsibility for loans in excess of $50 million!

The practice was seen as a cow because it took so much time and was such a hassle to get an approval signed. And rather than face the third degree, many employees chose not to make the trip. So the company was saving a dime but losing a dollar. Salespeople were not seeing clients face to face, while their competition was. That hurt business. Analysts were doing research by phone and fax rather than getting the real story firsthand.

Strong reasons to put that cow out to pasture? Not to the division vice president. His boss, the CEO, was continually expounding on the need to cut travel expenses. He had even set a goal for each division to cut them 33 percent by flying coach class and staying in B-rated hotels just like he did. So the vice president was less interested in getting rid of a sacred cow than in looking good to his boss.

We hear the same story at most cow hunts: "I've got all these great ideas for eliminating cows but I can't get my boss to buy them."

In this situation think of bosses as *customers* with specific points of view, needs, and agendas. Your job is to sell them. Walk in their shoes, see the world through their eyes, understand their concerns, challenges, and interests, and make sure your proposals address their experience. (See Chapter Eight, "The Customer Cow" and the "Caring" section in Chapter Seventeen for advice on this.)

In the above example, if you pitch to the vice president that face-to-face contact with customers is being compromised by an antiquated procedure and that travel is necessary to maintain a strong customer base, it won't work. Even though your argument makes good sense, you'll get "hosed" because it's not the vice president's priority.

You might suggest instead that streamlining the RFT process—including new, clear guidelines against excess—would save money all around. And make sure you emphasize cost reduction. You have to meet the boss's priority first if you want to achieve yours.

FUN HUNTS

One more point about sacred-cow hunts: Make them fun. Most people love the delicious irreverence of the cow hunts and the teamwork and camaraderie they produce. Keep that spirit alive. We can't say this enough. It's not a matter of pleasure for its own sake. The best cow hunts are fun because fun makes them the best cow hunts. With lightness and humor come creativity, energy, out-of-the-box thinking, and motivation. The more laughter, the less inhibition; the less inhibition, the more inspired the thinking. Most of us take work too seriously. Don't be afraid to enjoy your work.

Remember the key is not which cows you put out to pasture or how you set up the hunt. It's to develop an organization of hunters. Creating a hunting mentality throughout your company is the first step toward achieving a Change-Ready organization.

Seventeen

Building the Change-Ready Environment

DON'T PLANT SEEDS IN HARD GROUND

Good landscapers always prepare the earth before planting. They turn the soil, fertilize it, and then wet it down. Only then are they ready to plant.

It's the same thing when you're planting seeds of change in your organization. You've got to prepare the soil if you expect change to take root. Unfortunately, many corporations don't do the spadework. They go for the buy-in on a new process or system *after* they've introduced it. That's backward. And the results can be catastrophic.

When you create a Change-Ready environment first, resistance is minimized, and employees are more open to innovation and more likely to take risks. In the Change-Ready environment, new ideas blossom everywhere, even those places where you least expect them to.

Getting the buy-in to change after you've introduced it is working *bass ackward.*

FROM COP TO COACH

Just a decade ago managers focused on processes, products, productivity, and planning. They were the cops and organizers assigning tasks and making sure you followed the rules. Their word was law, and they ruled with an iron hand. When the manager showed up at your office it was the equivalent of the highway patrol pulling up alongside your car. Not anymore. They've gone from being cops to coaches.

Today's managers understand that whatever products and services their companies may produce, they're essentially in the people business. As coaches, their new job is to develop Change-Ready individuals and organizations. That means motivating employees to be excited about change, overcoming employee resistance to change, and creating a culture where innovation flourishes.

"I have to know as much about people as I do about computers if I want to be effective in this business," says one Hewlett-Packard manager.

Not everyone agrees with his assessment. When we're in the corporate trenches, hard-liners argue, "Change is no big deal. They're drawing a paycheck; they'd better toe the line. My way or the highway." Traditionalists protest, "We've got enough to do. Who's got the time to spend on nonbillable activities?" And technicians throw their arms in the air and swear that we're making too much out of the whole thing.

We ask them all to remember the last major change their organization undertook. Then we ask them to calculate transition, subversion, and morale costs. Usually that's enough to get them listening. Coaching employees to be Change-Ready is not a quick-fix process. But the payoff is immense. To the response "We don't have the time" we recall one executive's retort: "We don't have the time *not* to."

So here's that part of the puzzle that all the reengineering gurus and the reorganization mavens don't tell you about. The part about people and how to handle them when you're planning change. The part about how to make your managers into coaches so everyone can be a cow hunter.

THE RIGHT KIND OF RELATIONSHIP

Our research shows that Change-Ready environments have two essential characteristics: trust and caring. People need to trust the boss and the environment, and they need to feel cared about and acknowledged. In organizations where management treats its workforce with respect and understanding, tells the truth, and keeps its word, employees are more positive about change, open to innovation, and more engaged in the change process.

Trust emerges from relationships characterized by honesty, integrity, and reliability. In fact, these are the very words people use to describe a person they consider trustworthy. Caring comes from treating individuals with respect and empathy, and acknowledging their efforts and contributions.

TRUST

"C" grade. A grade of "C"—that's how managers polled by *Industry Week* rated the levels of trust in today's workplace. Bosses didn't fare much better. Their trustworthiness was graded at C+, with female managers assigning lower grades to their bosses than their male counterparts. That's a dismal report card for American business when you consider that resistance to change increases as trust in an organization's leadership decreases.

In his book *Credibility,* James Couzes, president of the Tom Peters Group companies, maintains that trustworthiness and believability are the foundations of leadership. Without them, a manager has no credibility.[1]

And says Roger Meade, CEO of Scitor Corporation, when you work in an environment of trust, everything flourishes.

But when you work in an organization without trust, how willing are you to take risks when you don't trust your boss to support you if you fail?

"The organization I work for lacks trust," said one respondent in an *Industry Week* survey. "You cannot rely on your co-workers because the company is forcing them to perform beyond one's limits. . . . Everyone is looking out for their own well-being and not the good of the company." Said another, "You can make the choice to trust each other, work together, and grow and succeed or to take the path of adversarial relationships and fail."[2]

Building blocks of trust. "Trust is a two-way street," observed one executive. "If you give your employees freedom and empowerment and hold them fairly accountable, they will be fair in return. If you show them that their input and decisions are trusted and valued, and truly mean it, you'll have the best people can give."[3]

Trust can't be bought; it's got to be built brick by brick over time. And not by mouthing the right words or platitudes. Trust is earned by individuals and organizations that demonstrate through their *actions:*

- *Honesty*—Can you believe what they say?
- *Integrity*—Do they keep their promises?
- *Openness*—Do they share what they know?

Lies have long lives. Trust is delicate. It takes a long time to establish and a split second to lose. A working relationship can crumble by not delivering on a pledge or by getting caught in deceit. And once lost, it is much harder to reestablish. Lies have long lives. Trustworthiness is probably a manager's most important asset. In feedback sessions for executives, "untrustworthy" is perhaps the single most devastating criticism, right above lack of intelligence and poor judgment.

There are many ways to undermine trust. Following are some typical Trust Busters with comments on how to turn them into Trust Builders.

Trust Buster #1: Talking But Not Walking

The 95/5 rule. "I really believe in empowerment," an IBM manager told his people, "but before you try anything new, run it by me first."

A *Fortune* magazine report on corporate chiefs who embraced cutting-edge management concepts such as empowerment, quality, and excellence noted, "What they didn't do—deep down inside—was actually give up much control or abandon their fundamental beliefs about leadership."[4]

In other words, they didn't walk the talk. There is a huge gap between knowing what to do and doing it.

James O'Toole, a professor of management and a leadership expert, puts it this way: "Ninety-five percent of American managers today say the right thing. Five percent actually do it."[5]

A survey conducted by management consultants Booz Allen & Hamilton supports O'Toole's opinion, "suggesting [this is] why programs like business process reengineering so often disappoint."[6]

After interviewing senior executives at major corporations including Ford, Merck, Proctor & Gamble, and General Mills, the consulting firm found:

"While companies talk big time about customer satisfaction, quality and other trendy indicators, they rarely measure those things. CEOs still consider cost control their top priority over customer satisfaction or superior technology. For all the talk about empowerment, CEOs at a fourth of the companies still get involved in tactical decisions like pricing and packaging changes."[7]

Peter Scott Morgan, a director at consulting giant Arthur D. Little, says that far too many managers "take actions that violate unwritten rules as well as their stated intentions. They preach the importance of teamwork, but reward individuals who stand out from the crowd. . . . They encourage risk taking—then punish good-faith failures. . . . It really is tantamount to managerial malpractice."[8]

This failure to walk the talk produces distrust of organizational leadership and accounts for much of the resistance to change in the workplace. People don't believe in their leaders, and it seems like they've got good reason not to.

Trust Builder #1: Model the Message

Walking the talk means that leaders' *attitudes and actions are consistent with their words.*

Rubbermaid CEO Wolf Schmitt, generally considered one of America's top business leaders, recently took 60 hours of training alongside other employees in one of his company's quality programs. "I had to visibly be a part of it," he says. "People look to see if you just talk about it or actually do it." He is also a member of three cross-functional work teams dealing with such basic issues as PC support and catering at the company.[9]

"I believe in the power of personal example," says Frank Pacetta, who as a Xerox sales manager took his district from near dead-last to first in his region and fourth in the nation. "You don't have to be a Knute Rockne and deliver a dramatic locker-room pep talk . . . but at a minimum, a leader has got to show his troops the route of the march and the destination. . . ."[10]

Another way to create trust is to show that you aren't above pitching in yourself when something has to be done. My father, Arthur Kriegel, owned a small business that manufactured travel accessories. Like most small businessmen, he was a one-man show. He handled the sales force, designed the line, purchased fabric.

Although he was tough and demanding, the workers in the factory loved and trusted my father and would always go the extra mile for him. One of the reasons was that when something had to be done, nothing was below him. He would work late, pack boxes, cut patterns, load a truck. Whatever had to be done, he would be in there working as hard as the next guy. By his actions, not his words, my father set the standard of what was expected. And he demonstrated that this standard was applicable to everyone.

It's the same story with Jerry Richardson, the CEO of TW Services, which owns over 2,000 fast-food restaurants. Richardson, the head of the Carolina Panthers, one of the National Football League's two newest entries, started his business slinging burgers in a Hardee's, so he's not above helping out in one of his restaurants during the breakfast rush. He owns a NFL franchise but you'll see him making biscuits, serving customers, cleaning up trash, doing whatever it takes.

Trust Buster #2: Not Telling the Truth

Several years ago National Public Radio's McNeil/Lehrer program reported a cover-up at the National Cancer Institute. One of the hospitals involved in a major study on breast cancer had falsified data. NCI had hidden this information from the public *for three years!* The institute had a justifiable reason, of course. It was trying to determine if the falsified data had skewed the study's results. And they didn't want to alarm people before they knew the full story. But the information leaked, as it always does, and patients and doctors were furious. It wasn't the falsified data that infuriated them, but the fact the institute had suppressed it for three years.

It turned out that the rigged data didn't change the results. But it didn't matter. Trust had been lost. Patients didn't know what to believe. And many women across the country were angry and distrustful of the medical establishment.

A similar thing happened in Vietnam when General William Westmoreland shaded the truth about enemy troop strength and battlefield successes. When the public found out, trust in the military was shattered and has never been entirely restored.

And, of course, there's Watergate. Lack of openness resulted in the downfall of one U.S. president and most of his cabinet. More than that, trust in government and politicians was compromised. That too has yet to be repaired.

Rumors running rampant. A major electronics firm was planning to restructure within six months. Many people were going to be terminated or retrained for new jobs. When we asked how employees were handling the change, management replied, "We haven't told them. What good would that do? It would only cause panic."

Their response made some sense. It's good policy to announce change as close to implementation as possible. The only trouble is that sitting on a secret that big won't work. Leaks always occur, and they quickly give birth to rumors. The only thing that runs faster through an organization than E-mail is rumors.

Someone in the company found out about the restructuring and told others. Restructuring quickly "turned into" massive layoffs, and everyone got nervous. Management tried to put out the fire and communicate what was really going on. But nobody believed them. Would you? Trust was shot. The lack of openness created dissension and zapped morale, and productivity plummeted.

Heard it on the grapevine. A similar thing happened to AT&T in the eighties before divestiture. Top management confided to Wall Street security analysts that the company was planning job cuts. But, as usual, the word got out. In fact, many of the company's employees read about it in the newspaper. You can imagine the result. Work virtually ground to a standstill while people agonized over what was coming. At least two workers killed themselves.[11]

Once the layoffs began, gossip ran wild, fueled by fears that went untempered by high-level reassurances. "No one in top management stepped forward and said the rumors weren't true. Nobody told us anything official at all," said a former manager. "So the grapevine went berserk."[12]

Surveys show that the more clogged the internal arteries of communication, the more active the grapevine. When communication levels are low, 80 percent of top- and middle-level managers say the grapevine is "very active."[13]

AT&T learned this lesson the hard way. Lack of an open and continuous flow of information caused rumors to spin out of control and create a far worse situation than if the truth were known. It's better to confront a situation head on than to allow rumors to exaggerate the situation and play on people's fears.

Trust Builder #2: Openness and Honesty

"Communication and trust go hand in hand," wrote one executive in the *Industry Week* survey. "If management is open with its employees and communicates what is expected, future plans, and goals, then the employees will usually respond. . . . Secretive management leads to employees who are unsure where they stand and unsure of their future."[14]

Nothing creates a trusting environment like openness in communication. Interestingly, the less managers trust their staff, the less likely they'll share information.[15] Yet a vast majority of managers still believe it's "important" or "somewhat important" to control or screen information. Why?

Part of the reason is philosophical, based in the autocratic management style of "Tell them only what they need to know." Another reason is that information is power. Having it confers status. Using it gives authority.

"In a command-and-control organization, people protect knowledge because it's their claim to distinction," says Levi CEO Robert Haas. "But we share as much information as we possibly can throughout the company. . . . You cannot ask people to exercise broader judgment if their world is bounded by very narrow vision."[16]

Tell it like it is. When asked what he'd like to be remembered for, Don Shula, the winningest coach in National Football League history, said simply that he always told the truth: "I didn't lie to anyone."[17]

General Electric's Jack Welch, one of the winningest leaders in American business, knows the importance of openness and honesty. "How do you bring people into the change process?" asks Welch. "Start. with reality. Get all the facts out. Give people a rationale for change, laying it out in the clearest, most dramatic terms. When everybody gets the same facts, they'll generally come to the same conclusion. Only after everyone agrees on the reality . . . can you begin to get the buy-in . . ."[18]

Welch knows that sometimes telling the truth isn't pleasant. "People always ask, 'Is the change over? Can we stop now?' You've got to tell them, 'No, it's just begun.' Leaders must create an atmosphere where people understand that change is a continuing process, not an event."[19]

Leadership guru Warren Bennis stresses, "Top managers must set the example by being open and confronting issues openly with subordinates . . . they must bring disagreements into the open and work through them. Self-disclosure earns trust from others who then feel safe to expose their own thoughts."[20]

Working out. Other corporations recognize the importance of openness and honesty. Billions are spent on desktop publishing, company newsletters, and closed-circuit interorganizational video programming for management to communicate with employees.

Like trust, openness is reciprocal. Communicating downward is only half the story. The other half is listening to what's coming back and being responsive to it.

"Trouble starts when people are afraid to talk to the boss and ideas don't reach the top," notes Orit Gadiesh, chairman of the Boston consulting firm Bain & Company.[21]

"We meet with people once a week for thirty minutes to let them know what's going on," says Ron Parks, manager for manufacturing operations and human resources at the Dana Corporation. "Even though we give employees the information, we want to make sure they understand. . . . The sessions generate many questions. Employees often ask why a decision is made. And they get an answer. If they aren't satisfied with what we tell them they can direct questions up the ladder—right up to the chairman."[22]

To facilitate "upward communication," Jack Welch initiated "workouts" at GE. These aren't sweat-and-stretch sessions at the gym but Q&A meetings in which people can and do ask Welch, or other execs on the hot seat, anything they want to know. That's right—*Anything!* The only rule: You've got to answer nondefensively. Workouts have been so successful that organizations of all types and sizes have been using them.

Lipton's open book. Lipton is not only the world's number-one tea company, but its food service division ranks among the best food operations in the country. A recent partnership to produce new beverages with Pepsi generated $700 million in consumer sales in its first eight months.

"The reason for our continued success and why we keep setting records is that we have an open environment. Everybody knows everything. There are no secrets. And this builds morale and team spirit," says Richard Kundrat, Lipton vice president and general manager.

Kundrat uses a special technique he created to foster communications. It's called the Focused Objectives Open Book. Everyone in the division, from mail room to boardroom, is required to record their annual objectives. At the end of the year they enter their results and accomplishments. Kundrat doesn't lock the book up in his desk, but places it in plain view for all to see. The open book eliminates secrecy, rumor, and false imaginings. No special deals for certain people. Everything out in the open.

The open book has created a culture of trust and cooperation. The words *help me* are commonplace.

"Having that book out there, for all to see, has created an atmosphere that we're all in it together, part of the same team, playing by the same rules," Kundrat told us. "As a result, teamwork, team spirit, and cross-team communication have increased. Everyone seems to want everyone else to make it. People are closer. They even get ideas by looking at the book and seeing what others are doing."

That little tea bag that Lipton sells zillions of is the perfect metaphor for trust. The more open the environment, the better everything flows.

Trust Buster #3: Copping Credit

"Why should I develop new ideas for saving money or building the business?" a manager for a telecommunications company complained to us. "Anytime someone in our department comes up with a new concept, the boss presents it like it's his. The hell with him! Let him come up with his own ideas."

Nothing breaks down trust, teamwork, and motivation faster than having an idea coopted by a superior. A copywriter who helped develop a memorable ad campaign for a well-known headache remedy told us, "Everyone on the product team—Media, Marketing, and

Creative—contributed to the idea, even one of the secretaries. It was great. We were all stoked.

"But when the account supervisor presented the campaign to the client, the only pronoun he used was 'I.' You'd have thought he did the whole thing himself. Boy, were we pissed. I tell you, no one ever trusted him again. The next time we came together you could have heard a pin drop. I know it was childish. But here's the thing all creative people dream about—a funny, visible, and very successful campaign—and this guy stole all the credit."

We've all known people afflicted with the "I" disease. They take—or, more literally, steal—credit for everything and anything, except of course the idea that doesn't fly.

Once bitten, twice shy is what happens when credit is stolen. When bosses coopt ideas they find that their staff's creativity suddenly and inexplicably dries up. And, as in the headache campaign, the people who get bit, bite back.

Trust Builder #3: "We" Not "Me"

Managers who grab all the credit for themselves may not realize that their actions diminish them in front of their superiors (not to mention their supervisees). Talking "me," not "we," at a time when teamwork is so valued in the corporate world leaves the wrong impression. And most people are sophisticated enough to see through the ego trip.

On the other hand, focusing on the team's effort elevates you from the role of manager to the role of leader. Instead of being a good individual performer, you're someone who knows how to run, direct, and guide a team. That set of skills gives you versatility and authority. Focusing on the "we" isn't false modesty, it's a good career move.

"We" is also an inclusionary term, whereas "I" is exclusionary. "We" says to the team that you recognize and appreciate their contribution, that, as Lipton's Kundrat stressed, "you're all in it together." Inclusion builds loyalty, increases morale and motivation. And people will go to great lengths to help *their* team win. Giving credit to the team not only makes you bigger, but it also makes your team stronger.

Most significant efforts are collaborative anyway. Few ideas or projects are the exclusive contribution of one individual. Collaboration comes in unexpected and often unrecognized ways. Someone gives you an article or tells you an idea. You bounce a concept off a colleague and get a different spin on it. Someone asks a question that gets you thinking. There are always more people involved in a project than those assigned to it. No one works in a vacuum.

Great leaders have the guts to take responsibility for their mistakes and the wisdom to share the glory with their team.

Trust Buster #4: Loose Lips Sink Ships

LOOSE LIPS SINK SHIPS admonished a popular World War II poster showing Uncle Sam with a raised forefinger pressed over his mouth. While I couldn't imagine how my family's conversation was going to influence the outcome of the war, the message makes sense for the workplace. Nothing breaks down trust like idle gossip and the disclosure of private information.

A telemarketing manager thought he could trust his boss with a personal problem and get some advice about his son, who'd been expelled from school for using drugs. It seemed that the boy had been selling them to other kids as well, and the manager didn't know how to handle the situation. Obviously embarrassed by his son's behavior, he didn't want word of the incident to get out. His boss agreed.

Guess what? The boss told a couple of his buddies about the manager's problem over a drink that night. Two days later it was all around the office. Everyone was sympathetic and some even had good advice. But the manager felt humiliated and betrayed.

Trust Builder #4: Batten Down the Hatches

People love to gossip. But no one trusts a gossiper. There is always the fear that anything you disclose will be repeated and probably heard on the evening news. No matter how tempting it is to tell someone what you've just heard in private, no matter how juicy the tidbit may be, let your better judgment prevail. If people don't trust that what they've told you in confidence won't go any further, they won't tell you anything.

Uncle Sam was right: Loose lips will sink your ship.

CARING

How to play hardball with something soft. Making others feel you care about them is a "core skill," says best-selling author and management consultant Gifford Pinchot. It is an essential part of the "new manager's" job, not an afterthought. "You make them feel they're considered meaningful."[23]

Caring is a soft concept that many in the tough business world disparage as cornball or naive. Caring is for teachers and social workers, not lean, profit-driven, corporate machines. And caring is too simple, too basic, to carry much intellectual heft. But in a world where businesses are modifying their mission statements annually, caring may be the single best soft concept you've ever used to play hardball.

When you ask your people to make a change, you're asking them to take a risk, a leap of faith with you. They're thinking, Will I still have a job? Will it be a job I want and can do? Will any of my friends survive with me? Will I move up in the organization or lose ground?

In companies characterized by high levels of caring, employees are more willing to take this leap of faith. They are more loyal, more willing to adapt, more responsive to challenges because they believe their interests are being considered. It's basic: They'll care about you because you care about them.

Employees don't cooperate when they don't feel cared about. Changes are generally met with suspicion and halfhearted compliance. Why? Would you go to the wall for a friend who didn't care about you? Would you extend yourself to a company you felt used you or treated you as a cog in its corporate machinery?

"Low-caring companies" fail to create a reservoir of goodwill to draw on when the going gets rough. Employees feel disconnected or resentful and will often sabotage the company's efforts. Organizations where workers feel alienated are plagued by absenteeism and lateness.

Investing in people. One of the most caring organizations we know is a 200-employee California company that produces products and services in program management, systems engineering, and customized computer information systems. Scitor stands out from the crowd in two ways: 13 years of continuous profitable growth and an employee turnover rate of 2.1 percent in a field that averages 16.5 percent.[24]

How do they do it? CEO Roger Meade doesn't pull punches. He is a leader who builds caring relationships. Says Meade, "Scitor is our people. Our success depends on them. Knowledge resides in their minds and feet. Too many companies fail to grasp that feet can walk out the door as easily as they walked in."[25]

Scitor—"to seek to know" in Latin—goes beyond the norm in putting its people first. There are no limits or tracking of sick days, no wage deductions for illness, three weeks of vacation for new hires. The company provides a care center for mildly ill children and in-home emergency care. They also offer flextime, job sharing, and benefits for workers who put in more than 17.5 hours a week. Beyond that, they run a variety of social events for employees, including chili cook-offs, ski and fishing trips, road rallies, and a huge social weekend, all expenses paid, at a premier resort.

To Meade such practices are not considered overhead. "They are investments that add value to the corporation, not costs or overhead—because people are your resources, not your products or equipment. Taking care of people's needs is the key to productivity."[26] It certainly instills loyalty. Scitor's employees average only 5 sick days a year, and the company retains 90 percent of all women who've taken maternity leave.

The Avon Lady takes a hike. By contrast, Avon, the cosmetics giant that pioneered door-to-door sales, is a good example of a company that lost its focus on caring in an attempt to hold market share. The 108-year-old company had always relied heavily on its sales force, which it rewarded with incentives like prizes and trips. But at the end of 1992 and with a new CEO, these practices changed.

The company began to emphasize direct marketing, but unlike its competitor Mary Kay—which forwarded commissions from catalogue sales to representatives in the customer's area—Avon cut its salespeople out of the process. They also cut 600 jobs and restructured commissions, eliminating many of their traditional incentives like birthday presents and anniversary pins. All of this created the impression of noncaring. Despite the changes, "Avon's pretax profit in the U.S. sank 10% in the first quarter of 1993, 7% in the second quarter, 36% in the third quarter and 29% in the fourth quarter."[27]

"I know it sounds picky, but I guess those things [pins, birthdays, etc.] gave us the feeling we were being noticed," reports Carmelita Caburet, a Detroit sales rep with $250,000 in annual sales.[28]

The company has since recognized its problems and made attempts at remedying them. Says CEO James E. Preston, "We walk a fine line—a balance—between supporting the core representative business and testing new concepts. We got out of balance last year [1993]."[29]

Preston has also hired a new head of U.S. operations, Christina Gold, who exemplifies the kind of caring leader we're talking about. Recognizing what was important to her people, she has reinstated the birthday presents, anniversary plates, and annual pins. "My number-one priority is to rebuild Avon's relationship with representatives," she emphasizes. She makes it her business to stay in close phone contact with her sales reps. "We just told them they're appreciated," she says.[30]

Caring, not coddling. Caring does not mean coddling your employees, or gratifying their every wish. It doesn't mean appeasing or treating them like your grandmother's fine china. It doesn't mean not making demands or never criticizing their work. And it doesn't mean not expecting them to perform at their highest levels. What it does mean is that if you're going to ask them to adapt to corporate urgencies you should make every attempt to adjust to theirs.

As Meade emphasizes, "How can you ask people to unselfishly

support the needs of the company, if the company won't support the needs of its people? It is simply not fair to expect your people to give to the corporation if you do not reciprocate and help them absorb the shocks in their life."[31]

Caring is good business. Caring isn't just the cornerstone of the Change-Ready environment, it's good for business. Workers who feel cared about will, in turn, care about the products they produce and the people they serve. That was Sam Walton's philosophy. "The way management treats the associates is exactly how the associates will treat the customers," said Sam. "Satisfied, loyal, repeat customers are the heart of Wal-Mart's spectacular profit margins, and those customers are loyal to us because our associates treat them better than salespeople in other stores do."[32]

Sam's in good company. Herb Kelleher, the dynamic head of Southwest Airlines, is another chief exec who knows how important caring is. In an industry where profits have been steadily dropping, Southwest leads in profitability with a workforce that is known for its loyalty to the company and its leader.

Herb shows that caring by maintaining close contacts with his people. "He is the sort of manager who will stay out with a mechanic in some bar until four o'clock in the morning to find out what is going on. And then he will fix whatever is wrong," says Steve Lewins, a Gruntal & Co. analyst who's been following Kelleher and Southwest since 1971.[33]

Says Herb, "I feel that you have to be with your employees through all their difficulties, that you have to be interested in them personally. They may be disappointed in their country. Even their family might not be working out the way they wish it would. But I want them to know that Southwest will always be there for them."[34]

This family feeling pervades every aspect of the company, eventually working its way back to the customer. When you get on one of their planes you feel like you're in the crew's living room on a Saturday night. The flight attendants tell jokes, they make announcements in rap, and you get the genuine feeling they're glad to have you aboard.

Caring relationships are characterized by three things: respect, empathy, and acknowledgment.

Respect

Respecting people sounds very good on paper, but putting it into practice is another matter when there's a deadline to meet or a job that's been bungled. Try respecting the guy whose inacccurate figures made you look bad in front of your boss. Yet that's when yelling and screaming are least effective. The guy already knows he's screwed up. Rubbing his nose in the carpet will only further undermine him. This is the time when encouragement is most needed.

Says John Barbera, president of Turner Broadcasting Sales, "When someone's down that's the time to get them up off the floor. That's the time to give them a pat on the back, not a kick in the pants."

Respect is about treating your people as human beings with needs, aspirations, and fears—not as interchangeable parts that can be used up and thrown out.

Respect doesn't mean "smile-at-all-times" management. If people do bad work you don't ignore or accept it. On the contrary, respect implies holding people accountable for their actions. You call them to task, you let them know they've screwed up, but you never attack *them*. One of our rules is: Criticize behavior, coach the person. *Be demanding of performance and supportive of the person.*

This distinction is everything. When you ridicule, demean, or put down people you create three problems:

- *You compromise your working relationships*—employees typically feel intimidated and angry.
- *You create confidence problems*—people will begin to second-guess themselves.
- *And you provoke defensiveness*—humiliated individuals stop listening and nothing gets solved.

The result: Performance suffers and people stop taking risks. What you get is a compliant staff with no creative edge. And no one to tell you when you're wrong. "Who will tell the lion his breath smells bad?" goes an Arab folk saying.

Law and order. One partner at a law office was so frustrated by a slew of administrative and clerical errors that she could barely contain her anger. The mistakes were mostly minor, like missing filing deadlines and sending materials to the wrong address, but they were exactly the kind that made her and the firm look bad.

The partner began showing her frustration by chastising support staff and micromanaging their work. Did the situation improve? No, it got worse. Everyone was so nervous about making mistakes and upsetting her that the number of errors increased. Time-sensitive work was delayed to get her input. People were afraid to initiate actions on their own, the pace of work slackened, and everyone seemed to lose focus, probably because they were always looking over their shoulders. The problem was not corrected until an office manager was hired to buffer support staff from the frustrated partner.

Warrior woes. The Golden State Warriors basketball team learned this lesson the hard way when they lost their best player after one season because of respect—or rather, lack of it. Number-one draft pick Chris Webber, whom the Warriors went to great pains to acquire, refused to play under coach Don Nelson, a brilliant tactician who is known to sometimes publicly ridicule his players. Seventy-four million dollars wasn't enough to keep Webber from walking away from Nelson's coaching style.

"Listen, I've had coaches that were absolute jerks, I mean they screamed at us all the time," says Webber. "But you still have to respect people. You don't yell at them 'Why did we draft you?' in front of little kids in the stands."[35]

When you're critical of the job someone's done, but not them personally, the working relationship remains intact. And defensiveness is reduced. But when you attack the person, as Nelson did with Webber and fellow player Chris Mullen when he didn't make the All-Star team, you create deep animosity that sometimes can't be repaired.[36]

Two choices. Here are two ways of commenting on the same failed business presentation: "You blew it. What happened? Did you have a fight with your wife or something?" Or the alternative, "The presentation was poor. It was too rambling and lacked a convincing rationale. I know you can do better."

Which feedback would you prefer? Which allows you dignity while at the same time offering ideas for improvement?

That nobody is somebody's mother. "Treat everybody as if they're somebody because they are," says veteran baseball manager Sparky Anderson, who's always got something to say and, after 50 years in the sport, has earned the right to say it. "I'm in a restaurant; the waitress could be my mother, could be my sister. If the food stinks, don't go back. But don't get all worked up and take it out on the waitress."

Sparky advocates treating everyone with a sense of dignity no matter what their position or circumstance. He's got a sign on his desk that might reveal why: THE WORLD TURNS OVER ON SOMEONE WHO IS SITTING ON TOP OF IT. You never know when it's your turn to take a fall.[37]

Thin skin at Oil of Olay. Procter & Gamble's CEO Edwin Artzt violates Sparky's dictum. He has been accused of using personal attack to intimidate his employees. When managers in Taiwan objected to introducing only one Oil of Olay skin product at a time, a former marketing manager reported to the *Wall Street Journal* that Artzt cursed and called them "imbecilic" and "stupid."[38]

The *Journal* also reported that P&G managers said meetings with their boss often turned into "public hazings." At a meeting of beauty products managers, Artzt berated the group for half an hour about mishandling one of their products, Noxzema cream. With a severe tone of disgust, he exclaimed, "How could you people be so stupid to get into this mess?"[39]

"I told Ed he was going to lose a lot of brilliant people who were too scared to stand up to him," says Louis Pritchett, a sales vice president who retired just before Artzt took over as CEO. "He thinks, 'As long as we've got these sons of bitches running scared, we'll all be fine.' "[40]

Cut from the same cloth is former Digital sales and marketing chief Edward E. Lucente, who was ousted in 1994 in part because of his abrasive management style. "People were afraid to tell him the bad news," said a *Wall Street Journal* source.

On a morale-boosting trip to Dallas, one attendee reported that Lucente invited employees to ask him about anything, but when a salesman requested elaboration on the company's software strategy, characterizing it as unclear, Lucente "took his head off, belittling him in front of the whole room. Needless to say, no one else asked anything."[41]

Creating anxiety among your employees may have limited value in specific situations (more on this later) but as a general way of managing over the long term it is grossly unsuited for the changing corporate environment. Employees should not be targets for your frustration or fall guys for your mistakes. Managers who use intimidation tactics inspire loathing, not cooperation.

And don't excuse denigration with the "straight talk so everyone knows where I stand" excuse. We've heard that defense many times, and generally it's just a whitewash for reprehensible behavior.

MacArthur's rules. General Douglas MacArthur had a set of questions he used to define true leadership. The core of his approach was respect for his subordinates. MacArthur asked:

- Do I heckle my subordinates or strengthen and encourage them?
- Do I lose my temper at individuals?
- Do I act in such a way as to make my subordinates *want* to follow me?
- Am I interested in the personal welfare of each of my subordinates, as if he were a member of my family?
- Do I correct a subordinate in front of others?
- Am I inclined to be nice to my superiors and mean to my subordinates?[42]

Surprised that a man known for his toughness and tenacity could be so sensitive to his subordinates' feelings? The general was also known for the loyalty of those who served under him.

Empathy

Standing in someone else's shoes. A manager in the controller's office of a large insurance company had the unenviable task of correcting billing and accounting problems in the company's various departments. His job was to go in, clean the dirty laundry, and get out as quickly as possible. Almost without exception he was met with hostility and suspicion. Though he saw himself as a resource, most people looked at him as an enforcer, a bad cop who was going to either create more work or make them look bad for mistakes in the first place.

Whenever he took a new assignment he felt he was going into battle and he geared up by becoming hard nosed and aggressive, a style that reflected the football player he once was. Naturally his input was resisted. People got defensive and ended up blaming accounting procedures or other departments for the problems. In some cases they took no corrective measures at all.

"What a job," he confided. "It's like going into a war zone and the strangest part of it is they're shooting at me, their ally. I'm there to help them out of a jam. If they won't work with me, they'll be in real trouble down the road. But they don't get it."

We listened closely and then asked the manager to step away from his frustration for moment and consider another strategy. Instead of going in like gang busters with an extensive list of problems and threats of dire consequences, how else could he approach the job? We asked him to put himself in the position of the department managers. What did he know about their situation?

"Well, the company's restructuring right now and a lot of those people don't know if they're going to be pounding the pavement next month or not," he said. "And a few of those managers are changing their assignments. They'll be out of their departments by the end of the quarter."

"What else?" we inquired.

"Many of them are putting in sixty-plus hours a week. Since the last reorganization they're being asked to do more with less. There's a lot of tension and grumbling going on."

"Anything else?"

"Just that a number of them have had run-ins with the CFO before and I'd say they aren't feeling too kindly toward the controller's office."

Bingo, the lights went on. Time pressures, job insecurities, overwork, people leaving, a long history of bad blood—these were things he'd barely paid attention to before. The lack of cooperation he was getting now made sense. By moving out of his own point of view to what those managers were experiencing, he could see how his heavy-handed approach had increased resentment and resistance.

From that point on the situation began to shift. Our manager started listening more than he spoke and observing the reactions and responses of the people he was trying to serve. His reasoning changed, too. He saw that unless he addressed the department head's suspicions and fears, he was not going to get anywhere. The idea was not to stand in judgment, but to stand in the shoes of others and then ask how they would want to be approached.

After six weeks the feedback started coming in. The manager was getting greater access to records and more returned phone calls. The department heads agreed he was concerned about their problems and more receptive to their complaints. In fact they were high on the guy and wanted to know if someone was "working" with him. If so, what magic had they used to transform him?

The magic ingredient. The magic is empathy, the second piece of the caring relationship. Empathy is the ability to think and feel into another person's experience. It is the same talent that allows a mother to know why her newborn is crying or a teacher to say just the right thing to help a student grasp a tough concept.

When your first response is to understand the other person's point of view rather than to dismiss, criticize, or analyze it, dramatic things begin to happen. Individuals feel you're on their side, that you understand and appreciate their concerns and sensibilities. Even if you later present another point of view, leading with empathy will create greater receptivity to your input. In fact, empathy forges a sense of connection that turns into unbelievable loyalty and allegiance down the road. If you're going to ask your people to work 70-hour weeks or implement a restructuring plan, you'd be wise to create that connection.

By empathy we don't mean commiserating, sympathizing, or guessing what someone else might be experiencing. In some instances, empathy is quite the reverse. When an employee returned to the office after the death of his mother, his co-workers made such a fuss that he wanted to run out the door. Not that their "tell me all about it" looks weren't well intentioned. Of course they were. But their responses were not what *he* needed or wanted. They gave him sympathy; empathy is something else. An empathic approach would have been first to gauge his feelings and then respond appropriately—in this case to offer condolences and let him be.

Empathy is the process of connecting to someone else's reality so that you can understand not only *what* she thinks and feels but *how* she got there, the pressures, concerns, values, and perspectives that shape her thinking. For example, to anticipate how the CFO will react to your new marketing plan, you need to stand in her shoes and realize the specific pressures and concerns that *cause* her to respond. This vantage point makes it possible to communicate effectively and to establish positive working relationships.

The empathic vantage point is the perfect tool for creating powerful and resilient relationships within an organization. While autocratic managing styles may get you what you want in the short run and require less time and effort, they don't build the kind of relationships that can weather the storms of change.

We sometimes ask managers to think of three direct reports that are difficult to supervise and three that are easy. Then we ask them to observe all six people for a week and list next to each one's name: How do they react to obstacles in their paths? How do they respond to criticism? What motivates them to act? What are their personal aspirations for the future? What do they value most?

In almost every case we find that managers have a tougher time filling in the blanks for those employees they have difficulty managing. They have more in-depth answers for those they find easier to handle. Does this result from difficult employees being harder to get to know? Maybe, but only in a small number of cases. If you're having problems dealing with people it's usually because you're not understanding them and consequently don't know how to speak their language.

A short course in empathy. We're obviously not the first to talk about the importance of walking in your employees' or even your customers' shoes. (See Chapter 8.) But it's also likely no one has told you a structured way to go about it. "Just rely on your intuition" is the usual way it's put. What follows is a cram course in developing the empathic vantage point.

Empathy begins with paying attention: listening to your staff, noticing the things that excite or motivate them, observing their body language, focusing on their choice of words. Think of the people in your organization you have the roughest time managing. Write down what you know about:

- Their *general work situation*. For example: their division is doing poorly; there is tremendous pressure to cut costs; restructuring threatens their job.
- Their *functioning at work*. For example: their last performance review was poor; they were passed over for promotion; they have trouble getting along with co-workers.
- Their *personal situation.* For example: they have a daughter who's a great athlete; they're having marital problems; they go to church or temple regularly.
- Their *patterns of speech*. For example: they commonly use sports metaphors to describe business situations or they frequently use words like *anxiety* and *stress*.

- Their *values*. For example: honesty is paramount; they want to make a lot of money; getting along with people matters most.
- Their *goals, hopes, and dreams*. For example: they'd like to own their own business someday; they want a large family; they're shooting for presidency of the company.

Consider your answers. Do you have a better sense of the person than you did before? In most cases just focusing on hard-to-manage employees with understanding rather than judgment produces new insight about them. And the longer and harder you focus on them, the more likely you'll be able to understand what it's like to be them, if for just a moment. Once you wear their shoes, you'll be much clearer on how to deal with them.

Acknowledgment

Have you ever worked for weeks on a report, trudging home regularly after 9 P.M. each night and not even taking a Sunday off? All of us have at one time or another. It's just part of working and we all survive it. A few even thrive on it. But what happens when that report you poured your lifeblood into isn't even mentioned by your boss?

"The man acted as if he'd never received the thing," an accounting manager who'd had this experience recently told us. "For two weeks he'd been putting pressure on me to complete it. I lay it on his desk and nothing. Not even a thanks. Two weeks later he still hadn't mentioned it. I felt like a damned fool and then I started getting angry. I won't be busting my butt again for that guy."

Maybe the boss was busy. Maybe it slipped his mind. Or maybe he just took the manager for granted. Whatever the reason, it's bad coaching. If you want your people to work hard for you, you've got to care about them, and there is no surer way to undermine that caring than failing to acknowledge their efforts.

Inexpensive and worth the price. The third piece of the caring relationship is the simplest: personal acknowledgment. We're not talking formal programs that reward exceptional behavior with plaques and news articles. We're talking simple, everyday recognition like "Good job," "You've made a real contribution," "Great ideas." Or a quick voice or E-mail message.

This kind of caring doesn't take much effort. But it does require sincerity. Just commend someone for their contribution and watch them shine.

Every day, not once a year. "Managers are more likely to take time to deliver criticism than praise. Many reserve praise for the annual performance review. If the only feedback is when they mess up, that takes a toll over time. It needs to be done every day, not once a year," says Robert Nelson, a management consultant and author of *1001 Ways to Reward Employees.*[43]

Many executives believe that high salaries, stock options, or formal incentive programs are the only legitimate ways of acknowledging superior effort. As important as these may be, they should be given in conjunction with ongoing recognition and approbation. People want their efforts to matter and their progress to be noted and measured. The pat on the back is immediate and personal.

Says Nelson, "Most managers think it's just money. Most people . . . want appreciation. They want to know what's going on with their job and how they're doing."[44]

"People give you their loyalty when they feel appreciated," observes motivational guru Zig Ziglar. "One study found that 46 percent of people who leave their job do so because they *don't* feel appreciated by management. Sometimes the most effective motivation is just to say 'thank you.' "[45]

The "pat-on-the-back diary." The owner of a custom hand tool company had difficulty acknowledging his employees' efforts. He had read enough about modern management to know it was important, but he found himself struggling for words, clearly embarrassed by his awkwardness. Turns out he didn't trust praise. He felt it was manipulative, a way to get people to do something they didn't want to do. That's how it had been in his family. And not only could he not give recognition gracefully, he couldn't receive it. He viewed all compliments with suspicion.

"I don't need to be told I've done a good job," he argued. "I know the quality of my work. That's enough for me."

But it wasn't enough for his employees. Performance reviews aside, they wondered where they stood with him. Did he see their extra efforts? Did he know or care that they'd worked on Sunday to meet a deadline? A low level of grumbling and dissatisfaction was always present on the assembly floor. There was a strong "us and them" bias in the workers' perspective.

We had the owner keep what we call a pat-on-the-back diary. He had to record every instance when he acknowledged a worker's efforts. At the end of the first month the diary had two entries.

"Only a couple of people did something worthy of recognition?" we asked.

"Well, I might have missed a few," came the response.

When we went back day by day over the 30-day period we found at least 22 instances where praise might have been offered. There were 11 other marginal situations that could have gone either way.

"The stingier you are with your compliments, the stingier your employees will be with you," we emphasized. "Validating their work is a way of making them feel cared about."

Next month, the diary jumped to 18 entries. The following month, 25, which is about where it plateaued. Nothing dramatic happened at the plant. Objective measures like production and absentee rates remained about the same, but when we interviewed workers we found they expressed more favorable attitudes toward the company. There was definitely a different attitude on the production floor.

As for the owner, he was feeling much less clumsy patting backs and was now a convert to the "church of ongoing acknowledgment." He made a point of telling us his kids were the true beneficiaries of his new attitude. How did we respond to his conversion? We acknowledged him, of course.

Pitney woes. When Marc Breslawsky, head of the 800-employee office-systems division at Pitney Bowes, asked for feedback from his staff, he got a surprise. He discovered that they saw him as a tough businessman with little warmth who rarely acknowledged good efforts.

"I didn't pat people on the back. I didn't say thank you," admits Breslawsky. "That wasn't my style. And if I had something difficult to discuss with someone, I didn't temper it by discussing their good parts. They felt I didn't care about them."

His subordinates imitated his style. "A lot of people saw me like that, and they treated their people that way," he says. Then Breslawsky saw the light. The feedback he got gave him an appreciation of the need for appreciation.

"I started telling people what they do well and being more open in my discussions, and the results have been amazing." Teamwork has improved, and the time it takes to develop new products has been halved, he reports.[46]

It's not what you know. Caring is not a warm fuzzy new age concept. It's good business. Employees treat customers exactly the way they're treated by their managers. Companies that care for their employees attract the best talent and keep that talent longer. Teams perform better when they're directed by caring leaders.

People don't care how much you know until they know how much you care.

Offer respect, understanding, and acknowledgment and you'll foster incredible loyalty, enough to propel you through incremental or transformative organizational change.

Eighteen

Turning Resistance into Readiness

No one likes change, except, as the old joke goes, a baby with a wet diaper.

"Change creates fear in established organizations and paranoia in the minds of executives hired to protect the status quo," writes Gene Landrum. "The new can only be created by destroying the old."[1]

But it's not only fear that drives resistance to change. Change means more effort. It means moving out of the comfort zone and overcoming the inertia that sets in with long-established ways of thinking and doing.

Suppose your car runs out of gas a block from the filling station. No use calling Triple-A to tow it 500 feet. You put your shoulder to the bumper and lunge forward, but the steel behemoth doesn't budge an inch. As your high school physics teacher said, a body at rest wants to remain at rest.

Well, humans are like that old junker: They gravitate to the status quo. It takes a lot to get them going. They're apt to whine, complain, argue, dig in their heels, anything to resist change. But once you get them over the hump, you're on your way.

Resistance is the hump in the middle of the road that few leaders know how to get people over. Most managers think all they have to do is reward or threaten their people. Or they hope resistance will simply disappear once they've imposed change. These are half measures, like putting on a clean shirt when what you really need is a shower.

Some of them may work, but only for a short time. If you don't get to the real cause of resistance, it'll bounce back to haunt you. Resistance is surprisingly resilient, and although most managers have ample training in job processes, they have little training in people processes. Especially in managing change.

The next step in developing Change-Ready people and teams is to turn *resistance* into *readiness*. No matter how many sacred cows you've "pasture-ized," no matter how well conceived your plans for change, if you can't overcome employee resistance (and your own), you'll end up with volumes of ideas, none of them implemented.

CATALYST FOR CHANGE

Failing to understand and deal with resistance head on will exacerbate the problem, making it that much harder to implement change. In his classic paper "How to Deal with Resistance to Change" (1954), Harvard Business School professor Paul Lawrence describes how failing to understand workers' resistance can sabotage the whole effort.

Engineers in a factory studied by Lawrence imposed changes on the production line. Workers got testy and sabotaged the new methods. They weren't resisting their new jobs, but something else entirely. Previously, they had placed their outputs on the table next to them in plain view of their co-workers. In the new system those outputs were carried away immediately, robbing employees of their chance for recognition.

The engineers misread the workers' resistance as opposition to the new tasks. They tried to reason with them by "repeating all the logical arguments for why the new changes made sense from a cost standpoint." That didn't work, of course. Cost issues were not a genuine concern of the workers; peer recognition was.

As a result of failing to understand and deal with the real resistance there was "a chronic restriction of output and persistent hostility on the part of the operators," reports Lawrence.[2]

Had the engineers from the factory understood the importance of peer recognition on the assembly line, they might have worked with, and not against, the resistance. For instance, they might have instituted other ways for the new system to acknowledge individual effort. Understanding *resistance* is the first step in transforming it into a *catalyst for change*.

RESISTANCE-TO-CHANGE COW

RESISTANCE IS PERSONAL

Why does one employee embrace restructuring plans while her best friend vigorously opposes them? Why is one person reassured by a detailed explanation of a reorganization scheme while another suffers sleepless nights?

To understand and deal with resistance you have to look at *individualized* reasons for opposing change, such as the fear of not being able to succeed under new circumstances or the loss of power or status. System-wide solutions to resistance are rarely successful. In the end the decision to resist or cooperate is very personal. Different people resist change for different reasons.

If you bully or ignore resistance, you're just creating far greater problems down the road. Quits, transfers, absenteeism, lateness, lower production, loss of quality, slowdowns, wildcat strikes, sullenness, and quarreling are all examples of resistance that was not handled.

FIREHOSES AND WET BLANKETS

When we're on the road we usually carry a small pistol. No, we're not gun enthusiasts or urban warriors. The gun is an orange plastic water pistol, and we don't use it for protection but to make a point.

FIREHOSING COW

Whenever we're helping organizations to reinvent themselves, there are always a few people in the room who can't wait to give five good reasons why the new thinking won't work: "It's not realistic," "Not in the budget," "It costs too much," and so on.

We call this firehosing because it dampens people's enthusiasm, douses the spark of creativity, and just plain puts out the fire, killing excitement and motivation on the spot. Firehosing is not legitimate dissent. The difference? Hosing is an automatic response that effectively ends the conversation. Genuine differences of opinion extend the dialogue, often resulting in more-informed solutions.

Our solution to firehosing is to take out that orange pistol and give the naysayers a dose of their own medicine. So get out your water guns. Here are some of the more common firehoses to watch out for:

- *Yeah, but* . . . This is code for "I think the idea stinks." Anything that comes after the *but* is *bull.*
- *The toos.* It's too hard, too complicated, too expensive, too quick, slow, showy, takes too long. Anytime you hear the word *too* it's *too* late.
- *They'll never buy it.* Who's "they" and why presume how someone else will react?
- *It's unrealistic.* Our favorite. Was Galileo unrealistic? Was Einstein? How about Alexander Graham Bell or Ted Turner? Realism is just a name for yesterday's thinking.
- *It's just a fad.* Yes, and so were the compact car, the microwave oven, the fax machine. Today's fad is tomorrow's household word.
- *It'll never work; can't be done.* If these naysayers are so smart how come they never come up with any ideas of their own?
- *If it ain't broke, don't fix it.* And if you wait until it's broke to fix it, you'll end up with nothing left to fix.
- *Don't rock the boat.* Huge waves of change are already rocking the boat and will sink it if you're not prepared to change course.
- *Don't stick your neck out.* An ostrich strategy that can't possibly work in a competitive environment. If you don't stick your neck out you'll lose your head.
- *It's not in the budget.* Of course not. This year's budget was made up last year, when circumstances were different.
- *Let's wait and see.* A delay tactic based on the hope that down the road the whole idea will be forgotten.

One way to deal with firehosing is with a blast from your trusty six-squirter and a laugh. Firehoses are distractions covering the real reasons for resistance. But they can often serve as a warning sign of a more entrenched level of resistance.

FROM HEEL DRAGGERS TO FENCE RIDERS

When Ralston Resorts merged Keystone and Arapahoe Basin ski resorts with its recently purchased Breckenridge facility, there was resistance. "First of all, Keystone and Breckenridge had been arch competitors," said executive vice president John Rutter. "Second, the two resorts had very different cultures and operating styles. When we tried to merge them we ran into a great deal of opposition."

Following are some resistor types that Rutter and other managers typically encounter when introducing change, as well as some quick tips for dealing with each.

Heel Draggers

These are the people who oppose change quietly through noncooperation. They'll nod their heads yes but they'll act no. Every manager's seen one of these, although they can be hard to spot for obvious reasons. Look for signs of opposition like lateness in completing new procedures or a plethora of questions after you've just given specific, detailed instructions.

Quick tip: Bring resistance into the open. Use gripe sessions where complaining is encouraged to flush out these heel draggers.

Saboteurs

Saboteurs are also silent resistors, but their actions are more aggressive. They not only drag their heels, they create real obstacles to your plans like holding back information, planting bugs in the new software, or conveniently losing important data—"So sorry." Saboteurs are dangerous because they can wreak havoc and you'll never see them; these may be the most troublesome of all resistor types.

Quick tip: Same strategy as with heel draggers. Flush them out by giving permission to criticize and vent. Once resistance is in the open, it can be addressed. Hidden, it is almost impossible to neutralize.

Fence Riders

They're cautious. They take a long time making up their minds. They don't want to make a mistake or go against co-workers. They track the prevailing winds before taking a position.

Quick tip: Blitz them with convincing, persuasive information to blow them off the fence. Reassurance and confidence building are also important, but you've got to get to them before the antagonists win them over.

Ostriches

Some people create change, some react to it, still others pretend nothing's happening. That's these guys. They're uninformed, haven't paid or don't want to pay attention. With their heads in the sand, they act like change will go away if they just ignore it. We're always amazed at how many people choose to remain ignorant about something that will affect their future.

Quick tip: Inform them very specifically, one on one, if possible. Get them actively involved. Put them in charge of gathering more information or organizing staff input.

Dissenters

They express honest differences with your plans and offer logical reasons for opposition. Their thinking is legitimate and often based in a different point of reference.

Quick tip: Don't close them off; incorporate their best ideas. You just might build a better mousetrap. Let them know you value their input. Meet their rational objections with rational responses.

Antagonists

They're vocal, loud, and annoying. These clubhouse lawyers seize the microphone and won't surrender it. Arguments can't sway them. They're unwilling to compromise or negotiate. They oppose change no matter how small simply because it's change. (For more on their motives, see below.)

Quick tip: Ignore them. Withdraw energy from them. Don't allow them the soap box. If all else fails, cut 'em loose.

FOUR RESISTANCE DRIVERS

Firehoses and resistor styles alert you to the deeper, personal motives that drive resistance. We've uncovered four:

- *Fear*—"What if . . . I lose my job, look stupid, can't adapt," etc.
- *Feeling Powerless*—"No one asked me!"
- *Inertia*—"It's too much effort, too uncomfortable."
- *Absence of Self-Interest*—"What's in it for me?"

Each one is a powerful force for the status quo. Each is an obstacle to Change-Readiness. And each must be addressed if your plans for change are to be realized.

DRIVER #1: FEAR—"WHAT IF I LOSE MY JOB, LOOK STUPID," ETC.

The "F" word. What's a four-letter word beginning with "F" that you don't mention in public? We're talking about fear, something everyone's got and no one admits to.

The chairman's worried about how the board will react to the new restructuring plan. The manager's afraid that flattening the corporation will destroy her power base. Workers worry that they'll be replaced by machines. Clerical staff are anxious they'll look stupid learning the new software. And so it goes down the line to the night watchman, who's scared about being replaced by a video monitor or a Doberman pinscher.

Fear is the most common cause of resistance and the most powerful one.

It frightens the best of us even though we try to hide it. "Tough guys," after all, don't get scared. Bogey and Cagney didn't. Cagney and Lacey didn't, Arnold certainly doesn't. Our role models, so the saying goes, don't get scared; they get even.

Bunk! Everyone, even the most macho athletes, gets scared under pressure. Hall of Fame basketballer Bill Russell, one of the toughest players in the sport, used to throw up before every game. Edwin Moses, who won over a hundred 440 hurdles races in a row including three Olympic gold medals, confessed that before each race, "It feels like I am being led to my execution."[3]

In a world that is changing so rapidly and in which nothing is predictable for long, fear is natural and normal. In fact, if you aren't feeling any anxiety, you're probably playing it too safe. And that's a reason to be scared.

Fear's Vicious Cycle

Occasionally most of us excel when we're afraid. But most often fear prevents us from performing at our peak. It causes many of the mistakes that ruin the quality of our work and creates much of the stress that ruins the quality of our life.

What makes fear so potent is that it is self-fulfilling as well as self-reinforcing. It *causes* the very thing you're afraid will happen. Once triggered, it gathers momentum and becomes highly contagious, spreading through organizations like fire after drought.

To enable your team to embrace change, you have to learn coaching skills for breaking this powerful resistance driver. Understanding how the *cycle of fear* works is the secret to neutralizing it. Like a cancer, fear can be stopped with early intervention. The sooner you recognize it, the easier it is to stop the cycle. If you wait too long, fear-driven resistance becomes entrenched.

A visual representation of the fear cycle is presented on the following pages, using two situations that might occur when change is introduced:

- *Situation One:* Making a first presentation to the new management team.
- *Situation Two:* Adapting to a cross-functional team structure.

Link #1—Imagined Consequences: Doomsday Scenario

When an individual feels afraid, a self-perpetuating cycle is set off. First come negative thoughts. Suddenly a difficult situation becomes positively catastrophic. A challenge turns into a calamity. In other words, the worst possible consequences are imagined. In situation one, you imagine you'll look bad or lose your job. In situation two, you won't be able to fit into the new work team and you'll look foolish trying.

Once these negative thoughts start flowing you lose your ability to maintain perspective on the situation. Everything gets exaggerated.

"If I don't come in under budget, it could be bad news," one manager told us in a classic example of catastrophic thinking. "My boss is a real SOB. He could decide to outsource my operation and I'd lose my job. I've got a kid in school, a mortgage, car payments, the works." By the time he was finished playing out his doomsday scenario, he had himself sitting on a curb drinking cheap booze out of a paper bag.

That's what fear does. It takes a simple situation and makes it do-or-die. It's your job on the line, your self-worth, your survival. Whew. That's a lot of pressure. And the vaguer the situation, the greater the room for negative thinking. Huge organizational transformations like restructuring or reengineering are characterized by ambiguity and uncertainty, causing imagined consequences to run wild.

Remember when you were a kid lying in bed in your darkened room? In the shadows, things weren't so clear and everything turned scary. The baseball cap on the chair came alive; the doll in the corner became a ghost. In an uncertain situation the same kind of thing happens.

Link #2—Fear Distorts Perception

When I lived in New York I would occasionally put on a pair of rose-colored glasses. Everything looked beautiful through these lenses. Well, fear is like putting on glasses with the opposite effect. These dark lenses focus you on everything that's intimidating. And they distort what you see to make it appear even worse. At the presentation to management you see scowling faces, Godzillas in three-piece suits. Face-to-face with your new team members, you read rejection in their eyes.

The Fear Cycle

Situation One
Making a first presentation to the new management team

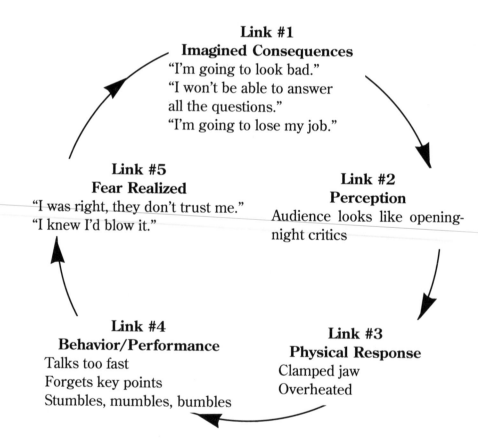

Link #1
Imagined Consequences
"I'm going to look bad."
"I won't be able to answer all the questions."
"I'm going to lose my job."

Link #2
Perception
Audience looks like opening-night critics

Link #3
Physical Response
Clamped jaw
Overheated

Link #4
Behavior/Performance
Talks too fast
Forgets key points
Stumbles, mumbles, bumbles

Link #5
Fear Realized
"I was right, they don't trust me."
"I knew I'd blow it."

The Fear Cycle

Situation Two
Adapting to a cross-functional team structure

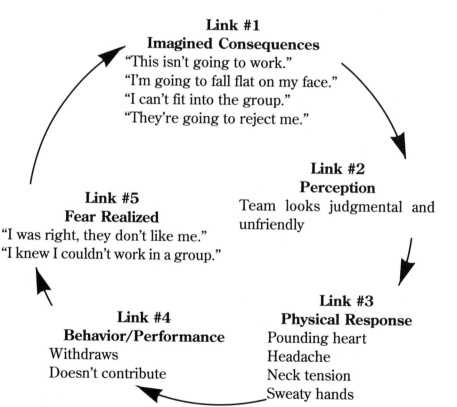

Link #1
Imagined Consequences
"This isn't going to work."
"I'm going to fall flat on my face."
"I can't fit into the group."
"They're going to reject me."

Link #2
Perception
Team looks judgmental and unfriendly

Link #3
Physical Response
Pounding heart
Headache
Neck tension
Sweaty hands

Link #4
Behavior/Performance
Withdraws
Doesn't contribute

Link #5
Fear Realized
"I was right, they don't like me."
"I knew I couldn't work in a group."

Most athletes know that fear distorts perception: The scared skier sees an intermediate slope as the face of Mount Everest. The apprehensive golfer thinks she's putting into a cup the size of a dime. The anxious tennis player swears the net is a foot higher than it should be.

But the same thing can happen to anyone tackling something new at work where the instruction manual looks like *Webster's Unabridged,* the new organizational chart seems like a jigsaw puzzle, and that important report you have to read by tomorrow appears to be written in Phoenician script.

And just to make matters a little worse, when you're caught in the fear cycle, your eyes are drawn to the very thing you'd like to avoid, like the face of the most critical, unsympathetic person in the room.

Link #3—Body Signals

Fear sneaks up on you. People don't realize the extent to which it affects their perceptions and performance. Physical responses or body signals are good indicators that they're caught in the cycle.

One person told us that when she's overscheduled and worried about meeting a deadline, her insides feel like steel cables, they're so tight. Another gets headaches across his forehead and can feel his heart pounding. Still another complains of a dry mouth and tight throat every time she makes a presentation.

Some of the more common "body signals" that indicate fear: clenched jaw, tight stomach, dry mouth, butterflies in the belly, quick temper, shortness of breath, clammy hands.

Link #4—Fight or Flight: Panic or Procrastination

Procrastination. When I signed a contract for my first book, all I could think about was that I had to write 75,000 words. So I jumped into action—called friends, went out to lunch, jogged a lot. Anything but face that empty, *blank* computer screen. And the longer I waited to get started, the harder it got.

Procrastination is one of the most common responses to fear. People will polish nickels or answer their junk mail, anything to avoid confronting the terrifying task, though they know that sooner or later it has to be done.

I've seen salespeople whose very livelihood depended on making cold calls spend hours filling out their expense forms and do other meaningless paperwork simply to avoid this fearsome task. And people with a deadline . . . forget it. How many times can you call the weather report?

Procrastination to Panic. Maybe somewhere inside our head is the hope that if we put off doing what we think will be too hard or too scary, it will go away or get easier.

"I do my best work when I'm under the gun," is the common rationalization. Nonsense! What people mean is that they finally *do* the work when they're under the gun. In other words they can't put it off anymore or they'll suffer grave consequences. By this time, though, procrastination has turned to panic.

Panic is not a place for high performance. You can't concentrate, you forget important things, you make mistakes, you get stupid. In the panic zone, you're likely to communicate poorly, get the "gottas" (see Chapter Four, "The Speed Cow"), and lose all hope of being creative.

Link #5—The Cycle Closes: Fears Are Realized

Panicking or procrastinating results in performing far below your ability level so the original fears you had are realized. Only now you have concrete evidence to support them.

The sad part is that when you're caught in the fear cycle your performance is not reflective of your real ability. It's not that you're incapable of adapting to change, but only that fears have compromised your performance.

How, then, do you stop the fear cycle? Two ways:

- by cutting fear down to size through "reality checks";
- by building confidence to face new situations.

Looking the monster in the eye. A Native American tribe in the Southwest used to say that fear was like a huge two-headed snake as long and thick as a giant redwood. There is no running from such a menace. It can easily catch and overwhelm you. To conquer it, the shaman says, you have to stand your ground and look it in the face. As it draws closer it will see its own reflection in your eyes, get scared, and slink away.

The wisdom works. Run from fear and it will engulf you like a fire. Ignore fear and it will attack you like a snake when you least expect it. Looking fear in the eye and seeing it for what it really is weakens the fear cycle.

Reality Checks—Cutting Fear Down to Size

Since almost all fears are exaggerated and irrational, they can be countered with a strong dose of reality. What is *really* true about the situation, your ability to deal with it, and the consequences of not handling it? Your worst nightmare or your deepest concerns are one thing, but *what is most likely to happen?*

Reality checks put the kibosh on catastrophic thinking, horrific fantasies, and exaggerated consequences.

The doomsday scenario—images of getting fired and feelings of shame—needs to be examined and defused. Here's how it's done.

A successful residential building contractor wanted to expand into commercial projects but felt unable to take the next step. "Every time I start thinking about expanding, I panic," she said. "It would mean buying new equipment, hiring new crews, changing the way I market myself. Who knows if all that would even work. And the thought of failing when I'm doing just fine right now seems so scary I don't want to think about it."

"What's the worst thing that could happen if the situation doesn't work out?" we asked (the first question in a reality check).

"I'm afraid I'll make some terrible blunder and go belly up. If that happened I'd lose everything—my trucks, my equipment, maybe even my house, not to mention the reputation I've been building for twenty years. Forget it. It's easier to just keep doing what I'm doing."

"On a scale of one to ten—if ten equals certainty—what are the chances of your fears being realized?" we asked (the second question).

She stopped for a moment to consider this odd question. "Hmmm, I've never looked at it that way before. It's probably only a four, or at the very most a five." Her whole body seemed to relax as she said those numbers. "That's not as bad as I thought. I saw myself in debtors' prison a minute ago," she laughed.

"But four or a five? That's a risk I'm willing to take. Even if the worst did happen, I suppose I could get a job working for another builder. My competition would probably be delighted if I closed the shop. They'd hire me in a minute. I mean I not only bring all that skill but contacts as well."

That simple conversation broke the fear cycle. Everything changed when she recognized that the consequences of failing, although serious, weren't nearly as catastrophic as she'd imagined. She had a business plan on her banker's desk within three weeks.

We've used the "worst-case-scenario reality check" with all types of people in all kinds of situations, and the results are similar. People realize that the chances of the imagined disaster are usually much less than they first thought. Fear exaggerates the perceived risk, making it seem much greater than it actually is. Reality testing corrects the distortion.

If all the things that we thought were life and death really were, a great coach once quipped, "there'd be a lot more dead people around."

Doomsday Check

Our research on peak performers shows that most people who thrive on change usually do a catastrophic-expectations check before taking on something new. They set out a worst-case scenario, evaluate the chances of it happening and the possible consequences if it does, and decide whether they can live with them.

The amazing thing, one hugely successful entrepreneur told us, was that doing this worst-case scenario, which he called his "doomsday check," "always gave me more confidence and actually increased my motivation, because I usually found out that the worst was never as bad as I had thought."

Here's how the "doomsday check" works in an organizational change situation. We asked a manager who was worried about losing his job to downsizing the "worst-thing" question. His response was pretty typical.

"I could lose my job and be out on the street. Jobs are tough to find for a guy who's turning forty-six this year. And I have a lot of plastic debt to cover."

So we asked him to rate the chances of that happening—question two. A smile broke out. "I must be crazy," he said. "I mean I've been one of the highest performers in the business unit and the feedback I've gotten is consistently positive. I'd rate the likelihood at four. Even if I lost my job I've still got options. I'd get a pretty good severance package and I know a lot of people in this business. I'd find another one. Maybe I'd start my own consulting business."

Again the fear cycle was broken when the manager acknowledged that his doomsday scenario wasn't likely and that he had other options. By asking people to quantify the risk of their worst nightmare being realized, we are shifting the way an individual looks at things from a fear-based response to a reality-based perspective. This shift makes all the difference in the way a person responds to the situation. Once reason is introduced, problem solving follows and contingency planning can be considered. As long as the individual is caught in fear, there is no room to see anything but doom and gloom.

Even if the person's situation is truly awful (they're likely to be laid off), making the shift out of fear can lead to productive discussion of other options and opportunities.

But What If . . .

Even if you use reality checks to break out of the fear cycle it still makes sense to have a contingency plan in place. No matter how well you assess a situation, sometimes the worst *does* happen. Your fears *do* materialize. You may not be able to control the big picture—the economy or your company's future plans—but you can control how well you respond to it. The only thing worse than the doomsday scenario is being unprepared for the doomsday scenario.

At a clothing company who called us in to help with its reorganization, one manager told us he was playing it safe. "They're planning a major downsizing and it's time for me to fade into the woodwork," he said. "No more high profile. No more risk taking. Just do my job and not call attention to myself. I'd like to still be around next year."

Everyone in his group agreed. Play it safe, do your job, and hope for the best.

"And what if you do get fired?" we asked. "What would you do then?" The question threw everybody off. No one really wanted to consider this possibility, though it was very likely some of them wouldn't be around in a few months. Most were hoping it wouldn't happen to them.

"Let's assume you will get laid off. Draw up a plan of action," we told a now fidgeting audience. After an uncomfortably long pause, they got busy. When they were done we asked them to share their plans with the group. Many had typical strategies like polish up the résumé, network at industry meetings, or call a headhunter.

But what surprised us was that quite a few had plans, like the salesman from Dallas, who said, "I'm tired of this peddling game. I've always wanted to go back to Arkansas and raise pigs." Or the HR manager who told us, "My husband and I have always dreamed about opening a little B&B up near Mendicino." Or the CIO who said, "I've really gotten into fitness and health in the past few years and would love to get into that industry."

Many of these employees did lose their jobs. But our follow-up showed that contingency planning helped people deal with the crisis situation. It mobilized them to take action more quickly than those who weren't in the group.

The interesting thing was that a fair number of people did change careers. That manager opened a B&B, though not in California. The CIO got a job with a health spa in the Caribbean. And one day we got a call from the Dallas salesman, who told us, "I'm back home now in Arkansas with five hundred pigs having the time of my life. It's a dream come true. I'm in hog heaven."

Preparing for the worst just might lead you to some unexpected or never-dreamed-of opportunities.

The national pastime. Most people are better at the doomsday thinking than they are at the contingency planning. Worrying—not baseball—is really the national pastime. We teach managers who are dealing with employee resistance a semantic trick that helps mobilize energy and turn worrying into planning.

Worry always starts with the two words *what if,* and then the horror movie starts rolling. You can stop that movie and shift anxiety to anticipation if you change the "what if" to an "if . . . then."

For example:

- *"What if* I get fired" is changed to *"If* I get fired *then* I will . . ."
- *"What if* I miss the plane" to *"If* I miss it, *then* I will . . ."

We did something similar when we asked the clothing-company employees to set up contingency plans. We moved them out of their play-it-safe strategy and into a more active way of thinking.

Changing worry to preparation is empowering. It frees up the energy that is stuck in catastrophizing and makes it available to create opportunity. It also increases confidence. You're less worried because you have a fall-back strategy.

An entrepreneur with a successful jewelry business used to have a safety net that gave her comfort. Years before, she'd worked as a waitress at a restaurant in Santa Fe. Whenever things were tight she would comment how she could always go back to that simple life and wait tables. It never happened, of course, but it gave her solace to know that no matter how bad things got, she'd always survive.

Creative worrying. Sometimes we encourage worrying. No, that's not a typo. We want people to worry. We want them to think about everything that might go wrong with a plan for change. And we mean *everything,* down to who'll put the paper in the copy machine. It sounds crazy after all that talk about reality checks, but we've found that this paradoxical intervention can occasionally work wonders.

After all the possible disasters are enumerated, we look at each one of them and create a strategy to deal with it. By the time we're done, every contingency has been explored. It's an incredibly energizing and upbeat exercise in problem solving that leaves people with two impressions: how out of control their worries can get and how every problem has a solution if you look hard enough.

We call it creative worrying, and it can put the brakes on fear-driven resistance.

Building Confidence

Reality testing cuts fear down to size, but it's only half a solution,. Building people's confidence, helping them believe they can manage change without failing, is the other half.

Even if employees believe a change is good for the company, they'll resist it if they feel they're not up to the task. If they perceive their skill and ability to be less than what they think is required to implement change, their fears will skyrocket and their confidence plummet. Neutralizing fear-driven resistance to change requires managers to help their people believe in themselves. Confidence is a fear killer.

Refocus Attention

One technique for building confidence is to refocus attention. Years ago when I was teaching skiing, I noticed that when faced with a challenging slope students would procrastinate with a third or fourth cup of coffee. Some got irresistible urges to wax their skis or call their travel agents—anything but start down the slope.

To get them moving I refocused their attention: Scared skiers look all the way down the hill or at the rocks or bumps they can't handle. By keeping their eyes glued on the things that petrify them, they supercharge their anxiety.

So I refocused their attention by asking, "Can you make one turn?" This instruction got them looking right in front of them and concentrating on what they *could do* rather than what they *couldn't.* They'd take that one "can-do" turn, stop, and then take another. After about five or six turns, their confidence increased and they usually were able to ski the rest of the run.

Looking at the moguls and rocks gave skiers a distorted view of the task in front of them. They didn't see the smooth part of the slope. Refocusing created a more balanced view of the challenge.

A simple rule in coaching yourself or anyone else is: *Can-Do's build confidence; Can't-Do's increase fear.*

Can-Do Training

To diffuse fear and build confidence at work, break tasks down into one "can-do turn" at a time. Once that's been achieved, move on to the next until you've got a string of accomplishments. The fear cycle can't get going if you introduce "doable" tasks early on in the change process (see "Driver #3: Inertia" later in this chapter for more on this).

I learned my first software program taking "can-do" steps. When I first opened the instruction manual I couldn't believe the complexity. I thought the program was supposed to be user friendly, but I felt like I was in a war zone surrounded by hostiles. How was I going to learn all those commands? How was I going to avoid pressing the wrong key and losing everything I'd written? The answer, I told myself, was one "can-do turn" at a time. Each day I read a new page and practiced what I had learned throughout the day. The software turned out to be quite simple. After a month I had mastered the program.

That positive experience not only helped me learn word processing, it increased my confidence in and my commitment to the computer. I began looking for other useful programs. I even found myself taking pleasure in mastering arcane commands. The old saying applies: *Inch by inch is a cinch; yard by yard is hard.*

More "can-do turns." Some changes aren't as clear-cut as a new software program. The sales staff at a pharmaceutical company had always sold to the purchasing departments of hospitals and other health-care-provider organizations. To keep up with the changes in the industry and to make calls more cost effective, the company decided to change its sales tactics. The new strategy called for salespeople to make presentations to purchasing committees composed of groups of physicians, nurses, pharmacists, and financial people as well as the purchasing agents. The company figured this would get the sales staff directly in front of all the decision-makers at once.

Panic set in. The salespeople were afraid they wouldn't be effective in this new situation and would lose business. They voiced concern about how they could appeal to all the different needs and concerns in a group setting. They were anxious that the personal relationships on which all sales are built would be undermined. So they continually resisted as long as they could, finding one reason or another to postpone the change.

Our strategy was to take one turn at a time. First we role-played, dealing with each committee member, and discussed the specific concerns of each: the doctors' focus on drug efficacy and research, the nurses' concern for ease of application, the budget director looking for the best price.

The second "turn" was to develop structured presentations to meet each of these concerns. We created overheads, slides, and handouts for the presentation. Then we rehearsed the format with real clients and got feedback—turn three. We videotaped the presentations for coaching review. It was all done one step at a time, enabling everyone to stay out of the fear cycle and get down "the new hill" quickly and easily.

Don't throw them in over their heads. In Joe Montana's first years with the San Francisco 49ers, the legendary quarterback rode the bench. Occasionally, when the team was so far ahead or behind, Coach Bill Walsh would put him in the game.

It wasn't that Walsh didn't believe in Montana's ability. It was that he wanted to build Montana's confidence by placing him in low-pressure situations. The strategy obviously worked. Montana excelled and his confidence soared. And, as they say, the rest is history.

Good coaches in any field put people into situations in which they can succeed. "I'd rather start players off slowly if I can," one coach told us, "to give 'em a few wins so they can build up belief in themselves."

When individuals feel that the situation is beyond their capability, they either give up or try too hard. Start out with a little less and you'll build much more. Start out a little slower and you'll improve much faster. Raise the bar, but not so high that the person will lose hope of ever clearing it.

Build on Strengths

Confidence is the key to performance. Focusing on people's weaknesses—even done out of a desire to help—saps confidence. Emphasizing strengths builds esteem and encourages people to do better in everything, including those things that give them trouble.

When you're introducing change, remind people of their competence. Show them how the skills they already have will help them to excel in the new task. But don't just lay on a lot of hot air and generalities. Be specific about how their skills will match up with their new assignments. And be honest; tell it like it is.

Remembering Past Successes

When employees are afraid of change, they often forget how well they've responded to it in the past.

"Remember how uncertain you felt when you first started this job?" we reminded the pharmaceutical salespeople. "And how much anxiety you felt making your first call? Now think about how you got through that. How you got up to speed. How you learned to be successful. You did it then, why not now!"

Bringing past success with change situations into the present is a way of building confidence. In coaching skiers, for example, I found they often stopped halfway down a challenging slope and scared themselves by looking at what they still had left to do. So I had them look back up the hill instead of down to see where they had come from. The response was almost always, "I can't believe I skied that!" And you could see the fear evaporate right before your eyes.

Looking back up the hill built confidence. When they looked downslope again they did so with more assurance. We're not talking about positive thinking. Focusing on past successes is *reality thinking*. You've done well in the past, and you can do it again.

Even when tackling a new situation you haven't faced before, there will always be familiar aspects and transferable skills. Nothing is entirely new.

Highlight films. We've done "building on past success" exercises with hundreds of athletes and started the practice of making personal highlight films for viewing in off hours. For instance, we had a professional basketball player who was in a slump make a three-minute video of his best moves. After watching the tape over a 30-game period, his point production increased 41 percent, and his steals per game went up 55 percent!

Another technique is to keep a written record of previous wins and achievements. Peter Thigpen, the former president of Levi Strauss's U.S. operations, observed, "Logging these small victories and referring to them when I'm feeling frustrated helps to remind me of my track record and my progress. It's a big help in relieving frustration and doubt and increasing my confidence."[4]

Baseball player Dave Winfield, a future Hall of Famer, is a great believer in highlight films. He used to encourage his teammates to make videotapes of their own best plays. "I include only hits and well-hit balls in mine, because when you're hitting the ball well, you're technically or fundamentally doing things correct," says Winfield.[5]

"I remember in New York [when he played with the Yankees], owner George Steinbrenner was very negative; he wanted every player to make a tape of all the errors they had made. Before the season started he wanted us to review all those errors and bad plays.

"No way, I said to the coaches. I'm not going into that room to watch that video. Put on the Three Stooges or something. I don't want any negative reinforcement."[6]

That in a nutshell is Winfield's personal philosophy. "You can't afford to let negative thoughts creep in," he says. "I don't try and analyze things from a negative standpoint. What we're trying to do is to instill, inculcate these guys with positive reinforcement." [6]

In other words, accentuate the positive and eliminate the negative.

Positive Framing

Baseball manager Tony LaRussa is one of the best at giving honest feedback that builds confidence. He does it by framing everything positively, even problems and mistakes. When a pitcher has a bad game, LaRussa's feedback might be something like this: "Your fastball had good movement; once you get a little more control you'll be unbeatable."

Compare that to "You were wild today. You've got to learn to control your fastball or you're not going to make it here."

Both point out the pitcher's "control" problem. But one uses the information to build confidence, while the other one uses it to criticize and threaten. Which one would you rather receive? Which would make you feel better about yourself before going into the next game?

We're not saying to avoid discussing the mistakes or errors employees make. But framing the error positively makes it easier for them to correct them.

À la LaRussa. When I'm asked to coach CEOs on how to speak effectively to large audiences, I always use LaRussa's positive-frame approach.

Typically most of these leaders stand woodenly behind the podium reading from a prepared speech. Even with good visual aids, they tend to drone on, directing their energy toward the page in front of them, not the audience. And their body language—so important for emphasizing critical points—is hidden behind the rostrum.

I always start by having them view a video of their performance and give themselves feedback. Like most of us, they usually notice only the negatives: "My voice was a monotone." "I went on too long." "I didn't make eye contact with the audience." "I wasn't very convincing." And so forth.

This type of feedback, whether it's true or not, can zap confidence and energy. Taking a page from LaRussa, I might convey the same information with a positive spin. "You have such a great voice," I might tell them. "It's strong and deep, but with your head down looking at your notes it sounds muffled."

Or "You have a terrific sense of humor and people really feel you care, but if you don't move around and make eye contact, it won't come across."

Or "You have a lot of passion and terrific gestures, but the podium blocks your energy from the audience."

I don't lie, sugarcoat, or even mince words about what's not working. But I frame the negative positively, to build confidence and communicate what needs to be changed.

Build on Mistakes

Whatever the change—downsizing, reorganizing, or just fantasizing—people are going to make mistakes. New situations create errors. Count on it. How you deal with those errors will have a real impact on employee resistance.

The Change-Ready manager deals with mistakes in a way that doesn't undermine people's confidence in themselves. Errors, as we discussed in Chapter Eleven, "The No-Mistakes Cow," can catapult you to greater heights. But only if you learn from them. Being a successful manager in a dynamic environment is not based on *whether* your people make mistakes, but on *how* you respond to them.

No one feels good about making errors. When they're significant, they usually create self-doubt, loss of esteem, and embarrassment, often undermining creativity and building resistance to trying anything new.

Many well-intentioned coaches try to boost confidence by telling people to shake off mistakes or forget about them. It's not that easy. How can you pretend nothing happened when the whole office is talking about it behind your back? Maybe you can manage to forget it temporarily, but when a similar situation occurs your old feelings will crop up again.

One of my early coaching jobs was with a health-care organization that had been receiving a great deal of negative publicity. To tell its side of the story, the company held several press conferences. My role was to help the new CEO manage those meetings without putting his foot in his mouth.

Well, he must have had a pretty good-sized mouth because as soon as an openly hostile question was asked, he choked on his foot. Flustered and furious, he responded defensively.

After the conference he was fuming. And like a good, but naive, coach, I told him to shake it off and move on. But when another hostile question came up at the next press conference, he had the same reaction. Clearly he had not learned from the first situation and repeated his mistake.

I changed my tactics. I had him remember the muffed responses he made in the meetings rather than try to forget them. "Go back to the moment you were asked that hostile question," I instructed him. "What were you thinking?"

"Two things," he said. "One was, This bastard is trying to get me. That got me angry. The other was that I didn't have the right response. That made me scared."

We considered the possible questions reporters might ask and all the most effective responses. The last option we came up with was a fall-back position: admit he was in a new job and didn't know the answer but would find out and get back to the questioner.

"How would you feel giving this response?" I asked.

"Fine," he said. "It's the truth. Hell, I've only been here for two months. I can't be expected to know everything."

At the next meeting, sure enough, someone threw a "gotcha" curve ball, one that we hadn't rehearsed. But the CEO played it beautifully, almost laughing as he said, "I'm a new guy on the block. You can't expect me to know everything." Then he threw it back on the reporter. "How long did it take you to learn the ins and outs of your job?"

Reviewing, Rethinking, Rehearsing

The trick is to turn mistakes into learning by *reviewing* what happened, *rethinking* new responses, and *rehearsing* them. This triple-R intervention allows you to deal with the problem differently and rebuild the confidence shaken by the error. The three Rs increased the CEO's confidence by replacing the negative memory with a positive strategy.

If you think of memory as an internal videotape that records experience, then:

Reviewing is watching the tape to see what you thought and felt.

Rethinking is figuring what changes need to be spliced into the failure experience to make it positive.

Rehearsing is running the new positive tape in your mind until it becomes automatic.

DRIVER #2: FEELING POWERLESS—"NO ONE ASKED ME!"

Don't tread on me. "People don't resist change as much as they resist being changed," says management consultant and author Christopher Hegarty. When change is imposed from the top, people feel powerless, victimized, and are often angry and resentful. Any *imposed* change evokes resistance to it. In fact, America was born out of such circumstances. The first colonial flag bore the inscription DON'T TREAD ON ME. And the Revolution's call to arms was "Taxation without representation is tyranny!"

In a now classic study Lester Coch and John R. P. French, Jr., (1948) divided factory-clothing workers into four groups. Two of the groups participated in changing work processes while another group had them imposed. The last group sent representatives to help create the changes.

Output of the group that didn't participate decreased by two thirds. Resistance developed almost immediately. "Marked expressions of aggression against management occurred, such as conflict with the methods engineer . . . hostility toward the supervisor, deliberate restriction of production, and lack of cooperation with the supervisor," wrote the researchers. "There were 17 percent quits in the first 40 days."[7]

Productivity in the groups that directly participated in the change exceeded previous levels. There were no signs of hostility and no quits.[8]

When people are involved in the change process it's no longer management's process; it's theirs. Ownership will make them work harder to make change work.

Today the buzzword for participation in the change process is *empowerment,* a term bandied about equally by line workers and CEOs. Everyone pays it lip service. Are they committed to the concept or just its appearance? Have they taken the "pow" out of empowerment?

Not just mouth music. Cindy Ransom, a middle-level manager at Clorox, isn't just making mouth music about empowerment. Four years ago she asked her workers to redesign operations at the Fairfield, California, plant. She gave them free rein to establish training programs, set work rules for absenteeism, and reorganize the factory into five customer-focused business units. That's not just marginal involvement, and the results weren't marginal, either. Clorox named Ransom's plant the most improved in the company's household-products division.

Says Ransom, "When I read about America losing its competitive edge, it really pisses me off. It gets me motivated to make a difference in my little corner. . . ."[9]

At Johnsonville Foods, a family-owned sausage company headquartered in Wisconsin, it's the line workers who run the show. They're making changes every day, adjusting profit goals, hiring and firing, buying equipment, writing budgets—all the while stuffing sausage.

"Everyone looks at what we're doing and says, 'God, that's kind of flaky, that's kind of goody-goody, warm and fuzzy,'" says Ralph Stayer, owner and CEO. "It isn't a soft or crazy deal. I'm a real hard-nosed, pragmatic guy. . . . Teach people to do it for themselves, this way you get a far better performance."

Stayer's been using participatory management for 13 years now and he's gotten pretty fair results: employee cooperation that's yielded a 20 percent sales increase each year since he turned over the reins, and a 50 percent increase in productivity.[10]

Managing by adultery. It's the same at Chapparal Steel, a classless organization that jokes that it "manages by adultery"—that is, it treats workers as adults with full authority to manage production. Employees are given extraordinary freedom and are expected to take the initiative. Their salary is even partially based on new skills learned, and 85 percent are enrolled in courses such as metallurgy and electronics so they can make informed decisions. Resistance to change is not an issue there.[11]

Sounds like a social experiment from the late sixties, doesn't it? The utopian factory of the future. Truth is, it makes perfect business sense. Chapparal produces steel more efficiently than any other mill in the country. It takes the Texas facility 1.6 hours of labor per ton, versus 2.4 for other mini-mills and 4.9 for larger, integrated producers.[12]

When Chapparal was designing a new mill for wide-flange steel beams, which are used in bridges and high-rises, the employees developed a process that yielded a final product in just 8 to 12 passes through the system. Traditional methods require about 50 passes.[13]

And it was the employees again—this time two maintenance workers—who invented a $60,000 machine for strapping steel rods together. The cost of the old, less efficient machine was $250,000.[14]

Empowerment's Price

Despite the obvious advantages, many managers continue to resist empowerment for various reasons, including the loss of their own control, power, and influence, a distrust of workers, and a lack of confidence that they'll handle responsibility well.

Another reason is that it takes longer. Dee Zalneraitis, the information group manager at the Hudson, Massachusetts, division of R. R. Donelley and Sons, the nation's largest printer, used to lock herself in her office and sweat out the numbers. Now she opens her doors wide and asks her staff how the company can save money. It works. They've come up with suggestions she hadn't considered, like eliminating business trips to unreasonably demanding customers.

But, says Zalneraitis, "It takes a lot more time explaining things. You really have to enjoy helping them learn."[15]

Empower at Implementation

The business world is still miles away from managers committed to empowering their people. Notes James Champy, co-author of *Reengineering the Corporation,* "We won't see them in great numbers for another five to ten years. But corporate America is definitely going in that direction."[16]

What to do in the meantime? Suppose you're a manager who has to enforce a new procedure imposed from on high. You know your staff should have been involved from the beginning, but your boss is from the old school. His refrain: "My job is making policy; yours is to carry it out." How do you deal with employee resistance in this setup?

Our advice: Find someplace for employees to establish ownership. It may not be at the conceptual level where the idea is created and refined, but at the level of implementation where it is put into practice.

We know one manager who exhorted his staff this way: "Okay, we've been shut out of the reorganization—no one asked my opinion, either—but that's over and we're faced with two choices. Let others institute the changes or get involved now and have input on the details. We can make our lives a lot easier if we influence how the new structure is put into practice."

In other words, decide where you *can* exert control and focus your people on this phase of the change process. Resistance will fall off in direct proportion to how involved employees are with implementation.

From victims to victors. Here's an example of what we mean. A major West Coast utility imposed a new software system on its staff. No one at the clerical level was asked prior to the decision. Everyone got a memo one day and that was that. The grumbling started immediately. People didn't want to learn the system. They felt the present software was just fine. Absenteeism rates started rising. There were a lot of unhappy campers at the watercooler. Sound familiar?

Even after the system was introduced through classes and hands-on tutorials, the resistance continued. Many employees became remarkably committed to finding bugs and shortcomings in the new program and complaining about them incessantly. A small revolution was taking form and productivity dropped.

Fortunately, an alert manager saw what was happening and turned the situation around. She called the group together and—without casting blame—acknowledged everyone's resentment at being shut out of the decision process.

Then she asked for verbal and written feedback on how the software could be improved and customized to work better in the office. She set up groups to send recommendations to management. Within a few months the staff began to feel that it could make an impact on the situation, that its input was being taken seriously. Resistance dropped way off.

The first part of the above example occurred; the second did not but it *should* have. And the truth is, without too much effort it *could* have.

No matter what the circumstance, there's always a way to empower people. There are choices to be made, actions to be taken, and feedback to be given. Employees want to feel like participants, not bench warmers. Nothing creates resistance so quickly as feeling disenfranchised.

Create a Dialogue, not a Monologue

Even if decisions are made by high-level management, it's important to lay out clearly to employees the rationale for decisions, the changes they can expect, possible consequences and opportunities.

The way you introduce change makes a world of difference in how people feel about it. If you drop a bombshell, expect employees to head for the fallout shelters. If they hear about it through the grapevine or rumor mill, that's even worse.

Many companies simply announce a downsizing scheme like it was a new health plan or accounting procedure. No input. No Q&A. No dialogue. It's not just the bad news, but the form of delivery that bends employees out of shape. No wonder people feel victimized and disrespected. The rumor mills start racing and the resistance starts rising.

A natural-gas company was buying out a pipe manufacturer. Management had decided on a restructuring effort to merge both businesses. Rather than report their plans in the corporate newsletter, the management team called a company-wide meeting and explained the situation. They opened the floor to questions and gave straight-talk answers. No pulled punches. They followed up the big meeting with a series of department-wide forums where specific changes could be discussed.

Major changes were implemented but employees were less resistant because they understood the decision in context *and* they felt treated honestly.

Process the Loss

Resistance to change is normal. When employees are committed to their work and have set personal and professional goals, imposed change is going to create strong reactions. Confusion and shock are typical first responses. People often feel disoriented, and everyone needs time to adjust.

Organizations should recognize this and provide a structure for employees to express their natural disappointment and sense of loss. Many companies bring in consultants to help process feelings. It's not the same as involving people in the creation of change, but it provides some help in moving them to acceptance.

At a private foundation that funds environmental projects, the executive director and founder, without warning, announced his reorganization plans to the management council. He wanted to change the structure of the place from top to bottom. The organization had expanded from 30 to 200 employees in the last year, and the old structure wasn't getting it done.

Council members went into shock. They were totally unprepared for the move and didn't know how to respond. There were threats of resignations and continuous squabbling. Members disagreed with virtually everything proposed, even changes they knew to be constructive. The place became impossible to work in. Finally, the director called in an outside consultant.

Her first move was to interview top managers and selected staff. She asked each to fill out an extensive self- and organizational evaluation on which they were to express their personal thoughts and feelings. She brought work groups together to do the same. Resistance dropped off. People began slowly to accept that change was needed, and the animosity and covert opposition receded.

No, not a miracle. Just a wise intervention that allowed employees to acknowledge their feelings and process them.

DRIVER #3: INERTIA—"IT'S TOO MUCH EFFORT, TOO UNCOMFORTABLE."

Have you ever bought a new piece of software that took you forever to install in your computer? I've got one of those sitting on my desk right now. It gives me 250 new fonts to play with and the capability of dressing up documents with borders and banners. I'll even be able to send out my own invitations—in color, no less. It's obviously a great piece of technology, but it's still in the box.

Why is it just sitting there? Well, consider the instruction manual. It's got the heft of a telephone book and it sounds like it was written by someone from a far-away planet in another galaxy. You know what I mean, the kind of *Star Wars* technospeak you heard in that intergalactic bar somewhere in space.

Here's the simple truth. To get that program up and running is going to take me a lot of time and effort, and I don't want to drive that steep learning curve. It's much easier to use my old program with its puny 16 fonts.

Inertia is the third resistance driver. Human beings are "inertiates"; we are governed by the desire to keep things as they are. By temperament we're wedded to the status quo, that which is known, comfortable, and familiar. Remember that gas-guzzling junker you couldn't get rolling? When your teacher said that an object at rest tends to remain at rest he called it Newton's first law of physics. He might just as well have named it the first law of resistance.

Not everyone fits this description, of course. There are people who just can't wait to break open the cellophane on their new software and salivate over the thought of reading a 200-page instruction manual. But I'm not one of them, and you're probably not either. Most of us prefer to live in the comfort of what we know.

Creatures of Habit

We're all creatures of habit. If you don't think so, try these exercises. Interlace your fingers and notice which thumb is on top. Do it again with the other thumb up. Feels strange, right? Like you lost your thumb. Now cross your arms. Try crossing them the other way. How does that feel? Try clapping your hands. Notice which one of your hands is the clapper. Now use the other one and notice the difference. Listen to how different it sounds, too.

There is a tremendous pull toward the familiar. Your body is accustomed to its usual way of doing things and will resist changing it. If you try something different, you'll feel a compelling desire to go back to what's comfortable.

The situation's no different at work. Change is resisted because it pulls people out of equilibrium. It means effort. When you're asked to do things differently, you've got to pay more attention, learn new things, respond with greater care. It's far easier and certainly more comfortable to stay with what you know than to learn about what you don't. There's safety in the status quo. You can go on automatic pilot. No unpleasant surprises. You've walked the terrain a hundred times. You can do it with your eyes closed. This is the comfort zone, the perfect place to zone out.

Driving on the wrong side of the street. It's tough to break old habits. What I remember about my first trip to London is not Buckingham Palace or Big Ben, but the horror of nearly getting run over so many times. If you've been there you know what I mean—they drive on the "wrong side" of the street. Day after day I'd step off the curb looking the wrong way only to hear the horns of a dozen angry drivers.

But that was nothing compared to driving on the wrong side of the road. I was okay on the straightaways but as soon as I had to make a turn I'd get confused, move into the wrong lane, and send pedestrians running for cover. I'm sure the British were glad to see me go.

Now think about instituting something as formidable as organizational change that requires a lot more effort than learning how to drive on the left side of the road.

Holes in the soles. I worked with a talented critic at a major newspaper who was required to produce two to three reviews a week. That's a lot of time at events and even more in front of the word processor. This particular critic possessed a keen intellect and a strong knowledge of her subject. She was handy with a phrase, too.

The trouble was she couldn't get herself to write the reviews on time. Her editor's deadline would come and go and she'd be struggling with the first paragraph. She knew the last possible moment she could hand in the material and still make the last edition—the true deadline—and invariably she'd come in seconds before.

But she was so good at her job that her editor was willing to tolerate her procrastination. She, however, was miserable. The late nights, last-minute rushes, the deadlines that ran her life took all the joy out of her job. She knew what she had to do but she couldn't do it differently.

"I know it's a pain but it's a familiar pain," she told me. "It's like an old pair of slippers with holes. You know it's time to get rid of them, they don't keep your feet warm anymore, but you still won't throw them away."

Many people know the old way doesn't work anymore, but the imagined pain and hassle of doing something different are too great. Though it may not be working, it seems easier to stay with the status quo.

The plant closes, nobody moves. The same principle operates in all those factory towns when the plant closes and nobody moves.

Unemployment rises dramatically, people lose their life savings and sometimes their houses, but they stick around anyway.

While it's true that many are glued to the town by family, social networks, and emotional ties, for others it's a matter of avoiding the effort of starting over again—not wanting to struggle with a new situation that may require new rules, expectations, and unknown challenges.

Change Fatigue

People in business are burned out on change. There have been so many new processes and programs introduced in the last decade that workers are on overload. Is it any wonder that they're unwilling to give up something that's familiar and comfortable? When everything's in flux, people are even more reluctant to surrender the stable and known. The power of inertia is multiplied.

The workforce has become jaded about change. Peter Scott Morgan, a director at Arthur D. Little, calls it "change fatigue." Says Morgan, "The eventual result is often widespread worker resistance to new initiatives, which frustrates management further. . . ."[17]

A West Coast commercial bakery typifies what Morgan is talking about. The bakery merged with a food wholesaler and implemented a reengineering plan to streamline operations and maintain its competitive edge. The new company was cutting edge. Cross-functional teams and a quality program had been put in place, and the bakery was introducing a line of gourmet breads to be sold to a new market—health-food and specialty stores.

When it announced the change in its computer system so it could network with retailers, the workers hit the roof.

"Are you kidding me?" said one disgruntled manager. "What do you think I've been doing here, sitting on my hands? If you change one more thing, I won't be able to find my desk. Why can't things stay the same for a while?"

Changing Perceptions

How do you wrench your people free of inertia's grip? How do you deal with the magnetism of the status quo, especially when employees are just recovering from your last change effort?

When people are presented with change, they distort how much effort it will require. They tend to exaggerate the difficulty involved, how long it will take, and how much learning is necessary. To deal with these errors of perception, it's a good idea to *use concrete and dramatic demonstrations that correct distortions and shrink the task down to size.*

That's what a medical software company did when introducing a new computerized recordkeeping program for doctors and hospitals. The benefits were obvious: less paperwork, faster retrieval, better communication, the elimination of voluminous files. But there was resistance from staff because the new software was seen as being too complicated to use.

To overcome this, the company ran an industry-wide conference that featured a convincing presentation of how easy the new program was to master. Volunteers were brought up from the audience and each was given a patient's chart. As everyone watched on the big screen, the volunteers followed the program's instructions for entering data. The simplicity of the new system was immediately obvious, particularly when compared to the old method of writing longhand in the charts.

When the volunteer entered the information correctly—which was most of the time—an exploding scoreboard lit up with bright lights and kudos. A CONGRATULATIONS sign flashed on and off. Too hokey? The audience didn't feel that way. They got into the act, laughing and cheering each volunteer. Everyone wanted to take a turn. The immediate result: People got behind the system.

"That was great fun," one of the nurses told us. "I didn't realize how simple the thing is to run. It's faster and kind of like a game, but best of all I won't have to decipher the docs' scrawl any longer."

How Much Change in Change

People also distort how much change is involved in change. We've seen employees react to restructuring as if management were turning the workplace into a foreign country where they don't speak the language or know the terrain. They assume everything will be different, from the coffee break to the work schedule. And this, of course, makes them inclined to resist the idea in the first place.

To correct this second kind of distortion, *leaders should not point out just what will be altered but also what will stay the same.* That bifocus puts a more balanced spin on plans for change and reduces anxiety.

When a telecommunications giant was buying out a small, regional phone company, the locals panicked. They worried that they'd have to relocate from Tulsa to the big company's home office in Alabama, a move no one wanted to make. They were anxious about adapting to the new company's culture, which was more conservative and authority driven. And they were concerned that their organizational structure would be changed, that they'd have to break up their work groups and separate from their friends. In other words, they worried about everything.

A vice president in charge of the transition was savvy enough to recognize and short-circuit their concerns at the reorientation meeting. Rather than focus on new policies and procedures, he began by highlighting the things that would remain constant: No one was going to have to move, operations would be maintained as before, the same work teams would be kept, managers and locations would stay as is.

"The reason you got bought out," said the vice president, "was because you've been so profitable over the years. You've been doing a good job and no one wants to break up a winner. The only thing that's truly going to be different is that we're now part of a big company and our home office is in another state."

The collective sigh of relief could be heard all the way to Alabama.

The more it changes, the more it stays the same. In most business changes, the fact is that a great deal *does* remain the same. At a Change-Readiness workshop for an educational supply house, we found salespeople grumbling about transformations in their jobs. With the rising need to cut costs and save money, many state universities—their biggest customers—were now using purchasing committees composed of product users instead of a central purchasing office. None of the sales staff liked the trend.

"It makes my life a lot harder," said a sales veteran. "I used to call on one person whom I'd known for years. We had a working relationship and an understanding. Now I've got to sell to a bunch of people I've never seen before. They've all got different interests and needs. It takes a lot more time and energy."

Her feelings were echoed by others. We couldn't change the situation, but we could change the perception of it. So we asked everybody to think about what hadn't changed in their jobs. "Well, they still need erasers," joked one of the participants. "The products we sell, they're still the same."

"The way they're used hasn't, either," said another. "And selling itself hasn't changed. It's basically creating a relationship and solving people's problems for them." And on and on they went until they'd listed about twenty things that hadn't budged an inch.

When the exercise was over, there'd been a subtle shift in perspective. Everyone preferred the old circumstances, but they had come around to a different view on what the changes meant. A few were even talking of the possibility that the new system allowed for increasing sales.

Blended Change

Another way to deal with inertia is *to blend in changes to the existing structure*. This is not always possible, but when it is, the effect is to reduce resistance by making change less difficult to implement.

When Paine Webber instituted a new software system, rather than throw away the old program, which the brokers knew well, they incorporated it into the new one. People still had the option of using the old system as they slowly gained familiarity with the new features. As a consequence, the pace of business remained constant while employees learned on the job and at their own pace.

It was a *good* strategy for getting everyone up to speed without constricting business, but it was a *brilliant* strategy for combating resistance to the introduction of something new.

Instead of starting from scratch, the company whittled the learning curve down to size by allowing employees to continue using the old system. If brokers ran into problems, their ability to do business wouldn't be compromised because they could fall back on what they already knew.

Once more, the rate of learning was placed in the hands of the brokers. They could regulate *when* they learned it, like during slack hours of the day, and that gave everyone the feeling that integrating the new program wasn't such a big deal.

Quick, "Doable" Tasks

Get your people involved in your plans for change quickly with "doable" tasks. The longer they contemplate the mountain, the higher it seems to get. The quicker you get them on the trail, especially the easy part of the trail, the more you'll reduce resistance.

Sounds logical, but often people are sent off to training programs where they spend weeks getting an overview of the system and months before they're actually using it. And they're generally expected to digest the whole "enchilada" all at once. When they get back to work, they've forgotten much of the information and have to rely on reference materials to remind them.

An alternative: Find specific activities they can do right away and implement change piece by piece. This reduces the steepness of the learning curve and the perception that the change is arduous. It builds confidence (see "Driver #1: Fear," earlier in this chapter) and communicates the message: "It's not as hard as you think."

"Before a meet I tell my nervous runners, 'Put one sneaker on, that's all, just one sneaker,'" says a former track coach we know. "If they do just that they're moving and that's the true beginning of the race."

A New York shirt manufacturer making the transition to computerization faced the task of introducing a complex computer-aided design system that would link up directly to the factory. The designers, used to drawing their creations on paper and sending them off to the factory in Tennessee, were overwhelmed by all they had to learn. Most had never used a computer before, and they made a lot of mistakes. The new system also required them to manage unfamiliar tasks like inventory, cost analysis, and suppliers. Management was having a tough time getting them to cooperate.

The solution was to use "doable" tasks, to implement one piece of the system at a time. The first week they just worked on the design area—cuffs, buttons, collars, and cut. These were jobs the designers easily mastered because of their familiarity with the basic tasks. By the end of the week they were experimenting with new ways to design by computer and showing some real enthusiasm for the system they had formerly resisted.

The second week they learned the part about suppliers, inventory, and purchasing. Again the computer-generated tasks were simple and straightforward, and because of their initial positive experience there was less resistance than expected.

The "doable-tasks" approach went on for another few weeks, and by the end of the conversion the new technology had been successfully completed with a minimum of bellyaching.

Unlike many change programs that are introduced with a lag time between introduction and implementation, this one "threw them in the water" immediately. The introduction and implementation occurred almost simultaneously.

Reducing lag time minimizes the potential for rumors, gossip, and dwelling on how hard the change is going to be.

Taking the Pain out of Change

At a big Southeastern utility they don't take resistance seriously. They laugh at it. Well, almost. When the company was introducing new services it held a conference and used skits to satirize the problems it was having with current programs.

Everyone fell over themselves laughing. But when the president showed up in costume, the place went wild. Scepter in hand, he bequeathed to them a whole new line of services while everyone roared their approval. Resistance to change evaporated the moment he waved his staff.

Humor is the key. It melts resistance like butter on a hotplate. It pulls people out of their narrow concerns and allows them to see things in a different light. The president could show them how the current level of service needed improvement without criticizing or blaming.

Humor dissolves defensiveness. Spend an evening in a comedy club and you'll find that the people who laugh loudest are the targets of the comedian's jokes. Humor is magic motivation. It's a great way to reduce resistance by taking the pain out of change.

Creating a Crisis

When fun doesn't work in getting people off the dime, try the opposite.

"Shock therapy, that's what they need," one Silicon Valley leader told us. He was referring to the complacency of his management team, and what he proposed to do was give them a wake-up call with a very loud alarm.

When people are glued to the comfort zone and you've tried everything else, you may need to raise their anxiety level.

That's what Lawrence Bossidy did at Allied Signal and Craig Weatherup at PepsiCo. They dealt with inertia by creating a crisis, making dire predictions, preaching doom and gloom unless changes were made. They pushed their people to respond to challenge by making it seem they had no other choice if the company was to survive. It's not pleasant but it works.

"Most organizations, like most people, won't change fundamentally until they absolutely have to," writes Brian Dumaine in *Fortune*.[18]

Creating a crisis makes action necessary, not just desirable. It lights a fire where the mildew's been collecting. Every psychologist has a collection of stories about people who won't quit smoking until they've had a heart attack or contracted lung cancer. Then they get motivated.

In a study of 40 companies, management professor Gibb Dyer found that before any could change, each had to hit bad times, and in many cases bring in a new CEO, before righting itself.[19]

When nothing else works against inertia, raise the stakes by raising blood-pressure. But be careful; this strategy has only a short half-life. Too much or prolonged anxiety downsizes performance. Reserve this tactic for getting people going, then back off when you're over the hump.

DRIVER #4: ABSENCE OF SELF-INTEREST—"WHAT'S IN IT FOR ME?"

Where's the Beef? "I don't see why he's so against the change," wondered the CEO of a large environmental engineering company. He was discussing his CIO's opposition to the company's plan to shift from a mainframe to desktop technology.

"It's going to make his job easier. Everyone won't have to come to his department to get information. And it'll save us money. Our people will be more productive. They'll have greater access and quicker access to data. That means more effective communication. I just don't get why an information guy would be opposed to this kind of move."

Most leaders are similarly perplexed by resistance to a change that clearly benefits the company. And that's the point. They are only looking at the change through that one lens. Sure, the company will benefit, but what about me, thinks the employee. Where's the beef?

"WIIFM"—What's in It for Me?

In the case of the recalcitrant CIO, what *was* in it for him? From his point of view, the new technology brought a loss of power, prestige, and influence. With mainframe technology he was in the driver's seat. People had to come to his department to get information. A computer on everyone's desk cut him out of the loop. Yes, the change was good for the company. But not so good for him.

One of the most powerful resistance drivers is "WIIFM," an acronym for *"what's in it for me."* Selfish motive? Yes. Not a team player? Yes. But how would you feel if you were in the CIO's place? Or if your position, power, or job were threatened by an impending change? It might be good for the company, but you'd be left out in the cold. If that were the case would you selflessly support the change and go quietly into the night? Get real!

"No worker was ever motivated by a change that would benefit the stockholders," one executive told us. Yet, that's how leaders think. They have a different agenda and a different perspective than the rank and file. If the stockholders' interests aren't being met, they're history.

Workers have a different agenda than stockholders, and they don't have the option of voting the leader out. But they can sure make it tough on the company if their interests aren't being served.

The truth is that when change is introduced people will automatically respond to it from their own narrow self-interests. If those interests aren't addressed, resistance will follow.

The Cost/Benefit Ratio

Change depends on the commitment and enthusiasm of the workforce that has to implement it. Whether it's a car or a castle, when you make any purchase you evaluate it by weighing benefits against costs. People think about change the same way. They evaluate the personal advantage of the change against the price to them.

Say the plant you're managing is moving and they want you to stay on. They're prepared to give you a raise in both salary and responsibility. But it means moving to Katmandu. Your wife would have to give up her job and the chances of her getting one there are pretty slim. Your kids have already changed school twice in the last five years; this would be a third change for them. And you don't speak the language. And your asthma would probably kick up at that altitude. And so forth.

So sure, it's a great opportunity and you'll get more money and a promotion. But do these benefits outweigh the costs? The cost-to-benefit assessment operates every day, 365 days a year. Sometimes it's obvious, other times hidden, but it's always there. And when you're introducing change, you need to understand and address it.

Miles up in the air. A large home furnishings manufacturer missed this point when it distributed to employees new credit cards for travel and other expenses. No big deal—a simple administrative change, right? Well not exactly. There was one small catch. The new credit cards didn't have frequent-flier benefits like the old ones. So now employees would no longer accrue free miles that they could use for vacations—a small perk they considered a big deal.

"I went free to Asia on my vacation last year using frequent-flier mileage. Next year it'll be a week in Staten Island," complained one manager.

Changing credit cards was probably a good budget-cutting measure. The error was not taking the personal cost of the change into consideration.

Long-Term Gain versus Short-Term Pain

Often the benefit to the individual is not immediate but long term.

"The new system, strategy, or structure will make our company more profitable over time," says the CEO, "and that will mean there'll be many more opportunities for each of you. But for now we all have to tighten our belts and pitch in with extra effort."

Wait a minute, you're thinking. I'm already working 60 hours a week, missing my kids growing up, spending zip quality time with my spouse. And my department was cut to the bone last year. I'm not sure I'm willing to wait for my reward down the road.

At a company that was reorganizing into cross-functional work teams, several people complained, "We're convinced that teaming is going to help us get to market quicker, but it also means going to more meetings and integrating new people. Frankly, we're meetinged out. None of us has time to do the work we're doing already."

In both situations, the short-term pain of changing outweighs the long-term gain of profitability and opportunity. Result: resistance. When the personal cost is perceived as great in terms of time, effort, and sacrifice, down-the-road benefits must be very compelling to get an enthusiastic buy-in.

Some of the most successful entrepreneurs are willing to surrender their personal lives and savings, putting it all on the line to chase their bright and shining dreams. Short-term pain is tolerated because the long-term gain is so tantalizing.

A general rule: *Long-term gain must far outweigh short-term pain to get a successful buy-in.* When benefits are abstract and far into the future, they must be extremely compelling to tip the balance in their favor.

Maslow's Hierarchy

All managers want their people to be team players. But no matter how altruistic you think people should be, the hard truth is that self-interest motivates most behavior. Many years ago humanistic psychologist Abraham Maslow created what he called a "Hierarchy of Needs."

He said that human beings develop needs in a sequential order and that "lower" needs must be satisfied before the next-in-order need can emerge.

Maslow laid it out like this: *physiological needs* (hunger, thirst) followed by *safety* (security, order), *belongingness* (love, affection), *esteem* (prestige, self-respect), and *self-actualization* (self-fulfillment).[20]

Looking at that list, we can see that team spirit and loyalty—an outgrowth of the need for belonging—shrinks in importance when measured against needs for safety and security. In other words, if a person's job is threatened or pay is cut, team spirit and loyalty go out the window. It's every man and woman for him- or herself.

Benefits, Benefits, Benefits

Can you imagine an insurance salesperson telling you how much his company will benefit if you buy a policy? Or that if you buy a car the salesman will win a contest? Absurd, but is that so very different from the CEO telling you that a restructuring will give the company an edge over the competition? Or that a quality program will help streamline services? Sure, there's a long-term benefit to the employee, but to most it raises the WIIFM question.

The first thing that enters most people's minds when a change is announced is the cost—the added time, extra effort, uncertainty, extra travel. And as already noted, the cost is usually exaggerated.

That's why managers need to emphasize the benefits of change—the what's in it for me—as strongly as possible. Focusing on personal benefit is necessary to counterbalance the perception of personal cost.

The key to getting someone to buy anything, from software to outerware, is to focus on *benefits, benefits, benefits*. How is buying into the change process going to help them get what they really want?

Don't make the benefit abstract by telling them something like, "This new program will really help your career." Tell them *how* it will do that. Don't say, "This new system will increase your efficiency." Tell them *how* it will do that and how much better it will be for them when their business unit runs more efficiently. In other words, make the benefits real, concrete, and personal.

Don't Be a Mind Reader

Don't make the mistake of assuming that you know what benefits are attractive to your people. None of us are mind readers. Something you consider important may not mean anything to them.

A new lunchroom with greatly reduced prices and a day-care center were the carrots dangled by a printing plant manager who was trying to sell his workers on a reorganization program.

"I bring my own lunch, for crying out loud," said one supervisor. "And when I don't, I'm not real keen to stay inside and eat. I want to get out of the plant and breathe some real air."

What the workers really wanted was flextime and the ability to set up work teams that would do their own scheduling. Interestingly, what they wanted was actually far less expensive than what the company was offering.

Personal personnel meetings. A finance manager at AT&T met with members of her team individually to discuss priorities relating to both their jobs and an upcoming restructuring. She got some surprises. Several people said they wanted the chance to get into sales and customer service. A few mentioned they wanted the opportunity to finish school and get their degrees. One wanted to pursue an evening MBA. Another hoped to go back to the South, where she was raised. Still another wanted more time with her family.

"I could have guessed some of these things," the manager told us. "But certainly not all of them. Talking to each person really gave me perspective on how different they are from each other. I used to think of them as a pretty homogeneous group. Now it's clear to me they're all individuals with their own needs.

"And that's helped me to manage this change better. I can talk to team members about the restructuring with very specific focus on how it will benefit them. I know how to appeal to each one."

Visualizing Benefits

Remember that CIO whose environmental engineering company was moving from mainframe to desktop technology? All he could see was his own loss of status and power. The numerous advantages of the new system meant nothing when measured against the threat to his self-interest.

To win his cooperation we used a visualization technique from our executive coaching sessions. Originally developed for athletes as a form of mental rehearsal, it is now being used to improve performance in many different areas, including the workplace.

The technique is simple. Relax and envision (see in your mind's eye) positive, successful, masterful images to replace the negative thoughts and feelings that come with fear. It's sort of like changing a bad movie for a good one in your internal VCR. The high jumper sees herself clearing a new height. The vice president views himself making a perfect presentation. The key is to make the positive "tape" as realistic as possible.

We had the CIO visualize what his department would look like if it transformed itself from an *information resource*—its role under the old mainframe system—to a *source of innovation* for the company. With just a little prodding from us, he imagined his team developing new information products and processes, creating new, interactive software programs, coordinating with the company's R&D effort, working with customers to determine future needs, and even forming joint ventures with high-tech manufacturers to develop innovative applications.

Then we asked him to imagine how all of it was going to happen.

Without losing a beat he came up with a step-by-step action plan. The whole experience was impressive. Not just for the scope of his ideas but for the attitudinal shift that had taken place. By looking into the future to see what might be, he could envision what was in it for him.

The Real Cost

With all this talk about benefits, there is one cost that should be mentioned and, in fact, emphasized: *the cost of not changing*. The consequences of not changing don't need to be exaggerated. The facts are that giants have turned to dinosaurs in every field because they kept playing by the old rules when the game was changing.

Maslow talked about survival being the primal need. Resistance dwindles rapidly when people understand that the company's survival, and by implications their own job, are in danger if they stick to the old ways.

Nineteen

Motivating People to Change

FOUR KEYS

When Keystone ski resort acquired Breckenridge, the first step toward creating a unified culture was to reduce employee resistance. But that was just the first step. Neutralizing resistance brings you back to square one. It gets your people receptive to change. To stay in the forefront of the ski industry, Keystone had to do more than that. It had to get its people excited about the possibilities that the merger created.

Overcoming resistance is about neutralizing negativity. Motivation is about lighting a fire. When people are burning with enthusiasm, they'll take risks, go the extra mile, and fully commit themselves to change.

Motivating isn't *only* about exhorting people to "win one for the home team," or taking the opportunity "to show the world." It's about presenting a powerful rationale for immediate action and giving clear responsibility to the players for its execution. It's also about knowing what moves each player on the team and using that knowledge to create confidence and commitment. And motivation is about painting a vivid and compelling picture of what is possible if everyone pulls together.

The four keys to lighting a firestorm in your company, team, or organization are:

1. *Urgency*
2. *Inspiration*
3. *Ownership*
4. *Rewards and Recognition*

1. URGENCY

"To inaugurate large-scale change, you may have to create the burning platform," says Allied Signal's CEO, Lawrence Bossidy. "You have to give people a reason to do something differently."[1]

If you're asking people to change, you have to show them that there is an important and timely reason for it. Urgency is created by offering a persuasive rationale for why change is imperative *now*. It requires projecting present circumstances into the future and seeing the dire consequences of business as usual—the cost of not changing. Without urgency, motivation often wilts like a delicate rose in the desert sun. Every car salesperson will tell you it's your "last chance" to buy that car at that price with those extras. Similarly, every doctor knows that the motivation to start that low-fat diet increases markedly after the first heart attack.

Fast-food emergency. Sometimes the numbers create urgency for you and all you've got to do is present them boldly. When we were consulting with a national fast-food company that was treading water while the competition was at the other side of the pool, we gathered up the data, made a few overheads, and projected them up on the wall for everyone to see.

There was urgency in indisputable black and white. Of the top seven competitors, this chain ranked dead-last in high-quality food, cleanliness, attractiveness of buildings, "a place I would take the family," a courteous staff.

Dead-last on all of the above and nearly last on many others. The data screamed for attention. We didn't have to say another word. There wasn't a single person in the room who didn't think it was time to call 911.

Levi's bad-raps itself. When Levi Strauss was preparing to restructure operations it took an unorthodox stance to create urgency. In one of its employee newsletters the legendary clothing company published damning criticism from its customers.

Federated Department Stores was quoted as saying that the only thing keeping the company from being truly "terrible" was the quality and appeal of its products. A spokesperson for department-store chain Mervyn's echoed, "If you weren't Levi's, you'd be gone."[2]

Now those are the kind of acerbic comments you'd expect from your competition when they're struggling to gain market share. Yet here was Levi's bad-rapping itself in its own newspaper so everyone would realize the necessity for change.

No walk down easy street. When the data isn't conclusive or the criticism less dramatic, the manager must interpret available information with an eye toward the dire consequences of clinging to the status quo. Toyota had a situation like this a few years ago. It was rapidly losing market share, and its sales growth was flat. Detroit's Big Three were on the ascendancy after a disastrous fall in the eighties. Despite these ominous trends, Toyota dealers thought everything was just fine. Their profits were up 150 percent due to greater efficiency and cutbacks in marketing and other costs.

How do you create a sense of urgency in dealers who were feeling "fat and happy"? How do you get them to see that today's blue skies might easily be followed by tomorrow's rain clouds?

Start by persuading your team that they're not strolling down easy street no matter how it looks right now. They're in dangerous territory with competitors looking to take them down or their own complacency threatening them from within. You've got to help them look beyond the short view to the larger picture, to gaze beyond their sandbox and into the whole arena. It's all about adding up the data in such a way that there's only one possible conclusion: Change or suffer serious repercussions.

We're not suggesting personal threats. CEO Bossidy cautions, "Scaring people isn't the answer. You try to appeal to them. The more they understand why you want change, the easier it is to commit to it."[3]

Life or death at PepsiCo. Craig Weatherup, president of a PepsiCo division with sales over $7 billion, had the same problem as Toyota. The numbers were impressive, with earnings up 10 percent and profits in the United States higher than the other colas'. Yet Weatherup looked down the road a piece and saw a dead end. In fact, he had his own burning-platform story, which he told his 30,000 employees at a number of intense three-day meetings held to drive home his message.

According to Weatherup, a worker on a North Sea oil rig faced an unenviable dilemma. Trained to wait for help and never to jump into the icy waters 150 feet below, he stood on the edge of the rig as a wall of fire rushed toward him. What to do? Without hesitation, he jumped into the inhospitable sea and miraculously survived. Afterward, they asked him why he jumped. The reply: "I chose probable death over certain death."

Weatherup saw the same choice for PepsiCo. It was a life-or-death situation for the company, he argued. Business as usual was certain death. Talk about high drama and intensity. That story got everyone's attention.

But that was just the beginning. Weatherup relayed a personal account of how David Glass, CEO of Wal-Mart, had told him bluntly, "There is nothing about the way your company does business with us that I like." Now, this is not the opinion of a candy-store owner who takes two cases a month; this is America's number-one retailer talking. "We're dead if we don't pay attention" is the not-so-subtle implication of Weatherup's message and, in fact, he went on to use the story as a way of laying out a careful and detailed plan for restructuring the company.

What happened? Employees bought into the urgency and "are changing the organization with gusto." Earnings were up 22 percent in the first quarter after restructuring.[4]

Look for Natural Leaders

Another strategy for galvanizing change is to look for natural leaders within the organization and win them over to the urgency of the situation. Natural leaders are people whom others look to for cues about how to react to change. Formal leaders who wield authority because of their position may or may not be trusted or respected. Natural leaders are. Their opinions matter, so getting them on your side may mean the difference between success and the dismal alternative.

Nowhere is this more obvious than on professional sports teams, where "clubhouse leaders" exude a winning attitude and a stabilizing confidence. When these players retire or are traded, their presence is sorely missed. Often the quality of the team's play falls off. That's what happened to the Oakland Athletics, a baseball team we've worked with over the years. Their natural leader for a decade was pitching ace Dave Stewart. As Stewart's talents declined with age, he still maintained a leadership role of immense proportions. His grit and clutch play were legendary. When he left Oakland, the Athletics' fortunes declined.

Using natural leaders to motivate others has been tried in many different kinds of organizations. Sports teams run mini camps for their clubhouse leaders. Some schools have leadership programs that identify charismatic students and train them in leadership skills. Adolescent programs in the inner city do much the same thing, hoping that the leaders they work with will interest other kids in their after-school programs.

Don't Cry Wolf

There are limits on the use of urgency. When it's overused or not backed by convincing data, it loses its effectiveness. Crying wolf can lead to disaster. The leader who is always conjuring up a crisis, or who sees doom down every path, is quick to lose credibility. Employees are astute about seeing through these alarmists because the alarm bell's been rung so many times before. In fact, they can be downright cynical about the leader whose redial button is stuck on "911."

When you're creating urgency make sure it's based on fact and not fiction. And use the strategy sparingly. When the platform's always burning, people become fire retardant.

2. INSPIRATION

Stoking the Fire

Urgency lights the fire. It creates the spark, producing the attitude and atmosphere needed to get people off the dime. Urgency creates an adrenaline burst of action. We've all heard stories of the grandmother who miraculously summons the strength to lift a car off her trapped grandchild.

But this spark will quickly burn out if it's not stoked. That's where inspiration comes in. After the initial burst, inspiration turns that fire into a sustained blaze. Urgency without inspiration creates anxiety and then panic. Inspiration elevates the spirit and provides direction.

To get your people excited about change, you've got to inspire them with an uplifting vision. Get them to aspire to greater heights, to go beyond previous limitations, to chase the "impossible" dream.

Passion

Inspiration turns ordinary people into passionate people. It gives them the courage to take risks, challenge the old rules, chase their dreams, and never give up. It creates a fire in the belly that fuels curiosity, persistence, and resourcefulness.

Passionate people have an uncommon fervor, an intense and eager interest. They're exactly what you want on your change team. They'll put in extra hours, work through your toughest problems, and infect everyone in your organization with change fever.

Passion sets knowledge on fire. A Silicon Valley executive put it this way: "In the information business you need your heart engaged to keep your brain at its best. Passion gives you the edge."

Enthusiasm

Enthusiasm is a low-budget word used to describe those with passion. Research shows that it is the single most important factor differentiating "outstanding" from "good" performance:

- A recent nationwide cross-industry study found that what distinguished "top" from "good" sales performers was enthusiasm— read *passion*.
- The prestigious *Endicott Report* confirmed that one of the three most important qualities for on-the-job success, especially in dynamic times, is "enthusiasm . . . passion . . . intense excitement."
- Television's number-one sports analyst, John Madden, a Super Bowl–winning coach himself, says the difference between the guys who make the Pro Bowl and those who don't is enthusiasm. And Madden himself is a great model for this quality.

Not Knute. Great coaches have the ability to inspire and uplift the team. They seem to have an intuitive talent for firing up their players, enabling them to surpass past performance levels and do more than they thought they could.

Hey, wait a minute. I'm pretty good at what I do but I'm not a Rockne or a Riley, a King or a Kennedy, you might be thinking. I'm just trying to get my people more positive about the changes that are coming down the pike and the opportunities they offer.

We can't say it wouldn't be helpful to have the passion of Martin Luther King, the charisma of JFK, the iron will of Margaret Thatcher, or the spirit of Eleanor Roosevelt. But it isn't necessary. The skills and strategies to inspire others are learnable. It comes down to two things: *the message* and *the model.* Some leaders inspire purely by the power of their words, others through the power of their actions.

The Message: Possibilities, not Probabilities

How inspired do you get thinking about reengineering, TQM, or restructuring? That's what we thought. These processes may be necessary and appropriate, but they aren't exhilarating, infectious, or uplifting.

To create passion you have to translate change into something that speaks to the best in people, the part that aspires to greater heights. "Inspiration has a *spire* in it," Larry Wilson, the founder of Wilson Learning and the Pecos River Training Center and author of the *One-Minute Salesman,* once told us: "Spire . . . the top part of a pointed or tapering object, as a mountain peak or a church steeple, gets people to look higher. To see the spire on top of the church or the mountain peak you have to look upward, which is what inspiration does."

Two-time Nobel Prize laureate Albert Szent-Györgyi asserts that all human beings have a natural drive to grow and make the most of their potential. Everyone is capable of acting from higher values. Everyone is capable of looking upward. The root of the word inspiration—*spirare*—means to "breathe into." When you inspire people, you breathe into them energy, life, and courage. You infuse them with determination and hope.

Inspiring people is not about offering probabilities. It's about *possibilities.* And as the Danish philosopher Kierkegaard once said, "There is no wine more intoxicating than the wine of possibility."

Heroic visions. In other words, inspiration is about creating aspiration. You have to get people to look higher than the bottom line, the next quarter, or the next paycheck. But how do you do that?

One way is to create a shared vision, a vivid picture of something people can aspire to. It has to capture the imagination with heroic goals that reflect the deepest expression of what people want to be. Or what your organization could be.

The more heroic, the more compelling. Take Lincoln's vision articulated at Gettysburg: "A new nation, conceived in Liberty, and dedicated to the proposition that all men are created equal." It's hard to see those words even after so many readings without feeling something running up and down the spine. The inspiring vision expresses a spiritual and idealistic side of us. It comes from the heart, not from the head. It is a lighthouse giving us direction, not a specific destination.

When William Paley took over CBS at the age of 27, the company had no money or stations of its own. It was insignificant in an industry completely dominated by NBC.[5] But Paley had an inspiring vision that pulled him and his fledgling organization out of near bankruptcy and transformed it into one of the most powerful media forces in the world.

Paley envisioned the audience at a time when there was no audience. He saw all those homes in America's heartland, isolated from each other, some without electricity, many without access to newspapers, connected by one common thread. He saw a country brought together by the electronic network called radio.[6]

A no less compelling vision was imagined by Apple founders, Steve Wozniak and Steve Jobs. At a time when computers were used exclusively by and for business, they foresaw a computer in every home. And their vision became a reality. In 1994 personal-computer sales outpaced television sales for the first time ever.

People's Jobs Are Too Small for Their Spirits

People get inspired when, in some way, they feel they are making the world or their community a better place. That is one of the reasons why companies like Patagonia, Ben & Jerry's, the Body Shop, and others have induced such fanatic loyalty and devoted effort from their employees. It's not only because they like the ice cream or the colorful pullovers. It's that they're making a difference by contributing to something larger than themselves, like feeding the hungry, helping the homeless, or saving the environment.

Feeding the homeless. To get rid of its "paper cows," Alabama

Power and Light destroyed files and records that had no current regulatory or operational use. But this was more than a mere paper-cow hunt. For every pound of paper destroyed, the company promised to donate a pound of food to the Birmingham Food Bank.

"This was such a fun campaign," said Clifford Capps, manager of general services. "The campaign was intended to bring attention to an important issue. By donating food to a good cause we gave employees an incentive to clean out their files. . . ."

The results were indeed inspiring. Alabama Power dumped *106,415 pounds of paper,* translating into *50 tons of food for the food bank!* That's making a difference in people's lives.

"A great weight-reduction program" is what senior vice president Bob Buettner called it, and one that helped the company to provide better service at a more competitive price.

Buettner figures the "Pound for Pound" program destroyed enough paper to fill up *2,723 five-drawer file cabinets,* taking up *15,793 square feet.* That's a lot of savings in storage costs.

The campaign was so successful that Alabama Power also donated $20,000 to the food bank.

Hopes, Dreams, and Aspirations

A vision doesn't have to be corporate; it can appeal to people's personal hopes, dreams, and aspirations. Even employees in the mail room or on the cutting room floor have dreams. Dreams inspire; they engage the spirit. Martin Luther King declared, "I have a dream!" He didn't say, "I have quarterly objectives."

Goals are not the same as dreams. Goals don't inspire. They're rational, specific, short-term targets that'll help you get there. *Dreams are goals with wings!* They arouse and exhilarate. If you know what your people dream about you can appeal to their deeper selves.

When people are inspired and passionate about something, nothing is impossible. They tap into inner resources, strengths, creativity that is normally not available. They accomplish things that previously seemed out of reach. And in the process they discover the most important thing; that the real limits are in our own minds.

Fuels for the Fire

When we ask people in our programs what inspires them at work, they tell us:

- "To be a part of something great."
- "To do something I've never done before."
- "To do something I didn't think I could."
- "To do something meaningful for people, the community, the world, the environment."
- "To learn something new and interesting."

Notice that not one of these motives is about money or base self-interest. They're all about going beyond self-imposed limits, and in some cases beyond the self entirely.

To inspire people when you're introducing a change, tap into the best part of them. Put the project into a larger context, one that has higher meaning and purpose. Instead of selling your team on the profits to be made off your new no-fat product line, inspire them with a vision of prolonging life and improving America's health. Instead of telling your engineers that introducing new technological processes will give them an edge in the race to build the information super-highway, inspire them with a vision of how their contribution to that highway will change the country's lifestyle forever. Or that it will create electronic communities in a world where people are increasingly alienated from each other.

In all of our speeches and seminars we talk *up* to people. We try to lift their expectations of themselves by relating to the best in them. We know that each of us is capable of far more than we're actually doing. We use, perhaps, only 30 percent of our capacity. We try to expand the way people define *what they may be* and *what they can do* by emphasizing that limitations are largely self-imposed and that overcoming them gives us a chance to use all our natural gifts. We talk about the importance of chasing our dreams and not being constrained by fears and what other people think is possible.

Above all, we speak to people's potential, not their past performance.

Your past is not your potential.

Raising the Bar

Another way to inspire people is to challenge them.

Just about every coach we've worked with from the pros to Little League uses challenge to bring out the best in players. "Raising the bar," whatever that bar might be, motivates athletes to try harder, to tap into some inner reserve that enables them to excel.

That's why a weak opponent causes teams to play at a lower level. There's no challenge to inspire them. And that's why a formidable opponent often calls up the team's finest effort.

Even off the playing field, there is something about a challenge that causes people to respond. Remember when you were a kid and a friend dared you to do something risky? Whether you accepted the dare or not, the words had a strange and powerful effect. You felt you had to respond to prove you had the courage, energy, desire, or commitment.

A challenge contains an inherent demand to test yourself. It is a chance to see what you're made of, an opportunity to realize your full potential. In its incredibly effective advertising campaign, the U.S. Army tapped into this innate desire with its challenge to "Be all that you can be." A lot of young people responded to it.

A "trashy" challenge. A physical challenge focuses our attention and strengthens our will. It gets the adrenaline flowing, releasing previously hidden strengths and resources. But those responses aren't limited to physical challenges.

Rather than buy new incinerators and acreage for landfill, the governors of seven New England states wanted to induce companies located in their states to cut their trash output. They knew that passing legislation would only create a firestorm of protest about reduced profitability. So for the past several years they've been using another approach.

They've run a "green dare" contest, which challenges companies to make substantial reductions in how much garbage they create. The result has been overwhelming. Forty-six companies, large and small, have cut a total of 1 billion pounds of garbage since 1990.

Procter & Gamble boosted the average recycled content in its packages to 36 percent. That included using 100 percent recyclable plastic in containers of Ultra Downy and Lemon Comet and 50 percent in containers of Tide, Bold, and Dash. Campbell Soup trimmed the weight of the steel used in its soup cans by 4 million pounds and its juice cans by 1.1 million pounds.

Baxter Healthcare, the medical-products company that generates $8.5 billion yearly, cut 11.6 million pounds of packaging and plans a 15 percent overall reduction by this year. It also plans to use more recycled fiber in its corrugated shipping containers and less chlorine-bleached paper and cardboard in its packaging.[7]

Friendly challenges. Many companies set up friendly challenges or contests between departments or teams to see who can sell more product, save more money, or come in under budget. These types of challenges get employees excited, often prompting them to work harder and more productively.

But most people get motivated by a challenge only if it is in their best interest or meaningful to them. A challenge that doesn't make personal sense or is way out of reach not only won't motivate people, it will drain their energy.

The Model as the Message—Walking the Talk

I remember doing some very difficult climbing in the Swiss Alps with our guide, John Barry, a retired engineer who was in his early sixties. The weather had been poor for three straight days, and everyone was having a tough time. We were tired and hurting and many wanted to turn back. The bitching and moaning about everything from blisters to backaches was increasing with every step.

When we stopped at midday for lunch, John, who had been especially quiet, sat by himself. After a quick sandwich he took off his boots and we saw that every toe on one foot had blisters that were raw and bleeding. If that had happened to any of the rest of us, we'd have been screaming for a stretcher. But he quietly patched himself up, put his boots back on, hoisted up his pack, which was considerably heavier than any of ours, and asked if we were ready. That was the end of our complaining.

People look to the leader for direction, both in terms of where they are going and as a model for the behavior it takes to get there.

"We need more walking and less talking," says Prudential senior vice president Ken Jenny. "There's too much talk these days—mission statements, meetings ad nauseam. Walking gets you to your destination; talking is for hanging out at the rest stops."[8]

It comes with the territory. When basketball star Charles Barkley declared he wasn't going to be a role model, just a player, he missed the point. It's not up to him. Anyone in a position of leadership is a role model. It comes with the territory.

Whether you like it or not, people naturally relate to you differently when you're in the limelight or have authority. Your words carry more weight. Your actions are scrutinized a little more carefully. Virtues or faults are projected onto you. You become a little larger than life. Barkley may have shunned the role, but those kids on the playground don't care—they still watch his every move—on *and* off the court.

That's why when leaders *live* the message they preach through their actions and attitudes, the impact can be inspiring. When the boss works into the night to finish the project, her efforts speak volumes to her staff. They'll be much more inclined to burn the midnight oil themselves.

Leaders must model the message. You can't expect people to take risks if you're playing it safe. You can't expect them to innovate if you're stuck in standard operating procedure.

Inspiring with dirt and toilet paper. "I make my living from dirt," observes Pat Shappert, head of housekeeping for the 1,900-room convention hotel at Opryland. Her passion and zeal for her job so inspires people that an intense competition has emerged among Nashville's hotel staffs. The cleaning team that can scour a bathtub the quickest or make a bed the fastest has become a source of regional pride.[9]

As vice president of purchasing for Service Merchandise, Inc., Larry Krieder buys everything from tapes to toilet paper. But the passion and zeal he brings to his glamourless job has attracted others. Staffers at Service Merchandise vie for positions in Larry's department. Once there, they "follow in his footsteps," adopting his work ethic and attitude. Krieder's inspiring attitude and unflagging energy has led to substantial profit. His department has saved the company almost $2 million a year, an amount equal to the profits of four of the company's retail outlets.[10]

We know that the old "If I can do it so can you" sounds trite and outdated. Maybe so, but it's still incredibly effective, especially for people who aren't generally focused on the future. That type of message, especially if delivered in a caring way, can be incredibly inspiring.

Substance, not Style

Professional basketball coaches with their Italian suits, slicked-back hair, and designer shirts and ties look like they belong in *GQ*, not the gym. Everybody is seeming to emulate super coach Pat Riley, who once did make the cover of *GQ*.

That's the problem. They're trying to imitate Riley's style. But when you look at the best coaches and managers in sports, you'll notice that they're all different. Tony LaRussa is a quiet tactician. Dodger manager Tommy Lasorda is exactly the opposite: loud and emotional. Bill Walsh was professional and distant. Mike Ditka was rough and tumble. But these great ones have one thing in common: They don't try to be what they're not. They don't try to adhere to a certain leadership style. Their ability to inspire comes from being who they are and maximizing it.

This is what we tell executives during coaching sessions: Be yourself. Find your own way of inspiring. Don't go for the pep talk if you don't have the pep. The key to being an inspired leader and model for others is to be the best *you* that you can be.

People want their leaders to be exceptional. So pick the area in which you already excel and become as good at it as you can be. Peak performers aren't good at everything, but they're *great* at one thing. Being the best you can inspires others to do the same.

3. OWNERSHIP

Research shows that owning your own business is one of the top three motivators, right up there with travel and financial independence. At our workshops some of the reasons people give for wanting to own their own business include: "To make my own decisions," "To be my own boss," "To have rewards related to results," "Not having someone looking over my shoulder," "To take charge of my future."

It's obvious from these responses that control over one's destiny is the main attraction of ownership. That's why you'll see individuals who own their own businesses burning the midnight oil when for someone else they'd put in the required eight hours and go home.

Barring profit sharing, the best way to create ownership is by giving employees as much control over their destinies as possible. In other words, they may not be able to own the company, but they can "own" their jobs.

That means empowering them with information, responsibility, and the authority to make decisions. And holding them accountable for the results.

As we've already emphasized, employee participation in the change process decreases resistance. It's equally true that this kind of ownership is a great way to get people excited about change. In fact, the more ownership, the more motivation.

The Essential Ingredient

Sal Runfola, operations vice president at Electronic Measurements, Inc. (EMI), maintains that empowering employees is the most essential ingredient in a successful restructuring of any kind. At EMI, a producer of medical power-conversion equipment, production teams routinely make engineering change orders. They create their own production schedules and evaluate their own performance. They even decide who gets hired.

Says Runfola, "They have direct contact with customers. They call customers up and ask, 'When did we ship the part and when was it received? Did it meet expectations?'

"In our sheet-metal transformers, teams are even soliciting outside business. They design the sales brochure and they get a commission. . . ."[11]

The result is a motivated and independent work team whose performance typically runs 150 to 160 percent above projections.

"Leaders will be those who empower others," predicts Bill Gates. "Empowering leadership means bringing out the energy and capabilities people have and getting them to work together in a way they wouldn't do otherwise."[12]

When the team calls the plays. "Our sales group was a team that called its own plays. I was the coach, but not even from the sidelines, more like from up in the stands," says Brian Casey, a former district manager for Fisher Scientific's safety division. "Aside from the quota, which came from the top, the team made all its own decisions. They not only set the overall goal, which was one hundred and ten percent of quota, but created strategies for achieving it.

"Each person had a role on the team. The high producer was the captain, who ran part of the meetings and held everyone accountable for personal quotas. One of the people who was great at marketing was in charge of developing new promotions and advertising. She even drew the team logo. My role was a supporter. I didn't dictate," points out Casey, "I facilitated.

"Since the team set the quota, everyone felt invested in how we did. Members assigned tasks and developed work plans based on each person's experience and level of expertise. When a person was new he was given a lower quota and taken on a few cold calls till he got his feet wet. If a team member wanted to do a promotion, the whole group consulted on strategy.

"The amazing thing was the level of teamwork. There's always gonna be competition, but it was good natured and people really helped each other out. We felt like we were in it together and that made all the difference."

Results: The team exceeded its 1993 goal by 110 percent, more than any other branch in the company. And that was in California in a recession year.[13]

Holding On While Handing Off

There's a rain forest's worth of paper on how and when to empower workers. Everyone says it's a good idea, a way to give more ownership to employees. But it's another of those things agreed on in principle and mishandled in reality. Often managers act like they're empowering while holding on to control. Imagine a quarterback handing off the ball but not letting go of it as he and the running back crash headlong into the line.

Examples of holding on while handing off: managers second-guessing their subordinates, looking over their shoulders, checking and rechecking work, advising them every step of the way, demanding frequent updates, or micromanaging in a million other ways.

Nothing is more de-motivating than being told you have authority to make choices and decisions and then having that power undermined by an anxious or distrusting boss.

Half-cooked tortillas. Scitor's CEO Roger Meade is the Joe Montana of Silicon Valley. When he hands you the ball you know it'll be tucked into the deep recesses of your abdomen. And he's not going to yank it back. Meade emphasizes that yes, he will discuss strategy with any of his employees, but no, he won't review or make decisions for them. He also doesn't ask for or require status reports. He lets work teams set their own goals and doesn't inquire how they'll achieve them.

"I give people the whole job and let them accomplish it. We just need to know what you're going to do. The how is up to you," he says.[14]

When his real estate manager wanted to lease office space, Meade wouldn't read the contract. He flat-out refused, telling him, "Any lease you put in front of me, I'll sign. Don't say to me, 'Did you consider it?' because I won't read it. As soon as you start doing that, employees [subconsciously] relax, because they know Roger's going to read it. When too many people get involved, no one knows who has authority or control, so everyone gets locked up. . . ."[15]

His thinking is echoed by Prudential vice president Ken Jenny: "Give them the whole enchilada. That's right, total responsibility for the job. If you don't give them all the information and all the control you'll end up with a half-cooked tortilla and no one will profit!"[16]

Avoiding Fumbles

Handing off the ball isn't always easy. Here are three steps to decrease the chance of a fumble. We use the acronym ERA to describe them:

- *Expectations*
- *Responsibility*
- *Accountability*

Expectations

Our paradigm: phoning for room service at the best hotel in town. After you order, the person on the line repeats the order back to you. The communication is direct with an agreed-upon vocabulary, and it's restated so that any errors can be spotted and corrected immediately. That's the way all expectations should be communicated.

But here's what generally happens. The boss is in a rush. She lays some papers on your desk, gives hurried, terse, confusing instructions without taking time for questions or feedback. Her last words before the elevator door closes: "Take your time, but get it on my desk by the ten-thirty meeting tomorrow." It's not likely she's going to get what she wants unless you're a mind reader. And most of us aren't.

The first hand-off rule is to *clarify expectations* to make sure you and your staff are on the same page.

The more clearly spelled out the expectation, the more successful the result. Use the repeat-back technique that works so well with room service. And don't just order a hamburger. Tell them exactly how you want it: medium rare with lettuce and tomato on a toasted, buttered bun. It may seem like overkill, but you'll save time in the long run when your order comes back to your specifications.

Casey at the bat. When Fisher Scientific was shifting its salespeople from regional offices to working out of their homes, Brian Casey was given responsibility for writing a home office guide.

"My boss told me he wanted the guide to be targeted for both the sophisticated and novice computer user. He also mentioned areas to cover, like how to prepare quotes, organize literature, communicate with the support staff, and manage the paper flow. He emphasized the tone he wanted—breezy and easy to digest. He gave me a budget and told me what resources I could use. By the time he was done I had a pretty firm idea of what he wanted.

"But he also gave me room to include my own ideas in the project, which I did. I researched the field, talked to a few experts, and read the literature. My favorite part of the guide was a section on what to do when your kid's listening to loud rap music and you've got a client call to make."

Casey's boss gave explicit instructions at the outset but then surrendered control. The execution and final content were up to Casey. The key to setting expectations is in the timing. Set them early, make sure everyone's on the same page, and then hand the ball off. After you've done that, get out of the way.

"Our initial conversation got me started by laying out a clear game plan. But once I took over the project it was up to me. No one was looking over my shoulder from the moment I left my boss's office," said Casey.[17]

Responsibility

Peter Principle to the contrary, people generally rise to the level of responsibility they're given. Whether it's writing a restructuring plan or implementing a new business strategy, responsibility brings out the best in people and motivates them to action.

We worked with the marketing director of a sports-medicine clinic with a staff of 20. The director wore many hats, as people do in small businesses, and he was often overwhelmed by how much he had to accomplish each day. One of his jobs was to send out a monthly newsletter to old clients and prospective customers touting the clinic's services and new technologies.

We advised him to let his assistant take over this job, but he wasn't sure. He offered the usual excuses: "It's too important to turn over to someone else." "I'll just have to edit everything she does anyway." "It'll take too long and it's too hard to explain." "It's easier to do myself." When he ran out of rationalizations he gave it a try. The results surprised even us.

Her first response was a flood of ideas. When we asked why she hadn't mentioned them before, she responded, "He'd never listen."

Though she got no more money for her additional duties, she seized the initiative. She read a book on guerrilla marketing and took a course in desktop publishing at the extension university. Then she set up a clipping file on health and sports medicine. She scheduled regular meetings with staff to hear their experiences with patients and learn about their new projects and ideas. Finally, she changed the design of the newsletter, making it brighter, bolder, and more attractive. Within six months the response to the letter increased by 45 percent. Business at the clinic was booming.

But the best part was that the assistant had been transformed. She walked around the place with a newfound pride and a great deal of energy. She was upbeat, curious, optimistic, and exploding with ideas. Her mood was contagious. The whole building seemed to resonate with her newfound vitality.

What's the voodoo behind responsibility? Why does it light a fire under people? It's as simple as this: When you give responsibility to individuals, you're indicating your belief in them. You're saying you trust them, you have faith in them, and you respect them enough to give them the reins—or the reigns, as the case may be.

In both of the above situations individuals weren't just delegated authority. They were elevated to a higher position, which increased their esteem and confidence. Now they "owned" their jobs, and that motivated them to work harder and longer. Here's the basic motivational principle: *Don't delegate, elevate.*

Accountability

Accountability gives responsibility meaning. Putting people in charge of the henhouse without making them answerable when the fox breaks in makes for an empty job and an emptier henhouse. There can be no genuine responsibility without accountability.

Think of parents who pressure their children to get high grades in school but at report-card time barely give a second glance. What's the message in that? You can bet the confusion won't be lost on the kids. Next time they'll think twice before hitting the books.

Or what about the manager who talks punctuality but waits to start meetings until all the latecomers show up? That regular five-minute delay becomes a regular fifteen. Soon everyone comes late.

He ain't heavy. Many managers have trouble with accountability. Some intimidate employees who don't perform well. They overdo the criticism and produce a staff of timid go-alongs. Others who need to be liked sugarcoat feedback or avoid it altogether. "He'll do better next time," "It was a tough assignment," "She's learning," are the kinds of rationalizations they use to avoid holding people accountable.

These *wanna-be-liked managers* are far more common than you might think. Most people don't want to be seen as the "heavy," and they're convinced that conciliatory feedback will save employees from embarrassment. In reality they're saving themselves from the distress of confrontation and the prospect of being labeled a drill sergeant.

In an executive coaching session, one manager in the auditing department of an insurance company admitted, "I don't like being seen as a hard-ass. When I deliver bad news I find myself backtracking, trying to put a prettier face on the situation. I've had people leave my office thinking they were doing just fine when my intention was to tell them to shape up. I know what I want to say, but I have the hardest time saying it."

Holding someone to a high standard can be of much greater service to an individual than a meager diet of faint praise.

Joe and Moe take a ride. You know the old story about Joe and Moe out for a drive. They're tooling down the highway when suddenly their car stalls. Joe turns to his partner and says, "That's one!"

They start the thing up and continue on their way until the car overheats. "That's two!" remarks Joe. Eventually the engine cools down and they get the jalopy going again but sure enough, something else happens. This time it's a flat tire.

"That's three!" shouts Joe and he pushes the car down a steep embankment, where it bursts into flames.

"What are you, crazy? Why'd you do that?" yells Moe. "We needed that car to get home."

"That's one!" says Joe.

Many managers take the opposite approach. They're counting twenty, thirty, forty, and still no action. Some have lost count altogether. Standards fall when there's no accountability and mediocre efforts are reinforced.

Pushover with a capital "P." The owner of a lighting fixture company had trouble giving negative feedback to employees. He hated to be criticized himself, and the thought of calling someone to task was a job he didn't relish. He avoided formal evaluation processes as long as possible, sometimes skipping them altogether.

"Every time I'm faced with one of those situations," he told us, "my stomach knots up. I'm afraid my point of view could be biased. Maybe I've blown the situation out of proportion or overlooked something. Maybe I'm overstating the problem."

His staff sensed his ambivalence. The consensus was that the man was a pushover with a capital "P." Even when they came in late or padded comp time, they knew they wouldn't be confronted. And, as you might expect, they often missed deadlines and meetings.

Even worse, they had lost respect for their boss, and this was reflected in the organization's low morale and chaotic operations.

Forgotten Homework

In the executive coaching we do with organizational leaders, we assign homework to increase personal awareness and highlight options for handling situations differently. We might ask people to observe how three of their direct reports react to criticism. Or to imagine where in their company they want to be in five, ten, and fifteen years.

To make a point about accountability we sometimes delay followup on the homework for a week or two. This never fails to produce a decrease in quality and commitment to the next assignment. It's as if these executives feel that "if they don't care enough to check what I've done, then I won't care enough to put much effort into doing it." It was the same in school. When the teacher didn't check the homework you were less likely to do it.

Accountability is experienced as interest and involvement. Without it, the level of motivation falls off.

4. REWARDS AND RECOGNITION

The most obvious way to motivate employees to get excited about your plans for change is through rewards. Every coach knows their special power. With enough M&M's you can get a six-year-old to spell "motivate."

In fact, American business is downright Pavlovian, elevating rewards—now called incentive systems—to new heights. The blue-plate annual bonus has been replaced by such sumptuous delicacies as opportunities to appear on the company's television commercials, Hawaiian vacations for the family, and employee-of-the-month awards with plaques and feature articles in the company paper.

Robert Nelson boasted 1,001 ways to reward employees in his book by the same name, but the number is probably closer to a million. Rewards come in all shapes and sizes and are only limited by management's imagination and pocketbook.

"Do This and You'll Get That"

But rewards aren't as simple as they seem. There are real limits to the "do this and you'll get that" formula. For example, when managers were asked if they would be willing to work harder and longer for more money, most answered no, they wouldn't.[18]

"While rewards are effective at producing temporary compliance, they are strikingly ineffective at producing lasting change in attitudes or behavior," claims author and social critic Alfie Kohn.[19]

"About two dozen studies from the field of social psychology conclusively show that people who expect to receive a reward do not perform as well as those who expect nothing," argues Kohn.[20]

For further emphasis, he points to what happened at a Midwestern manufacturing company where an incentive system for welders had been in place for years. When the company removed it, there was an initial drop in productivity followed by a rise in production that *exceeded* the original level.

To Kohn this is a clear indication that financial incentives aren't necessary to keep people interested. "The more closely pay is linked to achievement, the more damage is done," he argues.[21]

Kohn's right about the limits of financial incentives and the use of prizes and gifts to keep people interested in their jobs. They may be motivating at first, but after a while they can lose effectiveness.

Two Kinds of Rewards

There are two kinds of rewards: extrinsic incentives, like the corner office, money, gifts, and titles, and intrinsic rewards, which appeal to more abstract personal needs. People do things not just to get an object or the cash to buy things. They're also motivated by such intangibles as recognition, fairness, flexibility, creativity, meaningfulness, and freedom. These internal factors have more impact on readiness for change than traditional extrinsic rewards do.

Things—all intrinsic rewards—moved the writer to put pen to paper: freedom, opportunity, and the incomparable delights of self-expression. Could this be said as well of today's new generation of employees?

When American Express surveyed workers they found that what they wanted more than anything else—*including money*—was flexibility. Now some customer-service agents and credit analysts can set their own hours.[22]

Or consider the bitter 1994 contract dispute between unionized employees and management of the San Francisco Bay Area Rapid Transit District (BART). Workers said it wasn't money, but the way they were treated, that made them willing to walk the picket line. Their position was borne out by the fact that BART employees are among the best-paid transit workers in the country. Still they were dissatisfied.

REWARD COW

"They don't know you as an individual," said Rich Streeter, a train operator for 17 years. "They just want a body on the train."[23]

"If someone jumps in front of your train and commits suicide, they cart you away for a drug test," complained train operator Manuel Calderon. "Nobody asks, 'Are you okay?' Nobody offers you counseling. They just drug-test you."[24]

Some workers claimed management harassed them by constant disciplinary actions over small issues that did not endanger customer safety. Streeter reported that he was written up for not holding his head out of the train long enough to check that all passengers were safely aboard, although no one could tell him what "long enough" was.

Summed up one mechanic, "They treat us like we're second class."[25]

Social Needs

Social needs too can be the basis of intrinsic reward systems. Belonging, acceptance, identification—group-driven motives—are especially important with the new emphasis on work teams. Loyalty to the team or desire to pull one's own weight are expressions of these special motives.

Research indicates that when employees feel part of a team they are more inclined to give up their limited self-interest for the overriding welfare of the group. We've known individuals who've turned down higher-paying jobs to stay with their cohorts. And we've also seen people oppose change because it would break up their work unit and separate them from their friends.

"In many situations, team building is a substitute for pay raises and security," says Philip Breslin, a retired manager of labor relations at Bethlehem Steel, "because it provides me with an identification with a group of people all trying to accomplish a set of goals."[26]

One manager at Prudential puts it even more succinctly: "My motivation comes from my co-workers," she says.[27]

Fun at the fat farm. Ben & Jerry's Ice Cream knows about intrinsic rewards. They created a "joy gang" to find ways to put fun back into work. Perhaps their biggest success was "Elvis Day," when employees showed up dressed as the King. There were blue suede shoes, impersonators, cheerleaders, jumpsuits, sideburns, and one or two hounddogs. There was even a "snarl" contest.

The company also has a group of "joy ninjas" who once served "breakfast" at 10 P.M. for the second and third shifts. Another time they made the world's biggest milkshake.

Says owner Jerry Greenfield: "There was pretty much an agreement that things at work are tough, and that with all the tasks we have to perform, and the stress people are under, it would be a good idea to try to infuse a little more joy." [28]

Two-Tiered Rewards

When it comes to motivating people to change, the best strategy is to combine both intrinsic and extrinsic rewards. Use a two-tiered system to get the advantages of both: the short-term primitive power of the tangible incentive and the deeper and more lasting influence of the intrinsic inducement.

Mary Kay, the shop-at-home cosmetics company with annual sales of $613 million, unabashedly uses glitzy prizes to keep its sales force of 300,000 fired up. There are diamond pins to win, pink Cadillacs to drive, and five-star vacations to take. But the company is also aware that prizes alone won't do it. They take care of intrinsic rewards in one word: recognition. One might say they've developed it into an art form.

Every summer about 36,000 salespeople—or beauty consultants, as they are called—gather in the company's hometown of Dallas to give and get recognition. The most successful women are introduced by film clips similar to the kind used by major political parties to present a candidate at convention time. But achievement is roundly applauded at every level, not just the top. Color-coded suits, sashes, badges, crowns, and other emblems are worn to show how far each saleswoman has come. The level of emotion at these fetes of approbation is astounding. People cry, applaud, and cry some more. But when they leave Dallas they go with enthusiasm and a sense of belonging.[29]

PIP—Personal, Immediate, Public

To maximize the impact of extrinsic rewards, make them personal, immediate, and public: PIP.

Personal

At a chemical plant, management gave workers an expanded benefits package that was the envy of the industry. But the workers were not pleased. Why not? What they really wanted was more flexible work schedules. Management missed the boat by not paying attention to the kind of incentive that had value to its workforce.

Contrast that situation with a Hewlett-Packard manufacturing plant that keeps a special file in the personnel folder of every worker. Inside it is a listing of the employee's special interests, things that are important to the person. When someone makes a contribution to the plant, managers check the file and create a reward that is personalized. Some people get theater tickets, others baseball tickets or passes to Disneyland. The point is to offer incentives that fit the person.

We all know what it's like to open a holiday gift and find a scarf that would have looked great on your grandmother. Hewlett-Packard changed that with its file-within-a-file, and each of their special rewards cost the company less than $30 apiece. When it's personal, it doesn't have to be expensive.

Immediate

When a reward comes on the heels of an outstanding contribution it's got more punch. The longer you wait, the less impact it has.

Several years ago we worked with a company that used chips as incentives. Crude as it was, employees loved it. Anytime they made a contribution above and beyond their usual duties, they were rewarded with a chip redeemable for trips and prizes. It was Green Stamps at the office. Not only did the system create excitement and allow people to choose their own rewards, it had the advantage of providing timely feedback: "Do something good, get a chip." More than anything else it was the immediacy of the response that made it effective.

Teachers know that learning is improved by offering instantaneous feedback on whether an answer is correct. Educational software programs are built on this premise. If you get it wrong, the system tells you right away so the incorrect answer isn't imprinted in your memory bank. Get it right, and the program reinforces the learning with accolades and congratulations.

Public

Don't hide the good news. Tell everyone about it. Publicly announced rewards work extrinsically and intrinsically. You get the reward itself and the recognition that comes with the publicity.

Critics say that public acknowledgment of excellence creates envy and back-biting, and that employees are bound to grouse and grumble if one of their peers receives special notice. There is some truth to this. But the benefits of public acknowledgment far outweigh the risk. First, it sends a concrete message to your people about what you really value. Second, it often elicits a positive spirit of competition. At a big retail chain that held regular cow hunts and made a big deal about "hunters of the month," employees got into a friendly rivalry over who would hold the title next. Third, it can spin off new thinking. Public awareness of good ideas gets others to take them to the next step. In fact, this is how great ideas are born.

Cutting-Edge Goals, Stone Age Rewards

When you change an organization you have to change its reward structure too. Sometimes this is the last thing that gets attention, and a company can find itself actually reinforcing resistance to change.

Remember the national real estate company integrating interactive technologies with its basic business practices? The problem was that they had an information age strategy with a Stone Age reward program. The company was trying to wean its employees away from traditional sales techniques to a system that would have allowed consumers to shop for homes on-line. While it struggled with its agents' resistance to the new technology, it was still offering awards for the best newspaper ad and the cleverest brochure. The contradiction confused everyone and sent the message that the company was not fully committed to the interactive program. Incentive systems need to be rethought so they reward the future, not discourage it.

Reward Mistakes

Sounds crazy, no? But when change is necessary you don't want your people exercising caution and avoiding risk. Unless you encourage people to try—and that means making mistakes—you're going to end up with a whole lot more of the status quo. It's not honest mistakes that are the problem, but mistakes of inaction. If you're not making errors, you're probably doing something wrong. Change is hard to sell in a "no-mistakes" culture.

Setting up a system that rewards good tries, not just successful results, is a way to get people to risk changing and trying new things. Companies like 3M, known for its innovation, encourage their people to experiment with new ideas and concepts. They know that 60 percent of the time the idea will be a dud, but they're betting on the other 40.

"High Try" or "Best Shot" awards work well to get this message across: Change produces errors; errors produce learning; learning produces success.

Reward the Team

A district manager at a national food company was asked to come up to the dais to receive an award from the corporation president. Her team had introduced the most successful new product of the year, and after a few laudatory words the president handed her the microphone. Without hesitation she called everyone on her team to stand up and join her on the platform. Twenty-two people from Manufacturing, Sales, Design, and Marketing made their way up to the front of the room, where they were warmly applauded by the audience. The group wore smiles a foot long as they received public appreciation for their efforts.

What was so striking about the moment? When you want to motivate people to work together, you must reward the team, not just the captain. If you're going to use work teams to create change or your reorganization plans rely on them, you'd better attend to this simple principle. When the manager asked her team to share in the glory, she probably did more to solidify the group than a year of motivational speeches could ever do.

When championship rings are handed out in professional sports, everyone gets one regardless of whether the individual played every game or just rode the bench. From the coach's point of view, each player's contribution is important and should be acknowledged. From the player's point of view, nothing makes you feel more a part of the team than being rewarded as a team.

SACRED COW: TREAT EVERYONE THE SAME

It's nearly impossible to motivate individuals to change when your path is blocked by the sacred cow: "treat everyone the same." This remnant of the Judeo-Christian ethic of justice, the American tradition of fair play, and the union agenda of equity in the workplace holds that enlightened managers offer no special treatment. Everyone plays by the same rules.

While it's important to care about your people and treat everyone with fairness, the key to good coaching is recognizing and maximizing individual differences—not minimizing them. You don't manage the superstar the way you manage the journeyman. You don't motivate your creative talent the way you motivate your bookkeepers. Sometimes you need different rules for each person.

A nationally famous football coach who shall remain nameless was asked the secret to motivating his players. What he said struck us perhaps as much for its wisdom as its crudeness: "Some guys . . . you gotta kick their butt; some you gotta kiss their butt; some you gotta wipe their butt," he mused. "The key is knowing which is which."

Blunt or brilliant, raw or rare, the coach knew something fundamental: Different players require different handling. The same strategy used to motivate one player may be totally unsuited to another. Whereas one may respond to urgency, another may be more motivated by challenge. That's why our four keys to motivation are just the starting point. You've got to take the next step and ask, When do you do what to whom?

Jordan's Rules

The Chicago Bulls basketball franchise has been roundly criticized for creating special rules for superstar Michael Jordan. Coach Phil Jackson's response:

"My first concern when I got the job was trying to treat Michael as equally as possible on the court. That's what our offensive system is all about. But there is no possible way to treat him like every other player off the court.

"He cannot walk downstairs in a hotel without being mobbed. I've walked past his room and seen eight, sometimes ten service people outside his door, lurking to see if he comes out, flowers and candy all over the place. Unlike other players, he has to have people travel with him to filter some of this out. . . .

"There is a difference in the way he is treated, yes, but there's also a difference in the way he produces. A *big* difference. And that must be weighed. There are jealousies that other players must overcome. If they do we'll be a great team."[30]

What Motivates an Individual?

When I directed a mental-health clinic years ago I realized that the master's degree–level staff required a lot of direction and reassurance. Many of them felt uncertain of their abilities and needed to be continually supervised to feel comfortable with the high level of responsibility the work required. I soon found that what worked for master's-level staff was totally unsuited for the Ph.D.s. They resented this kind of direction, finding it intrusive and overbearing. They wanted to be treated as professionals. Independence and breathing room were essential to them, and they let me know it in no uncertain terms.

It's the same story for individuals. Some are motivated by bonuses and perks, others by unstructured work schedules and "room to be themselves," still others by power and achievement. It's like the coach said: The key is knowing what works with each.

The empathic vantage point (EVP) we mentioned earlier (in the "Caring" section in Chapter Seventeen) is the second approach. Learning to stand in the other person's shoes, thinking and feeling into their reality, is a skill all good coaches must either have or acquire. When it comes to motivating, it's as essential as the scripted pep talk.

"When Red Auerbach was coaching the Boston Celtics in the '50s and '60s, he yelled at certain players regularly because he thought that was the only way he could get maximum performance from them," writes Glenn Dickey, a sportswriter for the *San Francisco Chronicle*. "But Auerbach never ever yelled at Bill Russell because Red understood the prickly pride of the man."[31]

Says Auerbach, who coached nine NBA championship teams, "I always resented when people said to me, 'How did you handle so-and-so?' You handle animals, you deal with men . . . !"[32]

Taming the Green-Eyed Monster

Dealing with jealousy and claims of unfairness are all part of the process when you treat individuals differently. Our suggestions for taming the green-eyed monster:

• Fifth Business—Let everyone know they are valued and that each employee's contribution has importance. Even if they're in a support position, their role is essential. They are "fifth business," a theater term used to describe characters who have few lines but whose part is pivotal to the furtherance of the plot.

- Coach Individuals—Treat *all* your people as individuals with special needs and concerns. Let each one know you respect and care about them equally. Set specific goals with each. The more interest you show in your players as individuals, the less sibling rivalry you'll produce.
- Bottom-Line Rules—Initiate a set of *bottom-line rules* for everyone, regardless of status. John Madden had three when he was coaching the Oakland Raiders: "Show up on time, know the plays, hustle." But also create *top-line rules* that are specific for departments and individuals. People in sales and customer service, for example, might follow different guidelines than program designers.

THREE CASE STUDIES

Your company has been steadily losing market share, and top management is nervous. They've decided on a restructuring plan that changes the way the company does business, from the mail room to R&D. Rachel, Joe, and Tom have just been assigned to your work team. Your job is to motivate all three to embrace the plan for change.

Rachel Storm

Age: 37
Job: Sales rep
Years employed by company: 5
   Work habits: Ambitious to the point of being driven, works long hours, top 10 in sales department, prefers to work alone, responds to challenges, self-starter.
   Rewards: Likes expensive cars, fancy hotels, expensive clothes, excitement of the fast track.
   Personal characteristics: Attuned to her feelings, emotionally expressive, friendly but not close to peers, independent, optimistic, responds well to challenges, confident in her abilities.

Joe Slow

Age: 44
Job: Comptroller
Years employed by company: 20

Work habits: Reliable but unspectacular, good at detail, cautious—doesn't rock the boat, likes routines, keeps a cup of sharpened pencils on his desk, prefers clear, specific instructions, resists innovation and change, rejects risky assignments, bottom-line oriented.

Rewards: Interested in money—talks about "not having enough," other people's opinions mean a lot to him, team oriented.

Personal characteristics: Family focused, dresses conservatively, reliable, dependable, same street address for 24 years, logical and rational. Unemotional, traditional views, loyal to company, maintains friendships with employees—goes to their weddings and celebrations, marginal self-confidence.

Tom Teckie

Age: 28
Job: Mid-level employee—information systems
Years employed by company: 2

Work habits: Technology focused—spends hours in front of his terminal, brilliant problem solver, creative and innovative, takes initiative in areas of expertise, can always make a good system better. Maintains odd schedule—prefers late-night hours—refuses managerial work, mediocre communication skills, likes to work alone.

Rewards: Not interested in money or team values, appreciates freedom, flexibility, and good equipment.

Personal characteristics: Few friends in company—doesn't participate in company functions. Quiet, loner, grunge dresser, intuitive, analytical. Confident in his sandbox; shaky outside it.

If you've been coming from the empathic vantage point you'll know a lot more about these employees than the few pieces of information we've listed above, so what follows are general suggestions for motivating these three. As you can see, they're very different people with distinct values, work habits, interests, and personalities.

Consider Rachel Storm. How would you motivate her to change? What kind of language would you use to reach her? What kind of rewards? What kind of tasks would you assign her? These are the kind of questions any good coach should ask.

Rachel is a self-starter who responds to challenges, so creating urgency may be only a matter of selling her on the opportunities implicit in the plan for change. Emphasize the personal challenges. She doesn't need to be fired up—she already is—so direct that fire by painting a picture of how her ambitiousness will pay off in the company's future vision.

She's a motivated person; use high-octane words in your approach. Expensive vacations and cars are important to her, so extrinsic rewards should be emphasized and offered. But she's also drawn to excitement and fun. Focus on the thrill of new possibility. Give her tasks that stretch her.

It's a whole other world dealing with Joe. He's been with the company twenty years and worked his way up slowly and cautiously. He's conservative and slow to change and has been resistant to innovation in the past. Appeal to Joe's rational, bottom-line thinking by using language that is reasonable and arguments that are logical. Emphasize both external and social rewards.

Joe is concerned about money, so show him what he stands to gain and what the company stands to lose if it doesn't make the change. But he is also socially motivated. Appeal to his sense of team spirit and consider peer pressure as a means of getting his buy-in. Give him easy tasks that build his confidence and create comfort with the reorganization plan.

Tom requires yet another approach. He doesn't care about money or status. He's moved by intrinsic motives. Emphasize freedom and independence. Point to the opportunities for more "machine time" and developing new technology under the reorganization. Use language that is analytic and logical. Give him tasks within his area of expertise and appeal to his problem-solving abilities. Ask him for help in working out bugs in the new system. Downplay group interaction. Stress the possibility of enlarging his sandbox.

Treating your players differently isn't playing favorites, it's playing smart. By recognizing that each person is an individual with specific needs, dreams, and values, a manager can maximize every employee's contribution and motivate him or her to change.

As IBM founder Tom Watson advised, "Don't try to get your wild geese to fly in formation."[33]

Twenty

Developing
Change-Ready Traits

YOU DON'T HAVE TO BE A SUPERSTAR

Ted Turner, who conceived and created the first "all news, all the time" television station, is an obvious and highly visible prototype of the Change-Ready individual. Turner put up his billboard advertising business to buy a UHF television station. He mortgaged that to buy two professional sports franchises, the Atlanta Braves and Atlanta Hawks. And then he risked his $100-million-a-year organization to create CNN. Failing in an attempt to buy CBS, he nearly lost it all in his successful acquisition of MGM. For Turner, change is as ordinary as cornflakes for breakfast. The status quo? An anathema to avoid at all costs. Turner embraces new possibilities the way a thirsty man drinks a glass of water—in eager swallows and enormous gulps.

What traits do Change-Ready people share? And, more important, are they teachable? We've found that you don't have to be a super-hero to be Change-Ready; these traits exist in all of us. But like musical or athletic ability, they have to be developed.

Change-Readiness means feeling excited and challenged by change, anticipating and initiating it rather than simply reacting to events. Most organizations don't take the time to create a culture of readiness. They bring their consultants in just before and even after plans for change have been announced. That's like getting a boxer ready for the fight the day of the event. Not only doesn't it work, it often produces resentment and bitterness. No wonder many consultants complain they're targets, not facilitators.

Creating a Change-Ready organization involves challenging sacred-cow beliefs and assumptions, building an environment of trust and caring, conquering resistance, and firing people up. This chapter is the last step: developing Change-Ready people who will create your organization's future and take you into the twenty-first century.

To find out your Change-Ready strengths and weaknesses, how well you deal with the incessant demands of a world in flux, complete the Change-Ready Scale below, an abbreviated version of the test we use in our programs and workshops. (For a copy of the Change-Ready Scale and Program in hard copy or disk, see page 310.)

TAKING THE TEST

Focus on your performance at work. Answer each question honestly. Circle the number that most accurately describes your beliefs and behaviors as they actually are, not as you would like them to be or think they should be.

Change-Readiness Scale

1 = Strongly Disagree   6 = Strongly Agree

1. I prefer the familiar to the unknown. 1 2 3 4 5 6

2. I rarely second-guess myself. 1 2 3 4 5 6

3. I stick to my guns no matter what. 1 2 3 4 5 6

4. I can't wait for the day to get started. 1 2 3 4 5 6

5. I believe in not getting your hopes too high. 1 2 3 4 5 6

6. If things aren't going well, I'll find a way to make them work out. 1 2 3 4 5 6

7. I don't like dealing with issues that have no clear answers. 1 2 3 4 5 6

8. I like to establish routines and stay with them. 1 2 3 4 5 6

9. I can make any situation work for me. 1 2 3 4 5 6

10. I get thrown when something important doesn't work out. 1 2 3 4 5 6

11. I have a hard time relaxing and doing nothing. 1 2 3 4 5 6

12. If something can go wrong, it generally will. 1 2 3 4 5 6

13. I look in unusual places to find solutions. 1 2 3 4 5 6

14. I get frustrated when I can't get a grip on something. 1 2 3 4 5 6

15. I'm cautious in my acceptance of new ideas. 1 2 3 4 5 6

16. I don't worry about meeting other people's expectations. 1 2 3 4 5 6

17. Once my mind is made up, I don't change it easily. 1 2 3 4 5 6

18. I push myself to the max. 1 2 3 4 5 6

19. My first impulse is to worry about what can go wrong. 1 2 3 4 5 6

20. I make a little go a long way. 1 2 3 4 5 6

21. When an issue is unclear, my impulse is to clarify it right away. 1 2 3 4 5 6

22. I wait to see if something works out before I try it. 1 2 3 4 5 6

23. I focus more on my strengths than my weaknesses.
    1 2 3 4 5 6

24. It's hard to give up on something even if it isn't working out.
    1 2 3 4 5 6

25. I'm restless and full of energy. 1 2 3 4 5 6

26. Things rarely work out the way you want them to. 1 2 3 4 5 6

27. I've always been successful at living by my wits. 1 2 3 4 5 6

28. I hate to leave things unfinished. 1 2 3 4 5 6

29. I'm drawn more to comfort than excitement. 1 2 3 4 5 6

30. When I make a big mistake it doesn't phase me. 1 2 3 4 5 6

31. I'm uncomfortable in situations where the rules keep changing. 1 2 3 4 5 6

32. No matter what the odds, I never give up. 1 2 3 4 5 6

33. I'm more likely to see problems than opportunities.
    1 2 3 4 5 6

34. When looking for a solution, I exhaust every possibility.
    1 2 3 4 5 6

35. I don't like situations with vague expectations and goals.
    1 2 3 4 5 6

THE SEVEN TRAITS OF CHANGE-READINESS

The scale you've just taken measures the following traits:

- *Resourcefulness*
- *Optimism*
- *Adventurousness*
- *Drive*
- *Adaptability*
- *Confidence*
- *Tolerance for Ambiguity*

SCORING:

Resourcefulness

Add up your scores on questions 6, 13, 20, 27, 34. This total is your score. Optimal range is between 22 and 26.

Resourceful people are effective at making the most of any situation and utilizing whatever resources are available to develop plans and contingencies. They see more than one way to achieve a goal, and they're able to look in less obvious places to find help. They have a real talent for creating new ways to solve old problems.

Sitting poolside while on vacation I noticed two small boys playing with some palm fronds and string. It was clear these kids hadn't been to a toystore recently. Still, one had created an elaborate bridge across a tiny lagoon and a number of small "boats." The other had constructed nothing at all, content to use the fronds to splash water on his friend. The difference in the way they played said something about their levels of resourcefulness—the ability to make something out of nothing.

To resourceful people an apple might be useful as a paperweight; a pencil could be a backscratcher. Such elastic ways of considering things allow them to come up with a variety of solutions to a dilemma.

When people low in resourcefulness encounter obstacles, they get stuck, dig in their heels, and go back to feeding sacred cows. Very high scorers (over 26) might overlook obvious solutions and create more work than is necessary.

Optimal scorers know that every problem has a solution. If anyone can find it, they will. They're very handy when it comes to discovering innovative ways to deal with change. Since there are so many unanticipated difficulties when you challenge the status quo, they add value every step of the way.

Optimism

Add up your scores on questions 5, 12, 19, 26, 33. Subtract this total from 35 for your score. Optimal range is between 22 and 26.

Everyone has a pretty good sense of what this trait measures. Is the glass half empty or half full? One business owner took the definition further. He defined a pessimist as someone who saw the glass as not only half empty, but leaking. The optimist, he noted, was delighted just to have a glass!

Our scale measures whether people have a positive view of the future. Do they see rain clouds or sunny skies? Optimism is highly correlated with Change-Readiness, since the pessimist observes only problems and obstacles while the optimist recognizes opportunities and possibilities.

Some people say optimism can't be taught; it must be caught. Like a social disease, you get it by hanging around the right people. While there's no denying that optimism is highly contagious, we believe there's more to it than that. You can train yourself to look for positives as well as negatives. But does what you see determine your attitude or your attitude determine what you see? It works both ways. Optimism is a reflection of your frame of reference, and your frame of reference is influenced by your disposition. The good news is that you can modify either.

Optimists tend to be more enthusiastic and positive about change. Their positive outlook is founded on an abiding faith in the future and the belief that things usually work out for the best. Very high optimism scorers (over 26) may lack critical-thinking skills.

Adventurousness

Add up your scores on questions 1, 8, 15, 22, 29. Subtract this total from 35 for your score. Optimal range is 22 to 26.

"Life is either a daily adventure or it is nothing," said Helen Keller, whose spirit raised her above crippling disability and shaped her existence into an amazing journey.

Two ingredients capture this adventurous spirit: the inclination to take risks and the desire to pursue the unknown, to walk the path less taken.

Adventurous people love a challenge. They tend to be restless and shun the comfort zone. Routine bores them. They hate repetition and feel compelled to break out. They're always looking for new ways to do things. Adventurous people are great innovators and creators, pathfinders and scouts who go out ahead of the wagon train looking for opportunities and excitement.

Since change always involves both risk and the unknown, they usually perform well during organizational shake-ups. They are the proactors, the employees who initiate and create change. But very high scores (over 26) may indicate a tendency toward recklessness.

Drive

Add up your scores on questions 4, 11, 18, 25, 32. This total is your score. Optimal range is between 22 and 26.

Drive combines physical energy and mental desire to create passion. It's the fuel that maximizes all the other traits. If you have drive, nothing appears impossible. If you don't, change is, well . . . exhausting.

Drive is the individual's level of personal dynamism. It shows up in a person's level of intensity and determination.

Think of standing at the bottom of a mountain you've got to climb. There are at least forty switchbacks and some treacherous footing to negotiate. Plus the altitude and the weight of that rucksack on your back. What's your response? Low scorers feel worn out just looking up at that path. High drivers feel undaunted, perhaps even energized. It has less to do with their ability in the high elements than their energy and tenacity. And it's a long climb without those two.

"One [factor] that constantly emerges in psychological tests of greatness is level of drive," reports sports psychologist Jim Loehr, who has worked with some of the top athletes in the world.

"That's the single greatest predictor of all. How passionately is the person going after a particular goal? So many of the people who rise to greatness in sports don't feel they're genetically gifted. . . . You look at [basketball great Larry] Bird, and you don't believe he can be that great when he stands next to all these super Ferraris. Obviously he has something beyond genetic superiority."[1]

It's the same in business. To make some new procedure work, to overcome the myriad of problems that any plan for change unwittingly produces, you've got to have passion and determination. Very high scores (over 26), however, may mean you're bullheaded, obsessed, and heading for burnout.

Adaptability

Add up your scores on questions 3, 10, 17, 24, 31. Subtract this total from 35 for your score. Optimal range is between 22 and 26.

Adaptability includes two elements: flexibility and resilience. Flexibility involves ease of shifting expectations. High scorers on this trait are not wedded to specific outcomes. If the situation changes, their expectations shift right along with it. They adjust to the new circumstances with quickness and ease, so they rarely feel disappointed or let down.

Flexible people have goals and dreams like everybody else, but they're not overly invested in them. When something doesn't work out, they'll say, "Plan A doesn't work. Okay, let's look at Plan B." They can go in many different directions and generally have a lot of options working. Resilient people aren't thrown by failure or mistakes. They don't dwell on them and get depressed but bounce back quickly and move on.

Resilience is the capacity to rebound from adversity quickly with a minimum of trauma. One sales manager lost half her sales force in one afternoon; twenty-two people got the ax. She was back in the office the next morning developing a new plan to meet quota. It wasn't callousness, just the willingness to accept the new situation and make the best of it.

Like the manager, resilient people are nimble and fast on their feet. They're not weighed down by the status quo or stuck living in the past. Rigid people—low-scorers—don't accommodate to a shifting sea. They're caught in their nostalgia for the "good ole days," often opposing change if not by action then by attitude. Such people are dead weight when a company is in transition. They're always looking backward instead of into the future.

Scoring too high (over 26) in this trait indicates a lack of commitment or stick-to-it-ness. You may need an infusion of backbone.

Confidence

Add up your scores on questions 2, 9, 16, 23, 30. This total is your score. Optimal range is between 22 and 26.

If optimism is the view that a situation will work out, confidence is the belief in your own ability to handle it. There is *situational* confidence—"I know I can swim across this channel, learn this program, write this report"—and *self*-confidence—"I can handle whatever comes down the pike." This latter type is the kind of confidence the Change-Readiness Scale measures.

High scorers are generally individuals with a strong sense of self-esteem. But more specifically, they believe they can make any situation work for them. Psychologists call this particular belief an "inner locus of control."

While others see themselves as battered about by circumstances they can't control—luck, fate, recession, bad timing, a tyrannical boss—confident individuals see the same situations as influenceable. If they can't change things, they'll make the most of them. One way or another they know they'll prevail, so they don't feel threatened by change.

Another reason why change isn't forbidding to people high in confidence: They're unafraid of failing. Their belief in self is not based on a particular performance. Their ego isn't on the line each time they go to bat. When they fail they don't see themselves as a "failure," but as a person who has something more to learn. In fact, to the confident individual, failing is the road to mastery—that's precisely how one gets better.

There is a direct correlation between levels of confidence and receptivity to change. If people feel confident in their ability to handle a new task, they'll be more receptive to it and more positive about it. But it's possible that you can have too much confidence. Scores above 26 may indicate a cocky, know-it-all attitude and a lack of receptivity to feedback.

Tolerance for Ambiguity

Add up your scores on questions 7, 14, 21, 28, 35. Subtract this total from 35 for your score. Optimal range is between 22 and 26.

In a perfect world, there would be no uncertainty. Everything would be as clear as the full moon on a starless night. But we don't live in that world. So much of planning, marketing, and research is based on educated guesses and hunches of where the market will be three, five, or ten years out.

The one certainty surrounding change is that it spawns uncertainty. No matter how carefully you plan it, there is always an element of indefiniteness or ambiguity. You don't know what the competition is going to do or how the marketplace will respond. Sometimes solutions don't appear until well into the process.

When things are vague, in flux, or unclear, people who are uncomfortable with ambiguity get impatient and irritable. They want answers fast and they want them now. The result is that decisions are forced and made too quickly.

We've found tolerance for ambiguity in short supply, especially among hard-driving bottom-liners who tend to see things in black and white. They want results and get upset when things are not clearly spelled out.

Without a healthy tolerance for ambiguity, change is not only uncomfortable, it's downright scary. But too much tolerance can also get you in trouble. You may have difficulty finishing tasks and making decisions. If you scored over 26 you fall in this category.

YOUR PROFILE

You'll probably find you have higher scores on some traits and lower scores on others. This is typical of most profiles and indicates that some of your Change-Readiness traits are more developed than others.

What are your strengths? Where do you need improvement? Are you surprised by any of the scores? The scale has value not only as a personal measurement to evaluate your own Change-Readiness, but also as a training tool for managers to coach their players.

We've found it effective to use the test to provide 360-degree feedback for employees at all levels in the organization. Employees answer all questions with respect to a particular person and the results are then shared with that individual. The feedback is terrific, and there are usually more than a few surprises as employees find that others don't always see them as they see themselves.

The Change-Ready Scale is also useful in coaching teams to determine which players to pick and what roles to put them in. Adventurers are great starters, resourceful people are excellent problem solvers, optimists make good cheerleaders, and their input is especially useful when people feel discouraged.

Change-Readiness is an ongoing process. There is always room to grow and improve. One doesn't really ever stop expanding one's capacity to handle change.

COACHING FOR CHANGE-READINESS

Below are a sampling of exercises from our training programs to help people become more Change-Ready.

Coaching Resourcefulness

• *When is an apple not an apple?* To develop resourcefulness, we ask people to think of 10 uncommon uses for an ordinary object. For example, what could you do with a clove of garlic other than eat it? Some uses people have suggested: an amulet to ward off disease, an ear plug, a drain stopper, a toe separator for polishing nails, a bug repellent.

Giving permission and encouragement to go beyond conventional thinking is sometimes all that is needed to develop resourcefulness. We're always surprised at the ingenuity that emerges once the mental barriers fall.

• *Raft Building with a Twist.* In our programs we divide the group into competing teams and give each the materials needed to build a raft for crossing a small lake. Some groups are given no directions. Some are given materials with one important thing left out, like rope for lashing. Sometimes we leave out a tool, which must be "borrowed" from the competition. There's always a challenge that forces the teams to improvise. One group used T-shirts tied together to form rope to bind logs. They crossed the water high and dry and won the competition, but the drive home was a bit cold and damp.

• *Magic Weekend.* What would you do for two days away from home with only five bucks in your pocket? We told people to live by their wits for a weekend without using their credit cards or asking help from friends. Here are a few strategies that emerged: washing dishes for meals, giving directions to tourists at 50¢ a pop, earning food by folding clothes at the Laundromat, sweeping a store for supper.

All these exercises rely on a healthy sense of humor, a spirit of adventure, and a single piece of folk wisdom you probably heard as a child: "Necessity is the mother of invention."

Coaching Optimism

Many years ago a national magazine ran a double article entitled something like "Is Life Essentially Good or Bad?" Two prominent authors each wrote a piece taking the opposite position. I read both and had a classic experience of "cognitive dissonance." Each writer convinced me. But how could they both be right?

When I analyzed the articles, I realized that the conclusions reached depended on which evidence was considered. Both writers projected certainty because they had included only material that supported their perspective.

Your sense of the future is based on what you choose to look at. Optimists focus on positives; pessimists on negatives. Their attitudes are predetermined by what they happen to notice. And how they interpret what they see.

If you want to develop optimism in people, teach them to seek out and emphasize positive information and perspectives and to interpret what they see in a positive light.

• *Rose-Colored Glasses.* We have people practice looking with a positive frame of reference by asking them to tell us what's good about these typical negatives:

• Losing your job
• Getting a new boss
• Changing departments
• Getting transferred to Greenland
• The economy going down the toilet
• Your company downsizing

Impossible to frame the above positively? One manager said losing a job gave people the opportunity to try something new and different, perhaps something they'd always wanted to do. Another manager saw getting a new boss as an opportunity to start fresh and create the perfect working relationship. A third thought of the transfer to Greenland as a chance to learn about another culture and expand personal horizons.

• *Positive Flip.* Here's a variation on the above exercise. Make a list of everything that's not working in your life. Now turn it around and frame it positively. Examples: "Not making enough money" becomes "Motivation to seek out a better-paying job"; "Marriage in trouble" converts to "Big opportunity to bring romance back to your relationship"; "Intolerable working conditions" flips to "Will make the next job seem great."

We don't claim that these mental maneuvers offer real solutions to life's problems. Nothing is solved that simply. But they do help individuals to practice viewing events from a positive frame of reference, seeing opportunities where once there'd been only misery.

• *Twinning.* Because optimism is an attitude that can be caught, we ask individuals to specify three people in the company they think are especially optimistic. Then we suggest they spend a number of hours every day with each person on the list. What is the effect? What do optimists do that's different from what others do? How do they maintain their perspective when the situation looks grim? Imitation is not only the sincerest form of flattery, it may also be the easiest way to learn.

Coaching Adventurousness

• *Create Your Own Adventure.* We ask participants to think about a risky experience they have been avoiding. Something they've always wanted to do that brings a tightness to their gut and starts their pacemakers fluttering. Then, we give them 24 hours to do it. You'd be surprised at what people come up with. One person took a full-moon kayak trip on San Francisco Bay. Another did a routine at a local comedy club's open mike. Another registered for a bike trip to southern France. Still another sang ballads for an hour in front of a downtown department store.

When they return, we talk about what happened. How did it feel? What was exciting about it? What got in the way? What doubts and reservations surfaced? Then we asked people how they can be more adventurous at work and in their personal lives and what their next adventure will be.

In the end most individuals discover a part of Indiana Jones within themselves. Usually it's been waiting to express itself all along but too many fears, doubts, and obligations have kept it under wraps. The adventurous spirit exists in everyone. It just needs permission to come out and play.

Another thing people recognize is that adventure is as much about attitude as it is about action. A solo walk on the beach at two in the morning can be as compelling an adventure as skydiving from 10,000 feet. It's all a matter of how you view it.

Risking Practice. To become a better risk-taker you've got to practice. Sound crazy? Not really. The more you risk, the more you realize that the catastrophic consequences you expect rarely happen. In our programs we use a group format for risk-taking exercises, but below we've included a few designed for individuals.

• State an unpopular opinion.
• Act contrary to all expectations.

- Do something you've been scared to try.
- Confront someone you've been afraid to face.
- Introduce yourself to a perfect stranger.
- Point out your strengths to someone who underestimates you.
- Pasture-ize a sacred cow you've been afraid to round up.

Coaching Drive

For a moment think of yourself as an energy system. To keep running smoothly you need regular fueling, tuning, and conserving. The more attention you give to these requirements, the more energy you'll have when the going toughens. Adequate sleep, proper nourishment, relaxation, exercise, abstinence from drugs, these are all elements in maintaining a dynamic energy system. And energy is the foundation on which drive is built.

But human beings are more complicated than the average machine. Their level of drive is primarily affected by psychological factors such as desire, aspiration, and fear. "Following your bliss" isn't just the latest credo to descend on us from the self-help revolution, it makes motivational sense. There is a direct connection between excitement and energy level, between the mind and the body. When we're passionate about something, fatigue magically lifts.

Drive depends on how much passion you feel for what you're doing and how well you maintain your energy system. The exercises that follow are designed for building passion.

• *Passion Index.* We first used this technique in Hewlett-Packard management-training programs. Managers were asked to create a change project for their team.

After setting objectives and developing strategies, we asked them to rate their project from 1 to 10 on a Passion Index. Ten meant a blazing desire, one stood for cold embers. We got a wide spectrum of responses.

Try this exercise yourself on the various projects you're working on. In most cases we find that when people rate a project below seven, it doesn't get done. Without excitement for a task, you're only going through the motions. "There's too much hot stuff on my plate for a lukewarm addition," is how one manager explained it.

• *Raising the Mark.* Ask yourself how you can get projects that score below seven above mark. The Hewlett-Packard managers said things like make the project "more challenging," "riskier," "more of a breakthrough," "more creative."

Where's the passion in your job? And more importantly, how can you make it more meaningful so that it makes a difference? Look for personal challenges that excite you, creative work that gets your juices flowing, and things you just love to do.

After you've rated all your tasks on the index, look for a way to give priority to jobs that score over seven. Or begin your day with tasks that rank high. That'll start you off on a roll and help to keep you stoked throughout the day.

Another way to stay fired up even on the most mundane jobs is to challenge yourself to learn one new thing every day. Learning something new is exciting. It expands your capabilities, your possibilities, and you.

• *Dream Machines.* Passion is built on dreams. So what do you dream about? Some people gave up dreaming long ago and think of dreams as the stuff of childhood. Others are afraid of confronting the great distance between their hopes and their everyday lives. Still others are so busy rushing to meet short-term goals that they never set their sights beyond the horizon.

• *Sentence Completion.* Finish the following:

1. If I had unlimited wealth, I'd _____

2. If education and training were not an issue, I would _____

3. If I had all the time in the world, I would _____

4. If I had started out differently, I would have _____

5. If everything worked perfectly for the next five years, _____

6. I've always wanted to _____

7. If I didn't have all these bills to pay I'd _____

Responding to questions like these turns on the imagination and gets people thinking about possibilities. Once the imagination is awakened, anything is possible.

• *Mental Movies.* Close your eyes and imagine you're in your home or office watching a video. The tape begins with your name and a date-stamp five years from today. Then it shows your ideal life unfolding before you. All your major goals have been reached, all your wishes have come true. You're living your dream.

Run the tape without interference from your rational mind about whether these images are possible or not. No editing of the tape is allowed. No commentary, either.

Now write down a few key words that capture the essence of what you saw. Use these words to trigger the dream and rekindle your fire whenever you feel flat and without passion.

Coaching Adaptability

Flexibility and resilience are the keys to adaptability. The exercises below help people to stay mentally agile and clear of ruts and routines in their work and personal lives. Rigid thinking and actions are incompatible with Change-Readiness.

• *Changing the Rules.* This technique can also be used to coach tolerance for ambiguity. Two teams are given a game to play. We use volleyball because it's fun and almost everyone knows how it's played. After a few minutes we make a rule change, for example, the object becomes to keep the ball in play for as long as possible without either team getting a point. A few minutes later, we change the rules again, making it a requirement to hit the ball to every teammate before sending it over the net. A third change: no passing allowed, and so on. We even go beyond rule changes and vary the composition of the teams. After eight or ten of these shifts, the teams get pretty good at adjusting to new rules.

• *Breaking Habits*. Habit is the enemy of adaptability. The more inclined you are to set, rigid patterns of behavior, the more difficult it will be to remain adaptable. We recommend getting in the habit of breaking habits. Here are a few ways to go about it:

—Drive a different route to work.
—Serve dinner for breakfast.
—Wear your watch on your other wrist.
—Sleep on the other side of the bed.
—Change the way you write your name.
—Eat with your other hand.

Here are a number of exercises for keeping your most important muscle—your mind—flexible.

• *Describe an important situation (it could be personal, political, or social) from your own point of view.* Ho-hum. Now describe it from the perspective of a seven-year-old child, a visitor from another planet, the family pet. Making mental jumps like this keeps the mind nimble. It requires some agility to think like a gerbil. But it also challenges a person's usual and comfortable way of perceiving things.

• *What do X and Y have in common?* Juxtapose two things that seem impossibly unrelated and find the way they connect. For example, a dog and a mailbox. Both carry mail and have big mouths. How about a telephone and a hat? You can talk through both. Each is useful for hiding, if that's what you want to do, and neither should be brought to dinner. Now your turn. How about a trombone and suntan lotion? Pajamas and carburetors? Aspirin and lighthouses?

• *Use riddles to stretch the mental muscles into thinking "outside the box."* To break down the assumptions and paradigms that govern the way we think, answer the following:

—What gets wetter the more it dries?
—What's a reward for waiting?
—What can you put inside a barrel to make it lighter?

—In what place does Thursday precede Wednesday?
—What eats but never swallows?

Answers: a towel, a tip, holes, the dictionary, rust.[2]

Use these exercises before a meeting or brainstorming session and expect some breakthrough thinking.

Coaching Confidence

See the section "Building Confidence" in Chapter 18 for numerous ways of coaching employees to be more confident.

Coaching Tolerance for Ambiguity

Individuals with low scores on this trait tend to feel anxious and uncomfortable when things are uncertain or unpredictable. These days, that's all the time. It's the lack of control that people find hard to tolerate. But in every situation there's more under your control than you might think. The following exercises help to delineate what is and what isn't under your influence.

• *Taking Control.* Choose a new situation at work that requires action. On a sheet of paper, write down everything within that situation that is *in your control.* On the opposite page list all the factors that aren't. Look at the lists carefully. Can any items be switched? Ignore what you can't influence and focus on things that you can. Design an action plan(s) and place it to the right of each item. What happens when you concentrate on things you can do something about? How does your mood change? What happens to your level of clarity? What does this tell you about empowerment and helplessness? In every new situation there's more in your control than you first realize.

• *Out of Control.* Follow the same procedure as above, only this time focus on things that are out of your control. What kind of a response do you have when you think only about what you can't influence? What happens to your judgment? Notice how easy it is to exaggerate consequences. There is an obvious and direct connection between feelings of panic and attention to things you can do nothing about.

The following exercises help people to deal with ambiguity by giving up control.

• *Letting Go.* Blindfold people in a room with foam rubber or inflatable obstacles and ask them to find their way across the room. Sounds like a lot of bumps in the night, but the really strange thing is that people report they can "see" things better when they surrender to the dark instead of trying to fight it. Subtle degrees of shading, heat felt from near objects, and even air currents can be sensed if the individual stays relaxed and doesn't struggle to assert control.

We use this exercise to demonstrate the paradox of gaining greater effectiveness by letting go. It's a hard lesson for people to learn because the natural tendency is to try to take charge of the situation rather than flow with it. Especially when you start stumbling around.

• *Skiing on Ice.* Skiers, have you ever found yourself cruising along when you hit a long stretch of ice? Experienced Vermont downhillers know that the more you try to take control of an icy surface, the more likely you'll wipe out. So we offer this exercise. The next time you encounter ice, let yourself slide, don't try to control it. As you relax into the slide, you'll start to feel subtleties that you hadn't felt before, like nubs and ruts, rough spots, and snow patches that will let your skis get a grip so you can turn. Once again, the paradox: Letting go of control gives you more control.

CHANGE-READY TEAMS

Choosing Up Sides

When Bill Clinton sent ex-President Jimmy Carter, former Chief of Staff Colin Powell, and Senator Sam Nunn to negotiate with Haitian military leader Raoul Cedras, he created a team that was noteworthy for its expertise and experience. Carter had a proven record as a peacemaker and crisis manager. Powell, as former head of the world's most powerful armed forces, spoke Cedras's language. And Sam Nunn, a no-nonsense, tough-talking negotiator, could give the impression of congressional support for Clinton's policies. It was the right team for the right job, and it illustrated two fundamental principles of good team construction: balance and function.

One of the most important jobs of the manger-coach is to pick the players. You've got to have a sixth sense about who can work together because the wrong chemistry can destroy a group before it sits down to hammer out its first agenda. Even when the choice of using teams to produce a specific outcome is well conceived, if players lack the right set of skills the team is doomed. You can't use a running back to punt the ball or an accountant to engineer a new product.

Many people assume if you just put people together with a common goal, they'll eventually end up on the same page. Sometimes this happens, but usually it just produces the kind of dissension found in a committee of the Italian Parliament.

Balancing Act

The Change-Ready model offers another way to choose up sides. Instead of relying on "chemistry," an amorphous concept that's as hit-and-miss as a grammar-school bowling league, use Change-Ready profiles to create your team.

Assuming that you're starting with a pool of participants who have the necessary skills to do the job, a good strategy for creating team balance is to offset members low on one trait with those who score high on the same variable. In that way a particular member's weaknesses may be minimized. For example, a cautious—low adventure—individual could be paired with a high-adventure risk taker.

Balance has another value: It prevents teams from becoming too skewed in one direction or another. A group that is loaded with high-adventure players might take too many risks and find itself out on the proverbial limb. Or a team loaded with too many optimists might be reduced to Pollyanna thinking and naive solutions. We've seen teams with too many confident members get cocky and ignore danger signals out of sheer bravado.

The specific dangers of an imbalanced team are similar to individuals who score too high in one trait.

Too Much	*Danger*
Adventurousness	Too many risks, reckless
Optimism	Pollyanna-ish, rose-colored thinking, lack of critical judgment
Resourcefulness	Overlooks obvious solutions
Adaptability	Lack of commitment
Confidence	Brash, cocky, close-minded
Drive	Bull-headed, myopic, burned out
Tolerance/Ambiguity	Difficulty finishing and creating closure

Of course there are times when a team needs imbalance to accomplish its goals. Some teams, particularly those performing highly creative functions, require high resourcefulness and tolerance for ambiguity in all its members. A good manager will consider the group's task before choosing the players.

TWENTY-ONE

The Change-Ready Zone

TOO MUCH, TOO FAST

"There's no room left on our plate," the meeting planner for an international high-tech firm told me at a planning session for their annual sales meeting. "We're in an industry that's unbelievably competitive. We can introduce an innovation tomorrow and you can bet that in two weeks a competitor will leapfrog us. We've just started a Total Quality Management program to upgrade our operations and we're in the midst of a major restructuring. We're also introducing two new products within the next few weeks.

"And right before your speech the sales group is going to receive its quotas for next year. They're astronomical! Some people will have their quotas tripled! Most doubled! I don't know how they're going to do it," she said with a look of despair. "Or even if they will. There's just too much going on."

I wasn't surprised that this woman, and the vice president of sales, were acting like the doom-and-gloom duo. Both felt themselves to be under tremendous pressure and they showed it, frantically running around, not returning phone calls or following through on agreements. They looked like they hadn't slept in a week.

The company's mistake was in trying to do too much all at once. Taken individually, or even in pairs, none of the changes were impractical or impossible. But doing them all in one bold stroke seriously compromised the success of any of them. I also wasn't surprised that a year later the company was in serious trouble and was closer to skid row than Wall Street.

WHY CHANGE FAILS

The tendency for top management to try to accomplish too much too fast is typical of the madhouse nineties.

When you push too hard and too fast for change, you don't get more competitive or profitable, you get diminished quality, poor communication, and zero innovation. And the only increases you see are in the levels of stress and burnout. Very rarely do these massive initiatives succeed.

You can have highly motivated, Change-Ready employees, but if the *challenge* of the situation greatly exceeds their *resources*, the change effort will fail.

PERFORMANCE ZONE

The following Performance Zone map was developed from our pioneering work with world-class athletes and later with performers in many other fields. But it also provides a valuable model for maximizing organizational and individual effectiveness in any rapidly changing environment. Had the high-tech firm used it, there's a good chance it could have avoided its problems.

Maximum effectiveness occurs in the Change-Ready Zone when the challenge of the situation and the available resources are roughly in balance. The level of challenge is measured by how much change is needed and the learning, effort, and speed required to implement it. Resources are measured by team or individual competence, which includes levels of energy, motivation, and skill as well as available time and technology.

Too much challenge matched with too little resources lands you in the Panic Zone. Too many resources combined with too little challenge produces lethargy and the Drone Zone.

Keeping challenge and resources closely matched is crucial when introducing change. Sounds obvious, but our experience is that in the quest for quick solutions, this relationship is often misunderstood, overlooked, and underconsidered. Typically, management focuses on their strategy for change without real consideration of workforce resources. That's like a general making battle plans without accounting for the ability or readiness levels of his troops.

THE PANIC ZONE

The international high-tech firm with too much on its plate shows what can happen when the challenges of change exceed available resources. On the map, they're smack dab in the middle of the Panic Zone.

What does the workplace look like when employees are in the Panic Zone? Very much like a henhouse with a fox lurking nearby. Everyone's running around in a frenzy trying to do too much in too little time. People are nervous, pressured, and scared. They can't maintain focus and don't think clearly. Forget quality. People in a rush make more mistakes.

Creativity? No way. People are reacting, not reflecting. Under the gun, they're unlikely to come up with a brilliant or inventive plan. They just do the same old, same old a little faster. Communication suffers. It's hard to be clear, concise, and rational when you're racing around from one crisis to another.

Boosting challenge levels as a way to achieve an organization's change goals will backfire if the bar is raised too high. People do not realize a fraction of their capabilities in the Panic Zone.

Dr. Kenneth Pelletier, a professor at the University of California at San Francisco Medical School and an expert on workplace performance issues, agrees:

"In his eagerness to get things done as fast as possible, [the employee in the panic zone] may respond to challenges in a rote manner, causing him to make errors in judgment. And since he never takes time to consider new approaches to, or the implications of, a situation, his creativity will be inhibited."[1]

Time Trials

Often the change being introduced isn't demanding in terms of effort or new skills required. But the deadline pushes the project into the Panic Zone.

If you're asked to develop a plan for cutting health-insurance costs to employees that's probably within your capabilities. It's a different story, though, if the plan must be developed by the end of the week and it's already Thursday afternoon. Though you have the skills to produce the plan, the deadline has upset the challenge-resource equation and thrust you into the Panic Zone. Managers trying to keep costs down often put too few people on a project or assign employees who lack necessary experience.

When two of the largest food companies in the country merged, the new corporation had to consolidate their sales processes and procedures. It was a challenging task since each group had its own software and hardware, as well as different control and reporting systems. A tough challenge, especially with a one-month deadline.

What pushed the project into the Panic Zone was not the deadline but staff availability. Everyone was working on the consolidation part time. They all had other, primary tasks of equal or greater importance. After the first week the team was still having trouble scheduling an initial meeting that everybody could make!

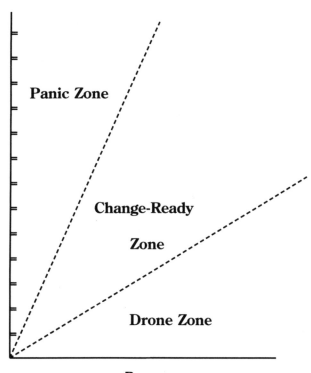

Challenge
Learning, effort, skill, and speed required to implement change. "How much, how fast, how hard."

Panic Zone

Change-Ready

Zone

Drone Zone

Resources
Team or individual competence; available time and technology.

THE DRONE ZONE

At the other end of the performance map is the Drone Zone, where resources far exceed challenges. Think of Detroit's Big Three riding high in the fifties on their tail-finned gas-guzzlers with the oversized grilles. They got stuck in the Drone Zone, playing it safe by making the same kind of car every year while the world around them was changing.

Companies end up in the Drone Zone when their leadership avoids challenges and stays glued to the status quo.

Detroit isn't alone. The list of companies that have bottomed out in the Drone Zone is like a Who's Who of American business. Giants in every field have been bruised and bloodied by their slowness to change. Household names like IBM, Digital, and Macy's, just to name a few, have ended up perilously close to extinction because they kept playing by the old rules, relying on past successes when the game had changed. And it's not only companies that get stuck in the Drone Zone. Individuals do, too, for the same reasons.

PLAYING IN THE "ZONE"

All of us have had at one time or another one of those fantastic experiences when everything falls into place and almost without effort or thought we perform far better than usual. These peak moments are so magical that we want them never to end.

It happens in golf when your swing feels natural and easy and the ball flies straight down the fairway. Or in tennis when you seem to know exactly where the opponent's ball is going before it gets there. In skiing it's those wonderful "breakthrough" runs when your body's in perfect rhythm and you feel in harmony with the mountain.

Athletes call these peak experiences "being in the zone," when all of a person's innate potential is turned into maximum performance. Playing in the zone usually happens when you're under pressure or responding to a challenge.

Peak performance isn't restricted to sports, of course. It occurs at work, too. Like your presentation to top management when you've got the audience in the palm of your hand, anticipating questions and responding with perfect answers.

Emmy Award–winning TV reporter Doug Kriegel describes being in the "zone" this way: "Sometimes when I'm rushing to meet a deadline, I get so involved in what I'm doing that I'm unaware of anything going on around me. I feel calm and get more done. Everything seems to flow. It's unbelievable. I've done my best work at these times."[2]

CHANGE-READY ZONE

Learning to play in the zone maximizes effectiveness when dealing with the pressure of change. You'll learn faster, adapt more easily, and perform better when you're in the Change-Ready Zone. Our research for the book *The C-Zone: Peak Performance Under Pressure* showed that people get in the zone most often when the level of challenge is matched to the level of resources.

Remember the merging food giants that needed to consolidate their sales systems but couldn't even get a meeting scheduled? Our job was to help the team out of the Panic Zone and into the Change-Ready Zone by either reducing the challenge or increasing the resources.

First we looked at the deadline, knowing that time frames are notoriously arbitrary. Not this one. Both sales forces were out in the field, so a new system had to be developed—fast. And a month, according to one of the managers, was stretching it: "I'd like to have it in a week; I'll settle for a month," is how he put it. Next we considered scaling down the task. "No way! We can't work with two systems," we were told.

Studying the resources side of the equation, we again hit a wall. "We can't spare any more people on the project," the manager assured us. So we suggested making the project a higher priority by having fewer people but making them all full time. That way there'd be more dedicated people-hours plus a more dedicated team. Management agreed, and the project was finished ahead of schedule.

If you've got a project in the Panic Zone, try the same strategy. Either decrease one of the challenge factors or increase available resources.

CHANGE-READY INDIVIDUALS

A franchisee for a major real estate company wanted to get ahead of the curve by moving his employees "onto the highway," as he put it. The problem was the huge variation in technical expertise among his 300 agents.

"Some of them are already on-line. Others don't even have a beeper and write their correspondence in longhand. They think the typewriter is high-tech. How am I going to get everyone into the Change-Ready Zone when their competencies vary so much?" he complained.

Our answer was to plot out a step-by-step continuum of skills from low- to high-tech. Low-tech started with "uses beeper" followed by "uses voice mail, computer, various software programs, E-mail, interactive databases" and so on, up to total systems mastery. Agents placed themselves on the continuum based on their competencies.

Then each was assigned the challenge of taking the next step along the progression. When they mastered it, they moved on at their own pace. That allowed them to control their speed of learning. If a person got stuck at any point, additional resources were available, like extra time for learning or special training.

The idea was to keep everybody in the Change-Ready Zone by balancing the two factors: challenge and resources. The plan worked. Within the year, most agents had reached systems mastery and were ready to deal with the next techno-change.

ZONE CHECK

A simple way to find out where you or your people are on the Change-Ready map is to do a "zone check." On a scale of 1 to 10, rate the challenge of the situation, including the degree of change, steepness of the learning curve, required effort, and necessary speed of implementation. Next, rate the resources available to meet the challenge, like team size, competence, energy, motivation, available time, technology, and information.

To be in the Change-Ready Zone the challenge should not be more than two points greater or lower than the resources rating.

Because a manager's assessment of the challenge-resource equation may be different from that of the team's, it's helpful to compare the scores of both. This process of discussing differences in perception creates a dialogue that serves several purposes. It gets everyone on the same page and shows team members that management is interested in how they view the situation. It also often results in developing creative ways of solving a problem or implementing a change.

RECHARGING BATTERIES

To prevent "change burnout"—the aftermath of too much time spent in the Panic Zone—a good coach will do what the pros do. Rest the players, give them a chance to recharge. A basketball game lasts 48 minutes. That's a lot of time to be running up and down the court in continuous motion. Even with time-outs and other breaks, superstars rarely play the whole game. *They can't if they're going to remain effective.*

Resting your players at work makes equally good sense. If someone's just coming off a tough, time-consuming project, don't assign her to another one before she's had time to recover. We all need to recharge our batteries, especially if we've been going flat-out for a while. Many companies give employees sabbaticals every few years. That's great, but you can also help someone recharge by resisting the temptation to dump another tough project in her lap immediately.

In sports like hockey, soccer, and lacrosse, a platoon system is used. A new line of players is brought in before the first team gets exhausted. It's a good way to keep your work teams fresh. Conserve their resources by taking them off the front lines every so often. Alternate which teams are carrying the heaviest load.

Let your tired players sit out for a short period of time. Assign them to something less demanding. Send them on a field trip to a place where they can bring along their golf clubs. But make sure you tell them why you're doing it. Star players and top achievers don't like to sit on the bench.

Scheduling a play afternoon, a party, or an off-site meeting helps people relax, rejuvenate, and recover. Apple Computer used to run Friday afternoon beer busts back in its heyday for just this purpose.

These measures should be implemented *before* you've got a group of Panic-Zoned basket cases on your hands. An afternoon of prevention works wonders to increase motivation and energy level and keep people in the Change-Ready Zone.

TWENTY-TWO

Change-Ready Review

People are the gatekeepers of change.
They have the power to open the door to change or slam it in your face.

Don't plant seeds in hard ground.
If you're trying to get people to buy in to change, you're already too late. Cultivate a Change-Ready environment first.

Good companies respond quickly to change; great companies create change.
Anticipate, don't react. Move before the wave. Change before you have to.

When you're through changing, you're through.

Change is a process, not a goal; a journey, not a destination.

Nothing is sacred—challenge everything.

Sacred cows roam in every conference room, office, and hallway. Don't just round them up, develop a hunting organization.

Twenty people in a room doesn't make a team.

Teams don't just happen. They have to be developed, facilitated, and motivated.

Speed kills . . .

quality, innovation, communication, service, and you. Don't let the "gottas" get you.

Don't compete; change the game.

Tilt the playing field in your direction. Go outside the lines. Reinvent the rules.

The biggest risk is not taking any; the biggest mistake is not making any.

If you're not making mistakes you're playing it too safe. You'll never win if you play not to lose.

Don't satisfy customers; surprise them.

Give them something they don't expect. Lead them, don't follow.

Technology is no magic bullet.

High-tech needs high-touch to be highly successful.

Cut your meetings; keep your croissants.

Meetings, like hot air, expand to fill available space. Cut them in half.

Be a coach, not a cop.

Create trust, not fear. Focus on possibilities, not limitations; strengths, not weaknesses.

Turn resistance into readiness.

Conquer fears, emphasize "what's in it for me," make the comfort zone uncomfortable, and turn every person into an agent for change.

Fire 'em up and get 'em moving.

Create passion with inspired visions, burning platforms, empowered employees, and personalized rewards.

Treat everyone differently.

Everyone marches to a different drum. Know what motivates every player on your team.

Play in the Change-Ready Zone.

Balance challenges with resources. Too much challenge: Panic Zone. Too little: Drone Zone.

Change-Readiness can be learned.

The seven traits are resourcefulness, optimism, adventurousness, drive, adaptability, confidence, tolerance for ambiguity.

Being Change-Ready means taking risks, challenging convention, and chasing dreams. It's growing, learning, and living life to the fullest; tapping into skills, strengths, and resources you never knew you had.

When you're Change-Ready you'll *do* more than you thought you could, *be* more than you thought you were. Making change your ally, not your enemy, will lead to a future of unlimited possibilities and make your life richer, more rewarding, and much more fun.

If you'd like more information on our Change-Ready programs and products or our Sacred Cow Hunts, contact:

Kriegel² Inc.
Star Route Box 284
Muir Beach, CA 94965
Phone: 415-388-7388
Fax: 415-381-0518

Source Notes

Chapter One

1. *Fortune* (October 4, 1993): p. 18.
2. 16th annual Cape Cod Institute brochure, 1995, p. 28.
3. Tandy Users Group speech, 1993 convention, Orlando, Florida.
4. Op/ed, *Newsletter for Organizational Psychologists,* 1995, p. 7.
5. *Fortune (*October 18, 1993): p. 66.
6. *USA Today,* October 25, 1993, p. 2b.
7. *Fortune* (April 12, 1995): p. 122.
8. *Op. cit.,* Cape Cod, p. 28.
9. *Fortune* (August 22, 1994): p. 93.
10. *Fortune* (October 4, 1993): p. 82.
11. *Wall Street Journal,* May 14, 1994, p. A1.
12. *San Francisco Examiner,* September 12, 1993, p. E3.
13. *Fortune* (April 17, 1995): p. 122.
14. Ibid., p. 128.
15. Ibid., p. 124.
16. Ibid., p. 122.

Chapter Two

1. *Fortune* (July 11, 1994): p. 60.
2. Greyhound Financial Conference, February 16, 1994.
3. *Wall Street Journal,* July 23, 1992, p. 1.

Chapter Three

1. *New York Times,* July 20, 1994, p. D1.
2. *Fortune* (April 10, 1989): p. 86.
3. *The New Yorker* (January 10, 1994): p. 59.
4. *San Francisco Chronicle,* October 6, 1993, p. D7.
5. Ibid.

Chapter Four

1. *San Francisco Examiner,* January 11, 1993, p. C7.
2. *Wall Street Journal,* November 16, 1994, p. B4.
3. Ibid.
4. *USA Today,* April 6, 1992, p. 5B.
5. *Fortune* (June 1, 1992): p. 135.
6. *Fortune* (August 22, 1994), p. 93.
7. Ibid.
8. Ibid.
9. Ibid.
10. *Fortune* (November 30, 1992), p. 71.
11. Ibid.

Chapter Five

1. *San Jose Mercury News,* November 20, 1988, p. 1PC.
2. *Fortune* (February 24, 1992): p. 78.
3. *New York Times,* January 17, 1994, Business Day section.
4. Ibid.
5. *Fortune* (February 24, 1992): p. 79.
6. *The New Yorker* (March 21, 1994): p. 80.

Chapter Six

1. *Fortune* (October 17, 1994): p. 204.
2. Peter Drucker, "A Turnaround Primer," February 2, 1993.
3. *Wall Street Journal,* October 28, 1993, p. B7.
4. *New York Times,* September 18, 1993, p. 17.
5. *San Francisco Examiner,* July 4, 1993, p. B1.
6. *New York Times*, July 19, 1993, p. C5.
7. *Wall Street Journal,* October 28, 1993, p. B4.
8. PepsiCo 1989 Annual Report, p. 30.
9. *New York Times,* November 3, 1994, p. C1.

Chapter Seven

1. *Success* (January/February 1994): p. 42.
2. *Wall Street Journal,* October 15, 1993, p. B1.
3. Ibid.
4. Op. cit., *Success*, p. 39.
5. *Fortune* (January 10, 1994), p. 106.
6. *New York Times,* January 16, 1994, p. F7.

Chapter Eight

1. *Fortune* (April 19, 1993): p. 118.
2. *Fortune* (Autumn/Winter 1993): p. 39.
3. Ibid.
4. *Fortune* (Autumn/Winter 1993): p. 53.
5. *Fortune* (May 1, 1995): p. 121.
6. *Fortune* (Autumn/Winter, 1993): p. 41.
7. Ibid.
8. *Fortune* (August 9, 1993): p. 42.
9. *Fortune* (Autumn/Winter 1993): p. 22.
10. Ibid., p. 52.
11. Ibid.
12. *New York Times*, February 20, 1994, p. 11.
13. Ibid.

14. Ibid.
15. Ibid.

Chapter Nine

1. *Fortune* (Autumn/Winter 1993): p. 10.
2. Ibid., p. 8.
3. *San Francisco Examiner,* November 21, 1993, p. E1.
4. *Nation's Restaurant News* (January 1, 1994): p. 122.
5. *Nation's Restaurant News* (August 1, 1994): p. 126.
6. *Fortune* (Autumn/Winter 1993): p. 24.

Chapter Ten

1. *Harvard Business Review* (July/August 1991): p. 85.
2. Ibid.
3. Ibid.
4. *Success* (April 1992): p. 161.

Chapter Eleven

1. *Fortune* (May 1, 1995): p. 49.
2. Ibid.
3. *Harvard Business Review* (July/August 1991): pp. 90, 91.
4. *Fortune* (January 24, 1994): p. 85.
5. Speech to Washington Business Group on Health, Washington, D.C., September 18, 1981.

Chapter Twelve

1. *San Francisco Chronicle,* September 27, 1994, p. 81.
2. Ibid.
3. Ibid.
4. *Wall Street Journal,* December 6, 1993, p. 1.
5. Ibid.
6. *Wall Street Journal,* October 1, 1993.

7. *Wall Street Journal,* October 2, 1991, p. A12.

8. *Fortune* (August 23, 1993): p. 54.

9. *Fortune* (February 22, 1993): p. 44.

10. Op. cit., *Wall Street Journal,* p. A12.

11. *Fortune* (July 25, 1994): p. 44.

12. *Wall Street Journal,* December 6, 1993, p. A1.

13. Ibid.

14. Personal communication, Peller Marion, November 8, 1993.

15. *Wall Street Journal,* December 6, 1993, p. A6.

16. Ibid.

17. Ibid.

18. *Time* (November 22, 1993): p. 36.

19. "MacNeil/Lehrer," November 2, 1993, New York Show 4789.

Chapter Thirteen

1. *USA Today,* September 28, 1994, p. 1A.

2. *Fortune* (November 15, 1993): p. 122.

3. *Fortune* (September 5, 1994): p. 95.

4. Ibid.

5. Ibid.

6. Ibid.

7. *New York Times,* September 29, 1994.

8. *San Francisco Examiner,* September 25, 1994, p. C2.

9. *Fortune* (September 6, 1994): p. 98.

10. Personal communication, Ken Jenny, July 16, 1994.

11. *Fortune* (October 17, 1994): p. 112.

12. *Fortune* (Autumn 1993): p. 112.

13. Ibid.

14. *Computerworld* (November 1991): p. 70.

15. Ibid.

Chapter Fourteen

1. *Fortune* (September 5, 1994), p. 86.

2. Ibid.

3. Pat Riley, *The Winner Within* (New York: Berkley Books, 1994), p. 16.
4. Personal communication, Laura Hotzler, July 26, 1994.
5. Op. cit., *Fortune*, p. 87.
6. Ibid.
7. Ibid., p. 86.
8. *Fortune* (May 18, 1992): p. 95.
9. *The New Yorker* (September 26, 1994): pp. 54-69.

Chapter Fifteen

1. *Fortune* (November 30, 1992): p. 64.
2. Ibid.
3. *Fortune* (March 21, 1994): p. 65.
4. *Wall Street Journal*, September 29, 1994, p. 1.
5. Ibid.
6. *Wall Street Journal*, July 14, 1994, p. B1.
7. Ibid.
8. Ibid.
9. Ibid.
10. Ibid.
11. *New York Times*, August 29, 1993, p. F9.
12. *Fortune* (November 30, 1992): p. 71.
13. *New York Times*, August 29, 1993, p. F9.
14. Ibid.
15. *Wall Street Journal*, January 13, 1994, p. B1.
16. Ibid.
17. Ibid., p. B2.
18. Ibid.
19. Ibid., p. B1.
20. *Wall Street Journal*, August 3, 1994, p. A1.
21. *San Francisco Chronicle*, January 12, 1994, p. E7.
22. Ibid.
23. *Profiles* (March 1993): p. 38.
24. Personal communication, Duffy Gilligan, March 26, 1994.

Chapter Sixteen

1. *Wall Street Journal*, January 26, 1994, p. A1.
2. Ibid.
3. *Success* (December 1994): p. 18.
4. Ibid.
5. *Wall Street Journal*, January 26, 1994.

Chapter Seventeen

1. *Fortune* (February 21, 1994): p. 56.
2. *Industry Week* (September 19, 1994): p. 28.
3. Ibid.
4. *Fortune* (February 21, 1994): p. 42.
5. Ibid.
6. *Fortune* (April 18, 1994): p. 16.
7. Ibid.
8. *Fortune* (November 14, 1994): p. 68.
9. *Fortune* (October 18, 1993): p. 67.
10. *Success* (May 1994): p. 64.
11. *Fortune* (May 23, 1988): p. 46.
12. Ibid.
13. Op. cit., *Industry Week*, p. 29.
14. Ibid., p. 28.
15. Ibid., p. 29.
16. *Fortune* (February 21, 1994): p. 48.
17. *Sports Illustrated* (December 20, 1993): p. 19.
18. *Fortune* (December 13, 1993): p. 83.
19. Ibid.
20. *Boardroom Reports*, December 1, 1991, p. 13.
21. *Fortune* (November 14, 1994), p. 58.
22. *USAir* (January 1989): p. 31.
23. *Fortune* (May 17, 1993): p. 46.
24. *Industry Week*, October 18, 1993, pp. 1, 3.
25. Ibid., p. 1.
26. Ibid.

27. *New York Times,* April 4, 1994, p. A9.

28. Ibid.

29. Ibid.

30. Ibid.

31. Ibid., p. 3.

32. *Fortune* (June 29, 1992): p. 103.

33. *Fortune* (May 2, 1994): p. 46.

34. Ibid.

35. *Independent Journal* (November 10, 1994): p. D4.

36. *San Francisco Chronicle,* November 24, 1994, p. E5.

37. *Sports Illustrated* (June 28, 1993): p. 64.

38. *Wall Street Journal,* May 10, 1993, p. 1.

39. Ibid.

40. Ibid.

41. *Wall Street Journal,* April 26, 1994, p. 1.

42. *Sports Illustrated* (November 8, 1993): Special advertising section.

43. *New York Times,* April 17, 1994, p. 26.

44. Ibid.

45. *Success* (November 1994): p. 180.

46. *Fortune* (October 17, 1994): p. 96.

Chapter Eighteen

1. Gene Landrum, *Profiles of Genius* (Prometheus, 1993), p. 33.

2. *Harvard Business Review Classic,* 1954, p. 91968.

3. Kriegel & Kriegel, *The C Zone* (Doubleday, 1984), p. 64.

4. Ibid., p. 75.

5. *Toronto Star,* September 20, 1992, p. G-10.

6. Ibid.

7. "Overcoming Resistance to Change," *Human Relations* (Coch and French, vol. 1, November 4, 1948), p. 512.

8. Ibid.

9. *Fortune* (February 22, 1993): p. 81.

10. *San Francisco Examiner,* December 2, 1990, p. D1.

11. *Fortune* (May 18, 1992): p. 88.

12. Ibid.
13. Ibid.
14. Ibid.
15. Ibid., p. 82.
16. Ibid.
17. *Fortune* (November 14, 1994): p. 53.
18. *Fortune* (June 28, 1993): p. 123.
19. Ibid.
20. Maslow, "A Theory of Human Motivation," *Psychology Review*, 1943.

Chapter Nineteen

1. *Fortune* (December 13, 1993): p. 84.
2. *San Francisco Examiner*, June 12, 1994, p. D1.
3. *Fortune* (December 13, 1993): p. 84.
4. *Fortune* (June 28, 1993): pp. 123–126.
5. Bennis and Nanus, *Leaders* (New York: Harper & Row, 1985), p. 87.
6. Ibid.
7. *San Francisco Examiner*, May 29, 1994, p. C3.
8. Personal communication, Ken Jenny, September 26, 1994.
9. *Success* (March 1994): p. 44.
10. Ibid.
11. *Sky* (January 1995): p. 28.
12. *Entrepreneur* (January 1994): pp. 224, 225.
13. Personal communication, Brian Casey, January 25, 1995.
14. *Industry Week* (October 18, 1993): p. 2.
15. Ibid.
16. Personal communication, Ken Jenny, September 26, 1994.
17. Personal communication, Brian Casey, January 25, 1995.
18. *New York Times*, October 17, 1993, p. 11.
19. Ibid.
20. Ibid.
21. Ibid.
22. *Fortune* (June 13, 1994): p. 52.

23. *San Francisco Chronicle*, July 20, 1994, p. A16.
24. Ibid.
25. Ibid., A15.
26. *Fortune* (June 13, 1994): p. 50.
27. Ibid.
28. *Inc.* (July 1989): p. 53.
29. Op. cit., *Fortune* (September 20, 1993): pp. 68-77.
30. *Sports Illustrated* (November 11, 1991): p. 118.
31. *San Francisco Chronicle*, December 10, 1994, p. D2.
32. *USA Today*, December 27, 1994, p. 2C.
33. *Sports Illustrated* (September 14, 1992).

Chapter Twenty

1. *Sports Illustrated* (February 14, 1994): p. 147.
2. Karen C. Anderson, *Kids Big Book of Games* (New York: Workman Publishing, 1987), p. 100.

Chapter Twenty-One

1. Kriegel & Kriegel, *The C Zone* (Garden City, New York: Doubleday, 1994), p. 14.
2. Ibid., p. 2.

ROBERT J. KRIEGEL, PH.D., one of today's hottest speakers on the business circuit, is a pioneer in the field of human performance and the psychology of change. His books—most recently *If It Ain't Broke . . . BREAK IT!* (1991)—have made numerous best-seller lists, including the *New York Times*'s, and have been translated into ten languages.

Kriegel is a commentator on National Public Radio's "Marketplace" and has done two specials for PBS. He has taught at Stanford's Executive Management Program and the University of San Francisco and was a member of the California Governor's Council. He has also been an advertising executive for Young & Rubicam in New York, where he managed Procter & Gamble, Johnson & Johnson, and Travelers Insurance accounts.

A former all-American athlete and pioneer in the field of sports psychology, Kriegel has coached many Olympic and professional athletes and done commentary on ESPN. *The New York Times* said his work "spurred a sporting revolution."

Dr. Kriegel gives speeches, and conducts programs, and does consulting work for corporations, associations, and government agencies around the world.

DAVID BRANDT, PH.D., is a clinical psychologist, organizational consultant, and executive coach who specializes in change and transition. *U.S. News and World Report* has called him an expert on contemporary psychological issues.

A former faculty member of the University of California at San Francisco Medical School and the California School of Professional Psychology, and co-host of "Psychtalk," a popular San Francisco public-radio program, Dr. Brandt is the author of two books, *Is That All There Is?* and *Don't Stop Now, You're Killing Me.* He has written numerous articles in professional journals as well as magazines such as *Sports Illustrated* and *Cosmopolitan.*

Dr. Brandt runs training programs and seminars on Change Readiness for companies and individuals across the country.